Pitmatic:

The Talk of the North East Coalfield

compiled by Bill Griffiths

This is the second volume of three resulting from the dialect project 'Wor Language', supported by the Heritage Lottery Fund. For more information go to www.worlanguage.co.uk

Published by Northumbria University Press
Trinity Building, Newcastle upon Tyne NE1 8ST, UK
www.northumbriauniversitypress.co.uk

First Edition Published 2007

British Library Cataloguing in Publication Data. A Catalogue Record for this book is available from the British Library.

ISBN-13: 978-1-904794-25-7

Designed and printed by Northumbria Graphics, Northumbria University.

Typeset in Original Garamond

Northumbria University is the trading name of the University of Northumbria at Newcastle. 181404

Acknowledgements

Direct Sources:

Firstly, thanks must go to those who have come forward to contribute words, sketches, stories, comments, poems and technical advice – and without whose participation the list would look very femmer indeed. Tony Sharkey, principally, for proofreading and frequent inspired improvements; but also Kenn Johnson, Geordie Darby, Steve Barnett, and many other ex-pit folk who have corresponded, talked and read with me, during the composition of this book. If faults are detected – please blame me and not them!

And thanks to those who have promoted contact – notably the Library Service throughout the region for hosting talks; local history and community groups; and the local press and radio stations.

Published sources:

Particular thanks for use of George Hitchin's *Pit-Yacker* (1962), Kathleen Teward's *Teisdal' en how twas spok'n* (2003), Dave Douglass' *Pit talk in Co. Durham* (1973) and Rob Colls' *Pitmen of the Northern Coalfield* (1987). A wide range of printed sources have been used and acknowledged in the list at the end.

Internet Sources:

A special thanks here to Harry Tootle, whose pioneering online dictionary of mining terms (http://website.lineone.net/~coalmining/) has been a particular help, and whose permission to quote has been most valuable. I have sampled and quoted many other websites, and hope that acknowledgement *in situ* and my thanks will suffice.

Manuscripts Sources:

Thanks to Beamish North of England Open Air Museum's Centre for Regional Resource Centre for use of the 'Geordie' wordlist of Michael Dodds; and for use of various transcripts of oral material being currently developed by Jo Bath.

Thanks also for the use of wordlists by Stan Oxley (via Joyce Oxley) and Geordie McBurnie (via Ada Radford), and to Tom Moreland for use of his unpublished memoirs. Robert Straughan's poems were kindly made available by his grandaughter, Sheila Armstrong.

MS D/Lo/B 265 (Yearly Bonds) is quoted by permission of the Marquess of Londonderry and Durham County Record Office.

Acknowledgements cont.

BL MS Egerton 2868 (James Raine's dialect word list) and *BL MS Lansdowne 1033* (vol. 99 of Bishop Kennet's Collection, Bishop Kennet's 'Etymological Collections of English Words and Provincial Expressions'), with permission of the British Library.

Bell-White MS 12 ('A Glossary for Newcastle, Durham and Northumberland') by permission of the Special Collections and Archives Librarian, Robinson Library Special Collections, University of Newcastle.

Illustrations

Besides prints from the compiler's archive, No. 3 is a diagram by George Butler; No. 4 is of Bedlington Colliery, courtesy of Bill Harris; No. 8 is a photograph of Derek Ezra's visit to Dawdon Colliery, also showing Harold Mountford (centre), William Campbell (right); No. 11 is Trevor Charlton, late Chairman of the Story of Seaham local heritage group, putting; No. 12 is a photo of a 3-D picture by J.Roddam; No. 13 is a print of the rescue attempt after the Seaham explosion of 1880, from the *London Illustrated News* of 18 September, 1880.

Thanks to J.D. Curtis for the cover illustration.

Abbreviations of place names

B'd Castle – Barnard Castle

B'p Auck – Bishop Auckland

C'd – Cumberland

Ch-le-St – Chester-le-Street

Cleve – Cleveland

D'm – Durham (county)

D'ton – Darlington

e – east

G'head – Gateshead

Hetton – Hetton-le-Hole

Ho'ton – Houghton-le-Spring

H'pool – Hartlepool

Ire – Ireland

Lx – Lancashire

n, N – north

N'd – Northumberland

Newc – Newcastle

N.I. – Northern Ireland

Nth – North of England

Sco – Scotland

s, S – south

S.Shields – South Shields

S'd – Sunderland

S'm – Seaham

Tyne – Tyneside

w – west

W'd – Westmorland

Yx – Yorkshire

Plus standard county name abbreviations

Note: in the context of distribution to 1900, reckoned via the EDD (English Dialect Dictionary), Nth imples counties of England from the Humber north; NE implies a combination of Northumberland, Co. Durham and Cleveland.

Abbreviations relating to language

AN – Anglo-Norman (also known as OFr, Old French)

Dan – Danish

Du – Dutch

Flem – Flemish

OE – Old English, the language of the Anglo-Saxons to ca.1100

ON – Old Norse, the language of the Vikings

CONTENTS

Foreword 3

Chapter 1: Introduction 5
- Memories of Seaham Colliery 7
- Pitmatic 10
- Adaption from a rural world 11
- Distribution and consistency 13
- Impact of modernisation 17

Chapter 2: The pit-surface features 21
- A coal mine 22
- Surface features 23
- The washery 33
- Distribution 36
- Spoil 39

Chapter 3: The shaft 43
- Sinking the shaft 44
- Maintenance 46
- Kibble and cage 48
- Operation 51
- The operator 54
- Signalling 56
- Unloading the cage 58

Chapter 4: Underground 59
- Areas 60
- Directions 60
- Passages and places 62
- Maintenance of passages 66

Chapter 5: Ventilation 73

Chapter 6: Drainage 81

Chapter 7: Coal 85
- Names for coal 86
- Sea coal 87
- Sizes of coal 89
- Stone and non-coal 91
- Seams 93
- Strata and cleavage 95
- Measures for coal 99

Chapter 8: The officials..........101
- Owners 102
- Middle management 106
- The Deputy's Kist 112

Chapter 9: Work practices 119
- Yearly bonds 120
- Cavils 123
- Pay systems 124
- Terminology of pay 128
- Shifts 132
- Start work 137
- Training 140
- End of work 142
- Celebrations 143
- Disputes 148
- …and Strikes 152

Chapter 10: Hewing 159
- Overall strategy 160
- Hand hewing 161
- Tools relating to working coal 167
- Blasting 169
- Filling the tubs 174
- The broken mine 175
- The goaf 176

Chapter 11: Putting 179
- Hand putting 180
- Tubs 187
- Rails 189
- The route to the shaft 191
- Sets 193
- Ponies 198
- Power assisted hauling 206
- Ropes and wires 207

Chapter 12: Automation. 209
- Automated cutting 210
- The electrical side 216
- Conveyor belts 219

Chapter 13: Safety & health 223
- Precautions and rescue 224
- Injury and illness 227
- Problems of pressure 230
- Problems of gas 235
- Explosions 242
- Reactions 244
- Lamps and lighting 250

Chapter 14: Everyday 255
- Everday terms 256
- Clothes 259
- Washing 263
- Food 264

Foreword

There have been dictionaries of mining terms before (Greenwell, 1849 and Nicholson, 1888), but few if any attempts to understand the work-skills and technicalities of the North East pits in terms of dialect usage, and how the language of work related to the wider language-world of the region and its literature of story and song.

Dave Douglass began such a task, with his *Pit Talk in Co. Durham* (1973), but dialect earned little attention in the following decades, despite the wealth of material available – at Newcastle Central Library's excellent local studies collection, and now at Beamish' Regional Resources Centre; plus many individual word lists and poems, published and unpublished in local libraries and private hands.

Bringing this range of material together into synthesis is not an easy task, and I have aimed to balance essential texts by Alexander Barrass and Tommy Armstrong with as as much new/unfamiliar material as possible. Inevitably, a good proportion of this new material gravitates around Seaham where I live. If the jokes, stories, songs and booklets from these local pits is anything to go by, then there should be a vast amount of the like out there, all over the Northern Coalfield, and the task of rescuing the pit literature of the last 50 years is only beginning. There is a certain urgency in collecting the stapled booklets of little presses, copying the handwritten diaries and songs stored away in family homes, and in interviewing and recording the talk of ex-miners around the North East, because the golden age of writing about the pits by working pitmen for working pitmen and their families is over. It is time to save and share what we can.

Regarding this book, there will be surely much to improve and add – with your help. Exactly, it is hoped its appearance will encourage many more than I have been able to reach so far to get in touch and volunteer their memories of working skills, their stories, poems, anecdotes and comments on word entries. What we cannot fit in here will be honoured on the website at: www.worlanguage.co.uk and help attest the remarkable vitality of the region's dialect and the inventiveness of its speakers.

Bill Griffiths
21 Alfred St
Seaham
Co. Durham SR7 7LH

Northumberland and Durham Coalfield. Area, 460 square miles; length from north to south, 50 miles; breadth, 23 miles at widest part; thickness of workable coal, 46 feet; number of seams, 16 to 20; probable available quantity of coal, 2,867,307,000 tons.

This old and important coalfield stretches over the greater portion of the counties of Northumberland and Durham. It extends from the River Coquet in the north to Staindrop (on the north of the Tees) in the south; and from Ponteland and Wolsingham in the west to the North Sea on the east.

James Tonge (1906) *The Principles and Practice of Coal Mining*, ch. 2. London.

Chapter 1: Introduction

Viewing the wooded countryside around Beamish Open Air Museum, or the grassy clifftops of County Durham's coast, you get no indication of the invasive ubiquity of coal mining in the North East in former times. Even the peaceful dales in the west, with their occasional (now scenic) ruins, were once the site of intensive lead mining, so that it should not be surprising to find William Egglestone's Betty Podkin, on her isolated Weardale farm, remarking:

> ...oor Peter...wurks ed Mister Bewmont's leed mines, 'n' hez cannie fare addlen [earning] ed prisent, 'n' see duz t' twee eldest lads;...maine feck o' mi other bairns gans ted new board skeäl, 'n' helps ma wud hoose wark, 'n' lads 'n' Peter Maniges t'geese, 'n' sheep when they're ed heäme, 'n' leaks efther t' gallowa 'n' seek like.
>
> (Egglestone, 1877, p.9)

Directly, or indirectly (as farms producing food, or cities providing finance, shopping and entertainment) everyone's lives were affected by the coal industry. And that in turn was a mark of the importance of coal to the nation at large. In the early seventeenth century it was said:

> ...the fore said sea-cole and pitt cole is become the general fewell of this Britaine Island, used in the houses of the nobilitie, cleargy, and gentrie in London and in all other cityes and shires of the Kingdom as well as for dresing of meate, washing, brewing, dying and otherwise.
>
> (qu. *HRCM*, ch.1)

From the 1740s on, coal was being used in the manufacture of iron; coal became the mobile source of power for industry in place of the fixed-location waterwheel. It was the mining (tin and coal) industry and its needs for power for pumping and winding engines that prompted the development of efficient steam engines (powered by coal!) and nurtured the science of geology. The demand for coal to power railway engines and ships and the nation's factories meant a massive expansion of coal production in the mid nineteenth century, till by 1900 it might be said that Coal was Great Britain. The dependency didn't end there: by-products of coke manufacture included gas for lighting and cooking, and an important chemicals industry.

Coal and coke remained important in the twentieth century, but the dominance of the home industry was increasingly challenged by the rise of the combustion engine, imports of cheaper coal, the discovery of offshore oil and gas, the need for a cleaner environment, and political distrust of the workforce.

Today, no chimneys evidence coal smoke; and those who remember the great days of coal are relatively few. There is no sign of the great collieries that dominated the landscape, and it is increasingly hard to picture the way of life that was mining. Scattered villages remain with their typical colliery rows, struggling for a new lease of life. And the very language that was the common speech of miners and their families is challenged by the continuing rise of International English.

Nonetheless, in a very real sense, the North East remains the product of coal – the distribution of its settlements, the pre-eminance of Newcastle upon Tyne, the family and social structures, even our sense of humour – are bascially part of the culture of coal. This book is centred on one aspect of that long tradition, the way words represented mining life and technology. The voice of dialect endures, if patchily: its intonation, its word preferences and local differences, for example, and it is possible still to recover much of the phrasing and terminology that marked out the miner.

But first, it wil be well to remind ourselves of what a mine 'felt' like. Here is a general account of working at our local colliery.

Memories of Seaham Colliery

Initial impressions on first day at work were a little frightening. Dirt, noise and strange smells assaulted the senses.

Once you were kitted out with your overalls, belt, boots and hard hat, you were introduced to your new marras. Everyone made you feel at home straight away, humour played a major part of this process. If you showed a weakness or had a physical feature out of the ordinary, this was seized upon and many lifelong nicknames were bestowed in this manner. You learned to give as well as you got.

This was no place for being 'precious', or being overly sensitive. The language was of the 'industrial' variety interspersed with a thousand dialect or slang terms – and this wasn't confined to the labour force by any means, most colliery managers and their officials could express themselves most colourfully.

Working 'at bank' was no less arduous than conditions underground in that the dirt and noise was a constant factor. Seaham Colliery Washery would not have been out of place in Dante's worst nightmares. You worked with the incessant racket of the belts moving the coal through the washing process. One of the main tasks was shifting the never-ending streams of slurry on the floors, with water dripping down your neck.

All these sensations continued unabated 24 hours a day and, during the peak times of coal production, all weekend too. However, overtime or a bit dot, was usually well subscribed, the money was pretty good compared to other local industries. A standing joke was aimed at colleagues who worked seven days a week as being in the SAS – Saturdays And Sundays! Sometimes arguments broke out if it was perceived that somebody may have been getting more than their fair share of overtime.

A few of the lads were what would be called 'Special Needs' these days, but there were no major problems because the stronger lads would look after these guys like big brothers. When the pit shut, I saw one or two of these fellas who had gone to pieces because they had lost that support from their marras.

A good barter system went on at most pits, based on mutual favours. If a brickie wanted some wiring done at home one of the leckys would come out and sort it in return for some pointing or similar. If someone couldn't offer a trade off, then the job would be done for a minimum rate – usually covering the cost of materials.

Practical jokes weren't uncommon at Seaham either, ranging from bricking up the inside of a locker to picking up a small car and turning it 180 degrees in the car park. A skeleton sat on the rafters in the fitting shops for a long time.

The locos used on bank to move the coal wagons down to the British Rail sidings, or the shale trucks to the harbour, were involved in many hair-raising incidents. Getting 'amain' was the term for a runaway train. This usually happened with a greasy rail and entailed the whole train careering down the incline until either the shunters on board managed to jump off and wedge some brakes on, or the driver regained control (usually with the help of copious amounts of sand). Now and again though the trucks ended the experience themselves by parting company with the tracks.

Mining was always a high risk industry, it was a lucky man who never suffered some form of injury and many paid the ultimate price, though in the latter years of North East mining fatalities were mercifully fewer as safety became the priority. Unfortunately, there were a couple of fatalities at Seaham Colliery through the Eighties, one on bank the other underground.

One Onsetter knew the old workings by heart and used to go off exploring alone, a highly risky business – not to mention eerie! However, he could tell you stories that would keep you riveted for hours.

Ghosts? Yes there were a few, inevitable for a pit the age of Seaham. The boy on the landing, the man with no features who rode the cage with lone miners, the sounds of the 'dreg' on the way and no trace on investigation, the apparition seen outside Christchurch gate from two different angles by separate people, the list goes on. Real phenomena, or the imaginings of tired and stressed workers? Including the two explosions, there must have been about 300 deaths during Seaham's span so who knows...

The last years were painful to watch. First the Board spent a lot of money on the Colliery, re-painted the car park, installed security cameras and imported lots of new equipment, all tried and tested methods of ensuring the balance sheet showed red! Then the trickle of transfers to the Vane Tempest Colliery, which grew larger until only a maintainance staff were left as custodians. Then the fateful day when they blew up the winding gear and killed 'The Nack' for ever.

(Steve Barnett)

Seaham Colliery itself is said to have become a virtual maze of passages and old workings, and it is not surprising that at nationalisation in 1947 its 'small circuitous roadways and drifts' led to its being considered unsuitable for major investment. In its later years the pit served as a washery and processing annexe to the Vane Tempest, with which it was connected underground. (The two pits were amalgamated in 1987.) It is a great pity that no practical model of its workings exists. Though hidden to the eye, a coalmine is surely as great a work of industrial architecture as any bridge or building – only in reverse!

Completely different might be the experience of a visitor, here a lady from the wages office:

> *You went down?*
>
> I went down, yes, I went down the pit. I was down for about three hours...
>
> Of course knowing a lot of the men [from their] coming to the pay window, when I was going round the pit people I met said "Oh, nice to see you Miss Turner", [and] dabbed my face. I was in such a state. I went down with Mr. Hardy, the Engineer, his daughter and her young man, and Mr. Jefferson, he was the foreman plumber. I had to go to Hardy's house and have a bath before I could come home. I was in such a state...
>
> Oh, when we got into the cage; talk about lifts. It's a wonder my heart didn't come out of me mouth. Mr. Hardy said "just step into this, step in here and just wait here for a little while". And when they knew somebody was going down, like Mr. Hardy's daughter and like me, from the office, what they would do [was] let the cage away, let this thing drop so far and then stop. You can imagine what it was like... He says "You'll be alright". I went down again, when it stopped. ["Are we there yet?"] He says "Oh no, we've just come down a few feet". I said "How far we've to go?" I've forgotten how far he said it was, how many feet. I can't stand it, I'll die.
>
> However, we got down to the bottom: couldn't see any thing, there was this dust road right away along... sort of done with arch girders; then there were props, [and] just [a low] roof, done with these wooden props, chocks...
>
> When I was down I saw little ponies, I could have wept, poor little things, spending all their lives down in the dark. When we went right into the face where they hewed coal, I hewed a tiny piece of coal, it was about as much I could do to lift the pick, but I had to bring this piece out, piece about as big as my hand...
>
> (Miss Turner, Beamish, 1983/235)

And over all, there was the darkness:

> *How did you feel the first time you went down?*
>
> Well rather funny. I didn't feel... I mean we always talk about pits you know and you think that it must have been imprinted on your mind, you see. I didn't take it as badly as I thought I might have done. Mind, the darkness – that hits you straight away. It is completely dark. You used to think the 'black out' [in the war] was dark. You can't imagine the darkness down the pit until you go down. You can't see a glint of anything once you lose your light. It is complete darkness which you never really got. Even in the 'black out'.
>
> (J. Agar, Beamish 1984/253)

It would be intolerable to let the traditions of mining be consigned to some similar darkness of neglect. Fortunately, publications on North East pits have become more frequent in recent years, each making a contribution to our perception of a complex working environment. Central to understanding the working of a pit is the language used, of object, action, skill, and this new study aims to broaden our preception of 'Pitmatic', and recapture something of the spirit as well as the technology of former times.

Pitmatic

The words 'Pitmatics' and 'Pitmatical' are surely formed by analogy with Mathematics, Mathematical, as a half-humorous half-serious way of describing the skill or practical craft of mining – Heslop in the 1880s gives "pitmatics – the technicalities of colliery-working" in his list of 'Northumberland' words. But it was also used to describe a type of speech and in the form Pitmatical is noted even earlier, in a newspaper report of a demonstration by miners in Newcastle in 1873. Here it seems to mean the everyday dialect of miners:

> A great many of the lads, especially from the Durham district, had evidently never been in Newcastle previously, and the air of wonder with which they gazed at the crowds, at the buildings, and especially at the fine folks who occupied the windows, was very amusing. If the quality criticized and quizzed them, the lads returned the compliment, and it was entertaining enough to catch snatches of criticism on the manners and customs of the upper ten thousand of Newcastle, reduced to the purest 'pitmatical', shouted across the streets, as the men and lads belonging to collieries swept by where I stood in the crowd...
>
> (*Newcastle Weekly Chronicle*, 19 April, 1873)

This becomes Pitmatic by 1885, and placed more precisely in the workplace:

> After a few minutes delay in the overman's cabin, thronged with men talking an unintelligible language, known, I was informed, as Pitmatic, we took our places in one of a long train of tubs, which, on a signal being given, started for the heart of the mine...
>
> (*The Times*, 21 August, 1885)

The next mention equates Pitmatic with dialect in general; it is not entirely complimentary:

> Happily, the younger miners, while possessing a liberal reserve of 'Pitmatic' for street-end and other familiar uses, are able to converse in a near approach to conventional English.
>
> (*Northern Daily News*, 31 May, 1919)

While a more technical context is suggested in this reference to Seaham Pit in the 1920s:

> I was also acquiring a new language. This was 'pitmatic'. It was a mixture of the broadest dialect of Durham and a number of words (often of foreign origin) used exclusively by pitmen when below ground.
>
> (George Hitchin, *Pit-Yacker* (1962))

When J.B. Priestley made his tour of England in 1934, he remarked on 'Pitmatik', in a similarly work (or is it a male?) context:

> The local miners [in Durham] have a curious lingo of their own, which they call 'pitmatik'... It is only used by the pitmen when they are talking among themselves... When the pitmen are exchanging stories of colliery life… they do it in 'pitmatik'...
>
> (J.B. Priestley, *English Journey* (1935), ch.10)

So does the word mean the technical language, the everyday language, or the 'private' language of pitmen? An element of all three, surely. Consider the analysis offered by a Partliamentary Commissioner in the 1840s when faced with the task of interviewing North East pitmen:

> The barriers to our intercourse were formidable. In fact, their numerous mining technicalities, northern provincialisms [i.e.dialect words], peculiar intonation and accents, and rapid and indistinct utterance, rendered it essential for me …to devote myself to the study of these peculiarities ere I could translate and write the evidence.
>
> (*Parliamentary Papers*, 1842 Commissioners Reports, vol.16, p. 514)

A multiple or open definition of Pitmatic may be vague, but the term has proved its usefulness by remaining current, and even today serves as a good shorthand for the dialect of the Great North Coalfield – a dialect which owes much to the mining way of life for its development, even though the pits are no more. Here we will be looking primarily at 'Pitmatic' as technical terms, with an awareness that these were often adapted from pre-industrial or non-industrial usage, and in turn affected the dialect of everyone in the region.

Adaptation from a rural world

The men who moved to work in the collieries of Tyneside and Wearside in the seventeenth and eighteenth centuries were drawn largely from the surrounding countryside. As Heslop (1892–96, p.xvi) puts it: "To these dalesmen [i.e. from Tynedale and Riddesdale] we owe the strong clanship of the colonies of pitmen and keelmen scattered along Tyneside and throughout the colliery districts".

Not surprisingly, they brought with them their particular customs and their language – retaining many features of the Old English of the Anglo-Saxons and the Old Norse of the Vikings. This speech contrasted notably with the more educated, metropolitan manners and English of the citizens of Newcastle. Though the talk of the pitmen and their families might seem novel and strange to city-folk, it was of course the more authentic, traditional speech of the region, and many of the words needed for the new technology of mining were in fact 'rural' words adapted to a new context:

Inbye, outbye – this is reported of directions and fields around a farm, e.g. on Teesside and at Barnard Castle.

Gate – from the Old Norse, meaning a roadway, used underground of main passages.

Goaf – again from Old Norse, meaning the bay of a barn with its wooden supports (and attested in that sense in East Anglia at least), becomes the part of a coal mine where the coal has been removed and only the structure of props holds up the roof. (Though in turn, the void emptied of props and support, ready to 'drop', suggests a further link, with 'gulf'.)

Cavil – to choose the work station by lot – was probably the same process used to allot shares of the olden common field since medieval times: "The most common method of working the meadows was to divide them into strips or 'dales', and these were allocated annually by lot or rotation, or on a more permanent basis" (Baker & Butlin, 1973, p.134).

Braffen – the standard term for a halter round a horse's neck, based on plaited straw, becomes a leather pad for carrying anything on shoulder (Seaham, 1930s).

Daytaleman – is explained thus in the 1820s: "a day labourer, chiefly in husbandry... a man whose labour is...reckoned by the day, not by the week or year. Daytalemen, about coal pits, are those who are not employed in working the coal" (Brockett, Newcastle, 1820s).

Hack – like 'pick' and 'mell' (hammer) were traditional terms for tools, from agriculture as well as from wood and metal working.

Stook – the last remaining section of a pillar of coal is the agricultural word for an upright stack of cut corn left in the field to dry.

Cansh – obstructive stone, was originally a 'step' of rock, sand or other obstacle in a waterway. ("Sha's gitten ov a kansh, i.e. the coble had run ashore on a ridge in the harbour" – Umpleby, Staithes.)

Bogey – "Agricultural. A low, two-wheeled sleigh-cart for carrying hay to the stack without the trouble of pitching. The 'pikes' are drawn on to this cart by a rope, the ends of which are wound round a windlass-roller at the front end of the cart. Also, a square wooden truck on four wheels, for the purpose of removing heavy goods a short distance, called also a 'tram'. Down the pit, a bogey with an iron pin about two feet long, at each of the four corners, to prevent the timber and rails from falling off, would be called a 'horney tram'" (Palgrave, Hetton, 1896).

Cat-band – both an iron band for securing cover of a hatch in a keel and a band on a corf to take a hook (Heslop, N'd, 1880s).

Rammel – Old French ramaille 'branches', source of rammel 'brushwood, rubbish', and in the pit, worthless stone mixing with the coal (Terry Hagan, Wheatley Hill).

Distribution and consistency

Before the term 'Geordie' for Tyneside language was fostered by Scott Dobson in 1969, Pitmatic was the only term available to describe popular industrial speech in the area ('Pit-yack' sems a relatively modern term, ?1950s).

The mobility of population in the North East in the nineteenth century – notably among colliery workers – would lead us to expect a measure of regional consistency in speech. As far as Pitmatic relates to technical terms, there is reasonable unity throughout the Great Northern Coalfield – strikingly so when compared to variants in other coalfields or even in Pennine lead mining.

Contrast with lead mines

The standard word for a lead mine, e.g. in the Pennines, was a 'groove', a pitman 'a groover' – linked to the Old English *grafan* 'to dig'. Wm Hooson's mining dictionary of 1747 (relating to Derbyshire) contains only a few words in common with our coalfield – corf, kibble – the majority of terms being quite alien, e.g. kyles, for 'small wedges' to keep the head on a tool; scrin 'the least or smallest kind of veins', etc.

Kathleen Teward's *Teisdal' en how twas spok'n* (Teesdale, 2003) includes a few terms on lead mining from Newbiggin-in-Teesdale that also contrast with coal mine usage:

Jagger (pony) – a small pony used in the mines [also listed by Hooson].

Jiggers – a moving wooden waterway in mining [later adopted in a coal washery also?].

Bros – a mixture of stone and ore.

Buddle – to wash waste from ore and lead [in a moveable wooden 'box' with water running through it].

A possible origin for 'bord' in coal mining is suggested as follows: "...a 'bord', meaning a gallery, owes its origins to the lead miner. Most Pennines lead seams were near vertical and to reach the ore, boards were wedged above the workings, to provide a platform from which the miners could work. As the exploitation of the seam progressed the next bite at the seam was described as 'the next bord'" (Temple, 1994, pp.11–12).

Nonetheless, it seems fair to conclude that the traditions of the two types of mine had not much in common. Each was a specialist job, in separate zones, with different ways of winning and processing minerals, that had evolved separately.

Equally alien are the terms for Cornish tin mining (from www.cornish-mining.org.uk), e.g.

Gunnis – a narrow linear excavation left where a lode has been worked, most commonly used when open to surface.

Leat – an artificial water-course, built to carry a supply of water to a mine.

Sett – one of a series of stone supports for a tramway, performing the same function as sleepers.

Stope – excavated area produced during the extraction of ore-bearing rock.

– though it has kibble and skip in common with the Northern Coalfield.

Contrast with other coalfields

While there is reasonable consistency in technical terms between coalfields, there is also a marked variation in familiar terms. The following examples are drawn primarily from Harry Tootle's online dictionary (where this aspect of the lexis is best illustrated), with some help from http://www.therhondda.co.uk/ – the North Eastern term is given first:

At bank – abin (Scots).

Bait – bag or bagging (Lancs); snap (Yorks); tommy (Teesside); piece (Scots).

Bank/top of shaft – mine head (Scots).

Banksman – puller-off (Mids).

Cauldron bottom or carving arse (fossil in roof) – "'kettle bottoms' in other coalfields", Sharkey; 'bell' S.Wales.

Bords – panels (S.Wales).

Chocks – clogs (Yorks).

Cow – backstay (Yorks), devil, dog (Lancs).

Creep/heave – squeeze (S.Wales).

Drag (brake) – 'snibble' or 'spragg' (Scots).

Foal or half-marrow – pusher (Somerset) (a small boy who helped the 'twin-boy' or 'carting-boy' to get a loaded 'put' of coal up an incline by pushing from the back).

Gavelock – coopreise (Yorks).

Heap – the colliery area (N.E.) – the colliery waste tip (Lancs, Scots).

Hedgehog (a twist or snarl in a rope) – kank (Mids).

Hewers – pikemen (S.Staffs).

Hoggers – pit drawers (Lancs).

Inbye, outbye – inwan, outwan (Scots).

Jowling – chapping (Scots), knockings (S.Wales).

Keps – fallers (Lancs), cage shuts (Scots).

Kibble – kip (Mids).

Kist (a tool box) – meaning a cabin in the pit (Lancs), a mobile water tank (Scots).

Marra – butty (S.Wales).

Onsetter – knocker (Lancs, Wales).

Pick – mandrill (S.Wales).

Pillar, stook – post (Derbys).

Pneumatic pick – jabber (Lancs).

Putters – hurriers (S.Wales).

Ripping – brushing (Scots).

Stone/spoil (waste rock) – attle (S.Wales).

Sylvester – buller/cronjie (S.Wales).

Token – motty (Lancs, Yorks).

Tram – horned danny (Mids).

Trapper – door boy (Somerset).

Vest, undersark – peeweet (Scots).

Water bottle – jack (S.Wales).

Though the evidence here is selective, it is perhaps enough to assert that as far as terminology is concerned, there was a measure of independence among the various coalfields. This is not surprising considering that commercial mining goes back at least to the seventeenth century in most areas, and that some 300 years of private, local ownership and operation preceded the linking-up of Nationalisation in 1947.

Variation within the Great North Coalfield

There were two pressures for local variation in the Great North Coalfield: firstly the expected variation between different localities with slightly different dialect backgrounds – this aspect was perhaps underlined in the nineteenth century by the local nature of the smaller pits and in the twentieth century by the relatively low mobility of the workforce between pits. A second force was of course the division of the coalfield between various landowners, such as the Earls of Durham, the Londonderrys, the Dean and Chapter of Durham Cathedral, and many smaller owners or lessees of mineral rights, with the result that mining terminology evolved slightly differently from pit to pit. This variation is best illustrated in everyday dialect terms (like synonyms for 'turnip', the divvent/dinnut division, etc.), but even here might not the 'boundaries' be a matter of colliery groupings, and the limiting of 'divvent' reflect the coherence of early collieries on Tyneside? As examples of variation in mining terminology we have:

For a pneumatic pick: windy pick (Dawdon), pompom (Seaham), jigger (Winlaton).

Bumpers (Nth Walbottle) – pullers (S.W.Durham).

Deputy (standard) – puffler (Sacriston).

Goaf – grove [sic] – "a space in a seam from which coal has been taken" (Wade, South Moor 1966); also 'gob' and 'waste'.

Spider (Glebe Colliery) for tram.

Mistress and midgey for an open lamp (putters' terms).

Clanney and chenny (Thornley) for a type of safety lamp.

Malgre these minor variants, Pitmatic, as far as it applies to the technical terminology of the pit, is remarkably consistent throughout the Great North Coalfield; slightly less so if a wider range of everday dialect is considered.

Imported, Invented and Diverging Words

'To mine' (to excavate, to dig) has had many applications beside the winning of coal: building stone, precious stones, mineral ores have been dug for since prehistorics times. The preferred medieval method of mining was to exacavate downwards from the land level and extract material in relatively safe and shallow 'bell pits' – the word 'quarry' is significantly absent from Old English. Mining as tunelling was certainly practised in the Middle Ages, usually in simple horizontal 'adits' into a hillside; yet when it came to putting mineral mining on a commercial footing in sixteenth century England, it was customary to bring over experts from the Continent.

> In 1452 Henry VI brought skilled miners of Saxon origin from Bohemia and Hungary and Edward VI granted mine leases to Germans in Northumberland and Westmorland... Queen Elizabeth in 1562 sent to Germany for miners for sorting, sieving and washing copper ore at a mine near Kendal... She also brought German miners to Derbyshire to introduce better methods...
>
> (Richardson, 1974, p.7)

Admittedly this benefitted metal mining rather than coal, but some technical innovations benefitted all, e.g. the introduction of the use of gunpowder in mining by Germans, here, in 1638 (Richardson, 1974, p.8). He continues "many Saxon words are still used in British mining, such as stope, stull, sump, stamp, trommel..." (p.8).

A few other common words come from non-English sources: 'corf' or 'scope' (basket) from Dutch, 'kibble' (bucket) from German, 'damp' (gas) from German, 'shaft' from Low German *Schacht*, etc.

Other words, as noted above, were adapted from everyday, sometimes specifically agricultural, language. But the developing technology of mining led to the need for new words for new devices. 'Tram' is believed to derive from tram as a beam of wood, part of a wheelbarrow frame; 'rolley' from the verb 'to roll'; 'rope' becomes applied to a steel cable. Other words evolved with the mine itself:

'Hoggers', originally footless stockings (so bits of coal couldn't get stuck in the toes of them) switched to become the flannel drawers most miners chose to work in by the 1900s. Hogger (singular), a pipe or hosepipe, became the word for the pipe conducting compressed air to the 'windy pick' in use at the coalface.

This special or separate development applies also the way some 'standard' English words became used in the North East pits... 'strike' rather than go on strike, 'buzzer' for hooter or siren, 'broken' meaning worked-through rather than damaged, 'dip' for downhill, 'hanger-on' for the onsetter not a mere follower, 'trapper' for trapdoor operator rather than trap operator, 'win' in the sense of gain or access to coal, etc. Such clashes with conventional English are a particular delight.

Impact of modernisation

Since modernisation was introdcued to the pits, during the course of the twentieth century, it might seem a standardisation of vocabulary would follow on. Changes, both as a result of new technology, and by way of discard of the 'old' did occur:

Main passages become 'arterial roadways' (Temple, 1994, p.18).

Take – "the area of coal allotted to a colliery after Nationalisation" (Temple, 1994, pp.19–20).

Surface – than on bank.

Shunters – not putters.

Roof supports – (usually powered) than props.

Hose – than hogger for air pressure pipe.

First shift – than fore shift.

Power-loaders or face men not hewers.

(With thanks to Steve Barnett, Seaham)

> Faceworker – in earlier days, a face worker could be defined as the man who worked at the coalface actually 'hewing' the coal, a 'collier'. With the introduction of the 'National Power Loading Agreement' in 1966 a whole new group of workers came under the definition of 'face workers', e.g. 'machine men', 'strikers', 'rippers', 'back rippers', fitters and electricians, etc.
>
> (Harry Tootle, 1995)

But some of the traditional vocabulary remained stubbornly in place in a changing world: canch for stone next the coal; bait (from the Old Norse for food) for the pitman's meal underground. The prinicpal roadway remained a 'maingate' (from Old Norse 'gate' for a road), the efficiently emptied space behind the coal-cutting operation was still the 'goaf', signals were still 'rapped' up and down the shaft, though sent by electrical button; and so on. Where tradition and the worker's imagination tended to fail was with modern equipment, which was generally known by its brand name, e.g. Dosco (road header), or Dowty prop.

One certain constancy was the pitman's combination of physical toughness and quick practical intelligence, reflected in the need to understand and communicate the complexities of everday work. As enduring has been a sense of humour: ranging from confrontation with the Devil in 'The Pitman's Rant' of the eighteenth century, through terms like 'foal' (for the most junior of putters) and 'cawdpies' (cold pies, i.e. a disappointment, for any accident to the tram), both from the early nineteenth century, to casual inventions like 'tomahawk' for a tommy-hack (a combined hammer-and-chisel tool), from the cowboy-and-injun days of the 1960s; and 'tadger' for an electric drill. The heavy irony of the phrase 'pitee aboot ye', expressing absolutely no sympathy, belongs here too. If it could be a ruthless world, the pit, it was also a brave one; character and language alike have enduring appeal, and our respect.

At large

The apparent conservatism of Pitmatic, as mine talk, surely assisted the survival of dialect in the community at large. Though Pitmatic in the narrower sense is the talk of miners at work, a male dialect in effect, and the preserve of a working pitman, yet the importance of coal mining to the region and the consequent status of the miner was reflected in the status of dialect – articles in dialect were included in most isues of the *Ashington*

Collieries Magazine published between the wars, and in a number of radio programmes in the 1950s.

In terms of word preference and frequency, word survival and loss, word invention, the pitman seems to have taken the lead, and left his special mark on the region's dialect. As a possible example, 'brattice' applied to a screen of canvas and the like, underground, to assist ventilation, from the early days of mining; in the collier's home it became any makeshift partition: "Sometimes in mining areas where the kitchen was accessed directly from the street or backyard a partition or 'bratticing' was erected to give some shelter or privacy to the room" (Davidson, Ashington); "brattish / brattice – a rough wooden or curtained partition to separate a front or back door from living areas, behind which outdoor coats and boots could be kept out of sight" (Gillian Wilkinson, Coundon, 1950s). In other homes it became applied to the storage area under the stairs: "Under the braddish – under the stairs" (Phillips, Cullercoats). The word 'brattice' predates the pits, but its importance there arguably kept it familiar in domestic use. Similarly 'rammel' may have passed through the transformation – 'brushwood', 'pit refuse', 'general rubbish'. Many words common and useful in the pit context – fettle, chum, dunch, marra, tew – surely survived the more securely outside the pits as well.

Other phrases from the pits have permeated common talk (examples from Tom McGee of Sherburn Hill):

"you're gettin yerself ahead of the buzzer" – getting above your station, being forward.

"gan canny ower the greaser," meaning mind how you go. "The greaser in question being a mechanism between the rails that lubricated the tub wheels and if care wasn't taken the tub could derail at this point" (Wheatley Hill).

"tak had" (take hold) as in steady yourself (in the cage) or use the handrail to take care of yourself.

"dropping off at the keps" – nodding, feeling tired. After a shift maybe.

Plus

"just ti thra a sprag in" – a spanner in the works (Darby, Seaham).

(Conversely, 'gob' from the outside world, seems sometimes to have replaced the more antique term 'goaf'.)

A remarkable example of Pitmatic meets Domestic occurs in Thomas Wilson's *Pitman's Pay*, where a celebratory feast is described in terms of a hewer tackling coal (mining terms italicised):

Splash gan the spuins amang the kyell —
Di'el take the hindmost on they *drive* —
Through and through the bowl they *wyell* —
For raisins how they stretch and strive.

> This ower, wi' sharp and shinin' *geer*
> They now begin their *narrow workin'*,
> Whilst others, eager for the beer,
> Are busy the grey hen uncorkin'.
>
> 'Tho' still they're i' *the hyel* a' *hewin'*,
> Before they close the glorious day,
> They *jenkin* a' the *pillars* down,
> And efter tyek the *stooks* away...

When Scott Dobson set about popularising 'Geordie' in the 1970s, it was the phrasing of pitmen he took as his central value, and his writing was more about the pit villages north of the Tyne than Tyneside itself (*"It's not ower far from Blyth and it's handy for Morpeth"*). This reflects a reality we can all appreciate: the economic importance of coal influenced the attitude towards dialect of all the coalfield population, male and female, young and old, so that what we think of as North East dialect today has been largely coloured by the language experience of the coalfield. The mining population acted as a sort of filter, and through them the main features of the dialect – its lexis, grammar, intonation and not least its humour – were developed over recent centuries, to the ultimate gain of all.

Chapter 2: The pit-surface features

A coal mine

The variety of names for a 'mine' reflect the preferences of local industries and national legislators, and evolving fashions of popular parlance.

Increasingly the standard words have become 'mine' and 'miner'. 'To mine' derives from the French verb 'miner' (to dig or excavate), whence the noun 'mine' and the person 'miner'; these were adopted in Middle English, and over the last century or so have gained in popular use to become the standard. The advantage, of course, is that they apply to the extraction of any mineral, not just coal.

Specific to coal, the formal term would be 'colliery', e.g. The Mines & Collieries Act, 1842, and the workmen 'colliers'. 'Colliery' is a formation from 'collier', ultimately from OE cōl, of any burning substance, so 'collier' could also apply to a charcoal burner. However, the term came to seem increasingly old-fashioned, and unions, in the later nineteenth century, usually prefered 'miners' to 'colliers'.

The extinct term 'delf' derives from the OE verb 'delf-an' (to dig), and is noted in the *Oxford English Dictionary (OED)* as "the ordinary name for a quarry in the northern counties". It relates to a time when mines and quarries would be surface excavations, 'dug' from above. Within the dialect period it is noted by Brockett as 'pits out of which iron stone has been dug' and by Heslop as 'small pits'. The following quotation seems to confirm its role in relation to ironstone mines:

> In several parts of the parish of Lanchester I have fequently observed that the surface of the earth is exceedingly irregular, with small pits, which the country people call *delfs*... these places are invariably attended with a statum of iron stone not far from the surface.
>
> (*Archaeologis Aeliana* (1822) vol.1, p.120)

Yet another term is 'groove'. While not impossibly from the ON gróf (a pit), it is in common use only from the seventeenth century and this suggests the influence of the Dutch word 'groeve'. It occurs as standard in the Mendips and the Derbyshire lead mines. Two references to its use in the North East are early, from Stanhope and likely to refer to a lead mine: "one groove work in the Helmeford", 1567; "Robert Rutter bur[ied]. He was hurt in a groove", 1625 (*Raine MS*). It is also reported from Middleton in Teesdale in the twentieth century (Teward, 2003). A lead-miner was thus a 'grover' – "a miner who works in an adit level or a lead mine; greaver (three syllables) in West Tyne" (Heslop, N'd, 1880s); or a 'groveman' (Marske, 1735, *Raine MS*).

And so to the regional standard, 'pit'. In the 1890s Palgrave announced: "Pit. The only word in common talk for a mine. So, a miner is always 'pitman' or 'pittie', and pit dress is 'pit-claes'". Brockett likewise favoured 'pitman', and 'pit crew' is noted by Tootle (1995). 'Pit' descends directly from OE pytt, and is first noted in the combination 'coll-pytt' in a charter of Cnut, 1023 AD, of land in Hannington, Hants (Sawyer, 960). Like 'colliery', 'pit' has fallen into disfavour.

A dismissive term for a smallscale operation is 'tatie pit'. An early nickname for a pitman was 'cranky' (Brockett: "a cant name for a pitman"); more recently, 'pit-yacker'.

Surface features

'Bank' is the common word for the surface level of the pit. In North East dialect 'bank' means hill or incline, but the use here seems to come from the phrase 'at bank' meaning 'up above' or 'on top', in contrast to the shaft bottom ("belaa, belaw – below, or in the pit", Heslop, N'd, 1880s).

Thus: bank – "the top or mouth of a coal pit" (*Bell MS*); "on the banck or surface of the earth" (*Compleat Collier*, 1707, p.37); "aboveground; the surface" (Nicholson, 1888); "the colliery surface near the shaft and at the level from which the cages are loaded and unloaded" (Tootle, 1995); "To 'work at bank' is to do the colliery work above ground" (Palgrave, Hetton, 1896); "...one would usually refer to the immediate top of the shaft as the 'surface', and the place where the tubs were loaded and unloaded as bank. Although it was very rare to hear of anybody having a job 'on the surface'. The more usual expression was that he had a job 'on bank'" (Tony Sharkey).

Some related phrases are:
"are ye gawn to ride t' Bank?" (*Bell MS*)

"the' rapped the cage ter bank" (Hay, Ushaw Moor, C20/1)

– an earlier version seems to have been – "drawn to the top, or *to Day*, as it is their phrase" (*Compleat Collier*, 1707, p.36).

Pithead/heap

A number of terms are used to represent the area at the top of the shaft, as well as 'bank':

pit bank or **pitheap** – "the elevated stage around the top of the winding shaft upon which the tubs or mine-cars were delivered from the cages" (Tootle, 1995).

pithead – "the pithead usually had two stories" (Darby, Seaham).

pit-head – "complex comprising baths, time office, token room and lamp cabin" (Douglass, 1973).

heapstead – "the elevated platform near the shaft above the surface upon which the tubs are landed and run to the screens" (Nicholson, 1888).

(Pit)heap, in turn, comes to apply to the whole colliery at surface level, perhaps because 'heap' can imply a horizontal group as much as vertical pile (compare OE 'on heap' in a crowd). An alternative explanation is that the term became generalised from the expresion the Coal heap (*Compleat Collier*, 1707, p.37), from a time when stocks of coal were piled up near the top of the shaft.

heapstead – "the head gear and buildings around the shaft area" (Temple, 1994, pp.19–20); heapstead – "the entire surface works about a colliery shaft. Including the headgear, loading and screening plant, winding and pumping engines, etc. with their respective buildings" (Tootle, 1995); "heep – mine surface buildings" (Dodd, Tanfield Lea); "as the cage reaches the heap" (Darby, Seaham).

Billy Purvis Recital

> *Just getting to work could be a feat in itself. Before special local terrace housing was built, pitmen lodged where they could, and tramped to work by the straightest route.*
>
> Dist thou knaw, mun, they tuik us afore the magistrates the tother week, mun? Die, thou sees, aw won'er'd what thor magistrator cheps was; Aw was flaid [afraid], it was he [He?]. Smash! Aw thowt, thou sees, he was summat immortal. But when they tuik us there, why, how, he was nowt but a man! Ah, god smash, says Aw tiv him, why thou's nowt but a man! You rascal, says he, what do you mean by going thru people's fields when there's a good lane for you? Injuring people's premises. Od's smash, whe's teld thou that? Aw's warned Jack Hume's been tellin' thou that noo? Never mind who told me... Why didn't you shut the gate after you? Why, mun, how could Aw shut ony body's gates after me, when Aw had twee picks ower yen shouther, an' a greet lump o'white breed an' butter, an' maw clogs an' hoggers [stockings] i' the other hand. How could Aw shut ony body's gates, man? You seem to be a strange sort of person; pray what religion are you? Why, Aw's a pitman!... Aw's warned thou's Mister Magi-strator, noo? What do you mean by that, sir? Why, Aw say, is thou a magistrate, Aw say? To be sure I am, you rascal! What do you take me for? Why, gosh cub, oney haud thee jaw! It's oney a nicknyem thou's gien thysel! Ay, smash a bit else, Aw's sure."
>
> (1816, from Robson, 1875, pp. 55–56)

'Plant' is another useful word for all the buildings, cabins and store areas that comprised the pit – "the machinery and fittings around the colliery" (Tootle, 1995). First noted in 1789, the word reflects a sense of something newly developed or put in place.

The components, according to Harry Tootle's dictionary, include:

banksman's cabin

battery charging station – for charging the batteries, worn at the waist, that powered the individual pitman's cap lamp.

backsmith's shop

cabin – another name for the lamp room on the surface.

fitting shop

joiner's shop – [Man leaving joiners' shop – sawdust all ower the back of his heed – "Why Geordie" says the yardman, "Yer brain's gorra leak, marra!" – thanks to Basil for that].

pump house – a building on the surface, or the place underground, where the main pumps for the colliery are situated.

token cabin – in modern terms, where the board was kept with numbered brass tokens relating to individual pitmen. His token would be issued to the pitman on going underground, to be returned when his shift was over. A quick means of keeping a check on anyone failing to return to bank. ["Token-cabin – an office on the heapstead where the tokens are hung up by the tokenman on their respective nails according to number or name" (Nicholson, 1888)] and **workmen's cabin**.

Michael Dodd (Tanfield Lea) adds:

pypyahd – for storing non-metalic pipes.

stak-yahd – hay store for pit ponies.

timma yahd – in pit.

wy kabin – weigh cabin.

Steve Barnett, re Seaham Colliery:

baths – (with baths attendants).

canteen – (with female under manageress).

control room – centre of communications – manned 24 hours.

medical centre – manned 24 hours.

time office

wages office and staff.

colliery office – here **surveyors**, who occasionally ventured underground… and coal sampler – checked specific gravity of coal.

planned maintenance staff – kept records of all underground machines – e.g. which scheduled for regular maintenance – would hand worksheets to overman.

lamp cabin and lamp cabin men.

Norman Wilson, North Walbottle Colliery:

> The pit yard also had a timber yard, and saw mill, and a system of rail track and sidings.
>
> It had what was called a land-sale, where coal merchants came and filled and weighed their own coal sacks to supply the public. It had a large slag-heap which burned continually; the heap was built up by use of an aerial flight, which was a cable-car system. There was also a small sewage farm.
>
> There was the main office, powder cabin well away in the timberyard, pithead baths, medical centre, canteen, lamp cabin, time office, weigh bridge, plumbers' shop, cutters' repair shop, electric shop, fitting shop, choppy house, joiners' shop, stores, engine sheds, blacksmith's shop and what we called the fire-holes – this was a shed along the end of the Lancashire boilers where the stoking was done.

In other words, there could be as many different structures or offices as there was any need for. Within the larger structures, there could be functional rooms, e.g. the locker room, where men preparing for work left their outdoor clothing. It was said that anyone turning up drunk for their shift would be hoisted on top of the lockers to sleep it off (or fall off!).

An account of Dawdon

Here is a description of the lay-out and working of Dawdon Colliery:

> Nearest the gate were the offices – they housed the Manager's Office and Manager's Clerk's – he protected the Manager from pesky callers, and would be a man, not a woman. Also the Under-Manager's. They all concentrated on organising underground work, that is, the production process. Also there would be a Training Officer alias Personnel Officer, the Draughtsman's Office and Administrator's Office (he was in charge over the office staff), the Surface Superintendent (an Under-Manager approaching retirement). On another floor would be the Head Engineer (or Mechanic) and the Head Electrician – they had specialist responsibilities. In fact, quite a lot of Capital Letters in that area.
>
> Further in were the Baths – there would be a Bath Superintendent and two helpers per shift (a Boilerman and a Bath Attendant – their job would be to clean the baths, guard the lockers, and so on).
>
> Next the Time Office, with the Head Timekeeper and assistants (called time clerks). The same office would house the Head of Wages and his staff. Mechanics and surface workers would clock on and off there, and for the miners, that was where tokens were handed out and collected. So there were racks of cards. But the tokens were kept on one long board, for speed of access – the men would come and pick off their two tokens (identical by number but of different materials, say brassy and silvery). They would hand one in as they went down, and the other when they came up. Then the men went to the lamp cabin to pick up their battery cap lamps – they picked out their own numbered lamp and self-rescuer

(a box to clip on the belt, with a filter that could help you breathe for say 20 minutes). Also there were oil lamps for a Deputy (it was his job to test for gas as he went round).

Next was the Powder Cabin – there some of the men would collected the dets (detonators); the explosives would be sent in separately in a special wagon (painted red) when there was some special task such as driving roadways.

Then the Mechanics' Planned Maintenance Office, where each mechanic would visit an Assistant Engineer to get their instructions for the shift – like what district or face they were needed on. And the Deputies' Room (or 'betting shop' – on account of all the internal telephones in their alcoves). This was where they maintained contact between bank and underground. Any small jobs or equipment needed could be phoned up to here at shift changeover. Then you would reach the tunnel to the shaft. There the miner would be searched for matches, go into the cage and ride to the bottom of the shaft...

Then there were the workshops. At Dawdon these were the Pipe-Fitters' Cabin (2 dozen men in all, spread out to work through the pit) – they looked after the underground water pipes – pumping water out, bringing clean water in for cooling the coal-cutting machines and the like. There was the Dowty Shop – these were surface-based men who repaired the Dowty props (hand-operated hydraulic props, like jacks). And a Painters' Shop – they produced all manner of DON'T notices, and repaired windows, and so on. The Joiners' Shop was very important – there was a sawyer's room as well – there they cut two-foot by 6-inch chocks into six inch wedges (the chocks were a convenient size to start from). Also they would produce 'mouse-trap' doors (the airlock sort), cupboards, tables, shuttering for concrete, and anything.

Wooden props came straight into the pit via the stockyard. Also there were men working on maintenance ('shaftsmen') and blacksmiths ('cagesmiths') – together they looked after the cage and shaft. 'Buntings' were timber guides for the cage. There would be a fitter, too, to look after the windy-power gates (pneumatic ones, that is), the wheels and ropes (wires). Them that specialised in wire ropes were called the blackhand gang.

There was a Blacksmith's Shop where they would straighten things that got mangled (not rails, though, they were just replaced) – and do all kinds of repairs. And make all manner hand-made items for the pit (and garden) – e.g. lifting chains for bank and underground...

There was a bricklaying squad. They could build walls underground if it was needed, and do work on building maintenance on bank. But generally a rough sort of work, nothing fancy. The Mechanics' (or Engineers') Shop was the largest of all. They looked after maintenance on bank and underground and included plumbers, fitters, etc. It covered all the machines from coal-cutters to canteen machines. They would remove gear-boxes and parts for repair, like drive-belts and that. All new machinery had to be dismantled and packed to be sent underground where it was re-assembled.

There was a welding shop: they prefabricated pipes, and chutes for where the coal changed from one conveyor belt to another, underground; and repairs – but if possible the damage would be brought to bank and repaired there.

There was a Compressor House – that was serviced from the Engineers' Shop. It held three compressors, one working, one standing-by, and one being maintained. This provided the power for the cages, for the coal-cutting machines, the windy-picks. There would be three men on 8-hour shifts, for one compressor had to be constantly in action. They kept the place polished and shiny! The compressors were powered in turn by electricity, though before 1960 the power was steam from coal furnaces ('fire-holes'). Also of course the power for the big fans that kept the air in circulation came from here.

The Stockyard was for timber (props, chocks, inch packing material for use with props), and wire-mesh, and any stores for underground. They moved them by forklift. The Engineering Stockyard used an overhead crane – here there was heavier gear: railway lines, wire meshing, cable, rolls of belting, all that sort. It had its own railway direct to the shaft.

And Loco Sheds: here were the diesel loco's for surface haulage like hauling coal wagons… Lastly there was the Granary ('choppy-house') – that was where the ponies' food was kept once, and the oats ground up ready for them, but now it's used by bricklayers. There would have been a Saddlers' Department too, but all that ended in the 1960s with electrification. And there was a canteen, and a really first class medical centre, them next to the baths. The water used to cool the compressors was led into a cooling pool – that was also available as a swimming-pool.

(Trevor Charlton, Dawdon)

Transcript of document placed in small tin in the fabric of the Engine House at Dawdon Colliery in 1935 and recovered upon its demolition

December 1935

This engine house was completed in november 1935. We are told that it will be in use for about 60 years. We are putting this note on the quarrels hoping it will be found and be of great interest to the finder. The following are the names of the persons mostly concerned with this work. Mr. F. Wilson (Manager), Mr. Jobling (Undermanager), Jack Winter (Master Shifter), Mr Wainwright (Engineer). W. Cooper, R. Johnson, J. Robinson, J. Osmond, G. Dunn were the stonemen. Jacob Shaw (Shotfire Examiner), R. Davidson and J. Thompson (Bricklayers), A. Shepherd., A. Darwin (Labourers).

This eng[in]e is now about 6 year[s] old and has been in use at 1st. north. E.L.M. the cable from 1st. North old engine house to the new engine house was brought in bye on 6 reels to the bottom of the E.L.M. bank, then reeled off on to tubs and taken into position by the endless haulage. This is the first time that reels have been brought in bye at this colliery.

Other items of interest. Dawdon colliery is producing about 3500 tons per day at present. The new cleaning plant has been erected nearly 2 years. The C.A.I.[L] (coal bye-product plant) in Dene House Road, Seaham Harbour, has just started [production] on a small scale. The old houses at the north side of the town have just been demolished. The M.F.G.B. are trying for a rise of 2/- a day for adult miners. A general election is just over and E. Shinwell [Labour] has defeated J. Ramsay Mcdonald [Nat Labour] by over 2000[0] votes in this division. Wages. There is 65% on the base rates. Stonemen are averaging about 9/- per day. Subsistance wage is 6/6^{d}. Minimum for adult coal Hewers about 7/- per day. All these include per centage.

(December 4, 1935)

Notes:

Quarrels – channels for wiring, etc. / ?tiles

E.L.M. – East Low Main

C.A.I.L. – In 1935 "A large industrial plant for the production of oil and spirit from coal opened near [Vane Temoest]". (McNee)

M.F.G.B. – Miners Federation Of Great Britain

Percentage – Bonus

As many as the buildings and offices were the many different workers. The list starts with examples from Dodd (Tanfield Lea, C20/2):

lektrishun – "electrician".

mekanik – "colliery craftsman".

pikk shahpna – "smith skilled in tempering steel".

pypman – "instals and extends pipes in mine".

stawkeepa – "in charge of mining supplies".

undastrappa – "underling".

wagin filla – [surface worker].

Plus:

electricians – "under separate surface foreman" (Barnett, Seaham).

fitters – "to deal with anything mechanical" (Barnett, Seaham).

runnin' fitter – "a fitter's deputy" (Wilson, G'head, 1820s).

saddler – "originally asociated with the gallowas' reins and such… became the provider to knee pads and battery pouches and anything else made of canvas or conveyor belting" (Johnson, Dawdon).

wagonway-man – "a general handyman, an experienced miner, who had a vague authority over the boys in his district" (Hitchin, 1962 p.65); "in Durham the 'doggie' was the wagonwayman who repaired and looked after the haulage districts and roads; he was not really an official but more like the chargehand in the factory system. His name I believe came from the dog nails which he used in repairing the roads" (Douglass, 1973).

and even the humble yardman:

> It was my name for a man that sweeps up and keeps the yard tidy. When coming off shift the hewers used to wind up (josh) the yard man (whose wages I believe was dependent on the tonnage hewn by the coalface men) indicating they had not taken much coal out that day and his wages therefore would be less.
>
> (Ivor Lee, Sunny Brow, circa 1910–25)

In the nineteenth century, surface workers "had very low status in mining communities" (Benson, 1989, p.28), perhaps because "working at the pithead was undramatic" (p.29). Simple tasks like picking stone from coal was left to "boys and girls, women, craftsmen and 'knocked-up' hewers" (p.28). Nonetheless they constituted a fifth of a pit's workforce in the late nineteenth century, and as longwall working was introduced there was an increasing role for the 'mechanic' and craftsman underground (*ibid.*, pp.28–29)

Important among surface workers would always be the blacksmith, who had his own forge, and much work to undertake for the pit (and for friends):

> My recollection …is that the blacksmiths did not shoe the ponies. That was done by the horsekeepers. The blacksmiths played a major role in the operation of a colliery inasmuch as they built, repaired and maintained most of the steel structures used on the surface and underground and they also had prime resonsibility for the statutory periodical recapping of the winding ropes.
>
> (Tony Sharkey)

As to women working in the pits, this was recorded in Gateshead in 1765, but they were no longer employed to work underground after about 1780 (Sir Timothy Eden, *Durham*, London, 1952, vol.2, p.384). Women were legally excluded from work underground in 1842 (Benson, 1989, p.31). The increasing sense of the pit as a male preserve flourished thereafter, though a welcome role for women was preserved in pit office work and (latterly) in the canteen. Surface work accordingly was undertaken by older workers – shifters (paid by shift) or:

daytal men – (paid by daily tally) – "daytal workers – lower grade of pit workers, but not casual employees" (Barnett, Seaham); "'datal' workers…under the old grade system was the lowest and worst paid class of work, except for surface work" (Douglass, 1973).

– and their lot prior to the pensions system of the twentieth century was not enviable.

Song 10: "Aw'm a poor aud shifter noo"
(Tune: "What gud can sweerin' de?")

At nearly aal things i' maw time,	
Aw think Aw've had a try,	
Frae what they craft aboot the shaft,	From…work at
Te what they de inbye.	do in the interior
Aw've worked upon the engine way,	powered route for tubs
Aw've even worn the blue;	?served in the militia
But, O! these things ar' past maw day,	
Aw'm a poor aud shifter noo.	part-time worker
Ay, man, these things ar' past maw day,	
Aw'm a poor aud shifter noo.	
As men can tell that sunk wi' me	sunk new pit-shafts
When Aw wiz i' maw prime,	
Thor wiz few that wor claim'd te be	
Maw equal at the time.	
Or when Aw had te drive a drift,	tunnel esp. in stone
Ne man cud did mair true;	could do it
But Aw've nearly work'd maw final shift --	
Aw'm a poor aud shifter noo.	
But Aw've nearly work'd maw final shift –	
Aw'm a poor aud shifter noo.	

Aw've gien the maisters soond advice	given...owners
When things war gannin' astray:	were going
At kanches work'd at bargan price,	stone obstructions...under tender
Myed mair than they wad pay.	made more
Aw've sketch'd thor plans for engin' plains,	
Aw've put their hitches throo;	overcome dislocations of strata
An' thus they've paid me for may pains –	
Aw'm a poor aud shifter noo!	
Ay, thus they've paid me for may pains –	
Aw'm a poor aud shifter noo!	
Thor shafts Aw've buntin'd, lined thor ways,	lined with wood
When nyen cud did but me:	none could do it
Aw've deun maw best throo aal maw days	done
Te work as brave men de.	
Te keep thor main air courses reet,	right
Aw've travell'd aud and new:	old and new sectors of the mine
But what care they for that the neet?	tonight
Aw'm a poor aud shifter noo!	
Ay, what care they for that the neet? –	
Aw'm a poor aud shifter noo!	
What mortal man that knew me young,	
Dreamt Aw wad ivor beer	would ever put up with
The maistor shifter's brazint tongue,	brazen/rude
Or lift his useless [gear]?	equipment
Wad work at clarty dams or owt	mucky barriers...anything
Thit met the flonky's view?	flunkey/arrogant servant
But a worn-out pitman stands for nowt –	
Aw'm a poor aud shifter noo!	

Ay, a worn-out pitman stands for nowt –
Aw'm a poor aud shifter noo!

Man's weel been liken'd <u>tiv</u> a leaf, — to
That bloomin' bears the blast;
Till, wither'd, <u>broon</u> wi' care an' grief, — brown
He's trodden doon at last.
But till that last, maw heart's enthrall'd,
Aw'll still be brave an' true;
For eternal <u>lowse</u> 'ill seun be call'd – — release
Aw'm a poor aud shifter noo!
Ay, eternal lowse'll seun be call'd –
Aw'm a poor aud shifter noo!

(Alexander Barrass)

The washery

Washing refers to "coal dressing or coal cleaning in the widest sense" (*HRCM*, ch.14). Basically, two processes are involved. Firstly, the separation of coal and stone and secondly, the grading of coal by sizes. Picking out stone was originally done by hand, and called waling. This could be done on a revolving picking table, or later a moving canvas belt. More recently, rollers were brought in, to crush large coals, and break down lumps that comprised both shale and coal.

An innovation from about 1800 was grading the coal by passing it over screens with bars spaced at about a half inch apart. This was necessary as there was no market for very small sized coal before the mid nineteenth century. While the screen was immobile, picking and grading could be combined, but the introduction of a jigging screen in the mid nineteenth century required the separation of the processes.

Typical of the twentieth century was a purpose-built washery, a process borrowed from the metal ore industry. Because of varying specific gravity, coal will tend to float while heavier shale will settle. The standard became a fixed (adjustable) screen combined with water in motion. The bits of shale and other rock would settle to the base of the tank to be cleaned out and dumped; purer water above this could be recycled. The merchandable coal would be stored on site to be distributed by rail or road (in earlier times by ship from the Tyne and the Wear to London).

Definitions:

Baum washer or **Baum jig** – a system for cleaning 'run of the mine' coal invented by Baum in 1892. "The coal was separated from the dirt by immersing it in water where the lighter coal rose and heavier shale and stone would sink" (Tootle 1995).

discard – "the non-coal element" (Johnson, Dawdon).

jigger – "shaking trough for cleaning coal" (Roxborough, SWDm).

to pick – to separate out: "picking coal" (Tootle, 1995).

pikin belts – "for removing stones from coal" (Dodd, Tanfield Lea, C20/2).

raised and weighed (usually weekly) – "the total mine output" (Johnson, Dawdon).

screening – "separation at bank of large and small coals by means of a grid iron frame, 3/8 to 3/4 in. width" (Colls, 1987).

screens – "moving belts at bank from which coal was sorted by hand" (Trelogan, New Herrington, C20/mid).

wail – to sort: "God whaling the tatties"– applied to thunder, 'Northumbrian Words & Ways' comp. Jean Crocker [und.] p.31, re Newham.

wailer –"a person employed on the pit heap at the mouth of the pit to wail or pick out the **stones** and **brasses** [pyrites] from out of amongst the coals" (*Bell MS*); "waila – cleaning coal in picking belts" (Dodd, Tanfield Lea, C20/2).

washery – "the surface plant where the coal is separated from stone and graded" (Temple, 1994, pp.19–20).

> The Washeries were next – properly the CPP (Coal Preparation Plant). It actually started with an Inspection House, a sort of 'dry-cleaning' process – to get some of the stone and dust out of the coal – the dust could be put to use if needed. Then the raw coal was fed by a belt uphill to the top of the washery, washed, screened and de-watered, then graded and loaded into wagons.
>
> (Trevor Charlton, Dawdon)

> Washery – manned by daytal workers – 1 washery foreman per shift, responsible to daytime Washery Manager. The washery a scene from Dante's Inferno. Washer was a centrifuge and shaker belts to separate shale and slurry…
>
> (Steve Barnett, Seaham Pit)

> When the tubs came to the surface, they went to the screens under their own power on a gentle gradient; first they went to the weigh-cabin. Each tub carried a token to identify the fillers - this was recorded along with the weight. Tubs would not be paid for if they contained too much stone. From the weigh cabin the tubs went into the tipplers. A tippler was a device which revolved the tub 360 degrees sideways emptying the coal onto what was known as a jigger. The jigger was basically a metal chute with a grid in it and it jigged back and forth (hence the name) so the dust and small

coal went through the grid and onto the appropriate belt; the rest went on a belt where the stones were picked out. It then dropped into 20 ton coal wagons (trucks). The men involved in stone picking were the elderly coming up to reirement, school leavers or perhaps those with work-related injuries or disease.

From the tipplers the tubs ran to the lowest point on the gradient where boys under supervision would remove the tokens; the tubs then went onto the creeper. The creeper was in effect a large chain with hooks on which caught hold of the tub axles and hauled them up a steep incline to put them back on the gravity system, so they could run away back to the shaft.

(Norman Wilson, North Walbottle Pit)

Th' Screenor's Dream

A letter in the Evening Chronicle *signed 'Screener', Hawthorn Road, Ashington, complained of his lot under Nationalisation, especially in comparison to the advantages Deputy Overman had received…*

Aa dreamt aa wus a depputty, an' haad a canny flat,
An' went t' work just when aa liked, an' wore a shiney hat;
An' tyuck a lad alang w' me, t' carry me aix an' saaw
An ' haad sum speshul knee-caps myed becaase th' place wis laaw. — low

Aa lit me pipe w' aad pund notes, an' hoyed away th' dottle, — tobacco residue
An' bowt meesel a bran' new car, an' let 'or oot full throttle;
Aa travilled far for hallidays, went sumtimes ower th' sea,
Oh! Whaat a time w' haad in France, th' Wife, an' Bairns, an' me.

Aa bowt a television, an' aa ask the nieghbours in,
Aa gae me radio-gram away for it myed such a din; — gave
Aa gan t' see Newcastle play, noow that aa've got a seat,
An' pity all th' poor lads stannin' theor upon thor feet.

Aa divvent need t' scrimp an' syev, w' feor an' apprehenshun, — save
For when aa'm aad an' finish work, aa getta greit big penshun; — old

Aa smiled becaase aa haad nee cares, neebody felt soreenor,
But when the 'larm went OFF – aa woke, aye – just a humble screenor.

(Robert Straughan, February 1953)

Distribution

Here we deal only briefly with the passage of coal after it has left the collieries.

Transport was originally cheaper and more efficient by river (the Tyne, the Wear) to a port (Newcastle, Sunderland), by water or later by railway. As colliers – the ships that carried coal to London and abroad – could not moor far up-river, it was necessary to transfer the coal out to the ships, hence **keelmen** – "men who moved coal from the staith to the ships in flat-bottomed vessels called keels" (Colls, 1987). It is hoped to deal more fully with this theme in the third book in this series – on coastal boats and fishing.

The erection of better staithes, that could take coal wagons out from the shore, so that coal could be dropped directly into ships' holds, led to the redundancy of many keelmen by the mid nineteenth century:

gears – "upright baulks or joists of wood put together in frame work on the shores of the River Tyne along the top of which lays the waggon way for the waggons to pass to deliver coals to vessels laying for loading. The whole Gears at one loading place is called a Staith" (*Bell MS*).

staith – "riverside place for transferring coal from tubs to keels, and later directly into ships: see keelmen" (Colls, 1987); "steeth – a coal drop for keels or ships" (Robson, 1849); "staith – often pronounced steeth or steith, a place to lay up and to load coals at... The word occurs in a demise from the Prior of Tynemouth, AD 1338" (Brockett, Newc, 1820s) [OE staeth, waterside].

Transport by sea remained economic in a few cases, e.g. at Wearmouth Colliery, where coal was loaded straight onto ships bound for South Thames Gas Board.

Railways initially linked more collieries with more ports (e.g. Hartlepool, Blyth). Bulk moving by British Rail was a feature of the second half of the twentieth century:

lohkoh – locomotive esp. steam (Dodd, Tanfield Lea).

tanky engine – "a smal(ish) steam locomotive used for moving the trucks on the colliery sidings. The driver was assisted in this work by one or more 'shunters'" (Tony Sharkey); "a slow tanky driver", *Ashington Col Mag*, February, 1935 [possible source of the phrase 'tanking along'].

waggon way – "a rail way on which the coals are conveyed from the Pits in waggons to the staiths on the Tyne, Wear, and Blyth" (*Bell MS*); "wagon-way – the railway upon which the coals are taken away from the screens.

The rolley-way is also called the wagon-way" (Nicholson, 1888).

Lorries featured in local deliveries:

Following the Bunker Round

Most miners, having worked a hard shift at the pit, were prepared to pay to have the [concessionary] coal put in. It was a job which had to be done properly – stones separated from the coal and the pavement swept clean – if you were to escape the wrath of the overseer – the miner's wife!

When I was a young lad in nineteen forty four,
My father was in foreign lands – a soldier in the war.
A soldier's pay was lowly – a shilling for a day,
And so I joined the other kids to earn a little pay.

Chorus:
We were standing on the corner just waiting for the sound,
Which meant money for a miner's lad – following the bunker round.   coal-lorry

It rumbled round the back streets pursued by pounding feet,
Of kids who needed sixpence to give themselves a treat.
The coalmen hit the sideboards, the air was filled with dust,   flaps
A job was there awaiting for the boy who could be first…

The race began in earnest, a ticket was the aim,   delivery note
With outstretched hand I made a grab, and thus I made my claim.
"Please missus, put your load in, I'll make a real good job,
And sweep and broom around the yard, and make it worth a bob."…

The coal-house hetch was opened, 'twas nigh on five feet high,
And fifteen hundredweight of coal from the shull did fly.   shovel

Verse	Gloss
The wife came out to see me and check the job was done,	woman
The shilling in my pocket would give a night of fun....	
I never saw the picture – I slept the whole show through,	
And in the morning I was there to join the motley crew.	
Who were standing on the corner just waiting for the sound,	
Which meant money for a miner's lad – following the bunker round....	

(Jim Moreland, *Just One Man*, Durham, 1980)

(The astute housewife would make sure to count the empty coal sacks after the delivery was completed – "the reputation of coalmen was similar to highwaymen!", Johnson, Dawdon.)

This next short extract comes from a poem on St Cuthbert's Fair at Durham, dating from the end of the sixteenth century. As the folk assemble in Durham City, one of the experiences they encounter is the 'cry' of coal-sellers:

Verse	Gloss
In Sylver Strete	
as I came bye,	
we hard colyares crye:	heard colliers
"By coles, by!	buy
By coles, by!... "	
Frome Brandan More	Brandon Moor
& Ranton also	Rainton
frome Feryfurth	?Ferryhill
& eke Brasede	Brasside
& thes are of Fendon,	Findon
a lytell her bysyde;	nearby
"pene fardynd;	penny farthing
masteres, ye pay no lese,	will pay no less
Ye pay no les!"	
They are raveris	robbers
rych & of great plenty.	

Such local scale distribution was called landsale – "Coals sold to carters at the colliery for direct delivery" (Tootle, 1995); "a land-sale, where coal merchants came and filled and weighed their own coal sacks to supply the public" (Wilson, Walbottle).

Spoil

The spoil or waste material would be stored locally in the nineteenth century – hence the spoil tips around Murton, not landscaped and grassed until the 1990s.

Definitions:

stohn heep – "surface deposit" (Dodd, Tanfield Lea, C20/2).

deeds [deads] – "colliery waste tipped on the 'spoil bank'" (Tootle, 1995, as NE).

fiery heap – "a colliery waste heap, which has caught fire by 'spontaneous combustion'" (Tootle, 1995).

> As for the coal dust, as carbonaceous as the other coal, and a ninth part of all that comes above the ground, it is woeful to see what becomes of it. A little of it is indeed sold to glasshouses, but if anyone will ascend a little eminence at night and look around him, he will see bright red fires in several directions pointing out to him the destruction that is going on.... By the burning of these heaps is formed slag, which is drawn off for the common roads in the country, and is also sent down the shafts to repair the horse roads in the pits.
>
> (*PP*, 1842, CR xvi, p.147)

> **Round Murton**
>
> On the outskirts of the colliery away from the houses a huge heap of discarded stone and shale and other unwanted rocks had accumulated over the years to spread and grow in height. From the top of this heap one could look down upon the houses and the mine below, or across the slopes. It was an unsightly area with a kind of harsh attraction, where colours of reds and browns in the rocks were added to by the wild growth of rose bay willow herb. Any grass which grew was coarse and knife edged. Boys were forbidden to play here as deep below the surface interior burning could suddenly burst out, and gasses poisonous and sulphurous could be emitted. It was to this forbidden area which Uncle John came in search of a kind of half burnt fuel, to be found by digging into the depths of the heap...
>
> I persuaded him to take me with him... We crossed the railway line and began the climb up the heap, to find on the top that some men had been there at dawn. Uncle John selected a place which gave promise and with his pick and shovel explored under the surface. The loose material had to be sieved and any likely pieces picked by hand to be placed in the hessian bags we had brought. It was slow patient work with varying results. A lucky strike meant that we could dig on to fill the bags, then while I hauled them back home, John would carry on digging.
>
> (F.N. Platts, *Canny Man*, pp.106–7)

The older spoil heaps were attractive places to go gleaning coal during strikes, with varying success:

> The 1972 coal miners' strike was a fun time. It was the first time that our moderate union had taken positive action, so it was more of an adventure than industrial action. The only real hardship that we endured through the entire stoppage was the need to supply heating material for the home fires. The wooded areas around Seaham provided ample dead wood for everyone. I have never seen so many men walking around with bandages on their left hand. The skills they purported to have, with regard to using a bow saw on the tree branches, were not all that they believed them to be. The strike definitely helped to clean up the wooded area of the district.
>
> Keith Adamson had found a hidden supply of coal fines (coal dust), on the South Hetton railway embankment. One o'clock in the morning saw, us up the fields with our bicycles, and six empty sacks. Having filled three sacks each, we loaded them onto our chosen mode of transportation, and (two sacks through the crossbar, one on top) pushed them home. After emptying the sacks of coal dust into the fuel-bunker, I went to bed a happy man. The following morning, after lighting the fire, I put a shovel full of my ill-gotten gains on the glowing embers in the hearth, and the fire was immediately extinguished. On further examination of my spoils I discovered that what I thought was coal was actually black soil!
>
> It's an ill wind that blows no one any good. The following year, some of the best onions I have ever grown, flourished in that medium of black gold.
>
> (Tom Moreland)

The beach in turn became an accepted place to hunt for coal, either tiny pieces brought down as spoil, or perhaps pieces shed in the process of loading colliers and their setting off…

> Along the coast road between Sunderland and Seaham Harbour we came upon quite a number of men riding or wheeling bicycles loaded with two or three small sacks of coal. I heard afterwards that these men descend very steep and dangerous cliffs near Seaham Harbour and pick up coal from the shore. They were going to Sunderland to sell the coal. Those people who still believe that the working folk of this country live in an enervating atmosphere of free bread and circuses might like to try this coal-picking for a day or two, just to discover if it is their idea of fun.
>
> (J.B. Priestley, *English Journey*, 1935, ch. 10)

With automation of production, especially from the 1950s on, the quantity of spoil was too great to be accommodated onsite, and because of the washing process could take a semi-liquid form. This would go to a settling tank, where the sludge accumulated: "in many cases it is found that the calorific value of the sludge is less than the heat required to dry it" (*HRCM*, ch.14) – in other words, it was not worth recycling. Instead, in East Durham, it was pumped directly into the sea, or dumped on the beaches along the coast, notably the Chemical and Blast beaches near Seaham, and at Easington; while special ramps of spoil (now eroded) gave lorries access to the beach level.

Alternatively: there could be an aerial ropeway. "An overhead system for transporting coal or colliery waste. The system consists of buckets or carriers running along overhead cables or steel ropes supported on towers..." (Tootle, 1995). The emplacements for such an aerial ropeway can be seen on the coast near Easington; the working apparatus featured memorably in the film *Get Carter* (1971). (An aerial ropeway was known in Byers Green as an 'aerial flight' (Tony Sharkey)).

> To give a bit more detail: the coal would drop into a V-shaped wash-box – stone and shale would sink. Then various grids would separate the coal onto special elevators and there would be de-watering screens and classifying screens. The waste water that was left would be re-cycled, you could recover small industrial coal from that and all. The coal meanwhile would go straight into wagons ready for dispatch, or sometimes be diverted to a stockpile. Slurry went directly by pipe into the sea; or was put in settling tanks; when the clarified water was drained off the top, then once a week the residue would be washed down the pipe into the sea. Shale was put in a wagon and tipped over onto the beach.
>
> (Trevor Charlton, Dawdon)

> Originally shale loaded on red wagons – by rail to cliff edge and tipped. Coal via hoppers to trucks – a gang of lads ('shunters') would hand-shunt wagons into sets. They lived in 'Dilly' (old brake van). Loco crew and driver would pick up set (shale or coal) – to weighbridge – weighman (a white collar worker) checked full weights – tare-man checked weight of returning empties. The tare was the unladen weight of wagon. Sets of coal trucks shunted into sidings at the 'Polka', waiting till 'the man' picked them up. 'The man' was a BR loco – so-called as fully-grown size compared to colliery engines. Thus: "Bloody hell, there's a man in!" – exclamation on seeing BR loco ahead on same track. Shale went by separate lines to the harbour.
>
> (Steve Barnett, Seaham Pit)

Chapter 3: The shaft

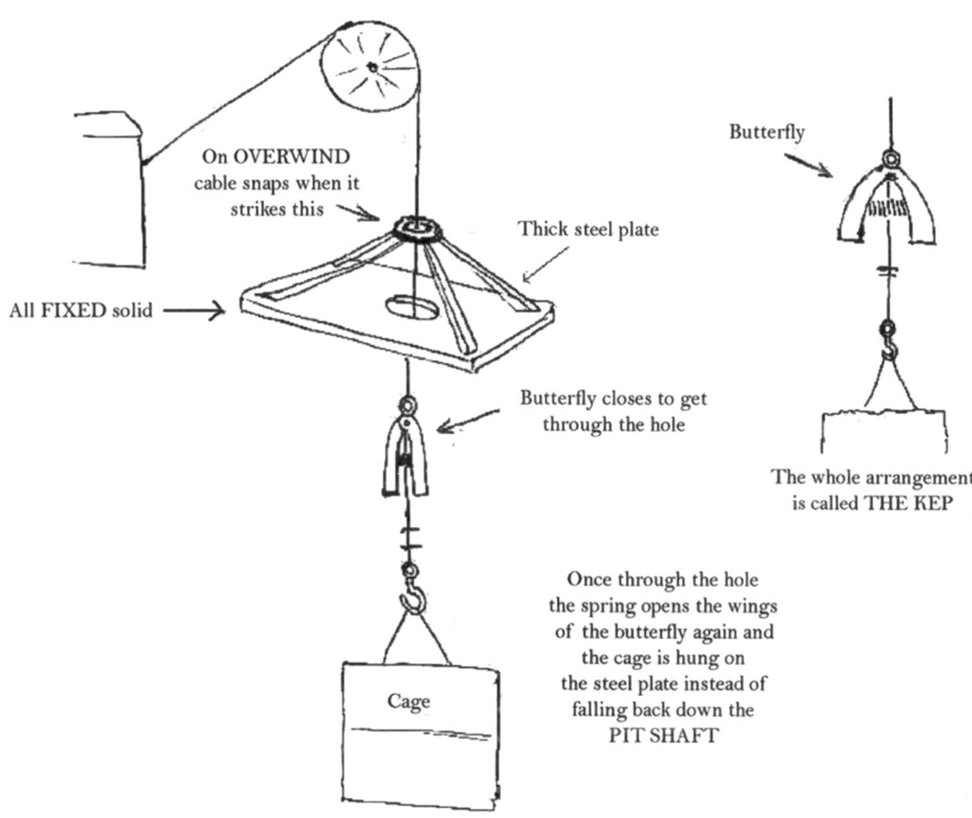
On OVERWIND
cable snaps when it
strikes this
Thick steel plate
All FIXED solid
Butterfly closes to get
through the hole
Once through the hole
the spring opens the wings
of the butterfly again and
the cage is hung on
the steel plate instead of
falling back down the
PIT SHAFT
Cage
Butterfly
The whole arrangement
is called THE KEP

Sinking the shaft

Medieval bell pits were excavated from the surface to a depth of some 25 feet. As the name implies the working widened at the bottom, within the limits of what was practical and safe. Examples at Hexham were sunk 8–10 yards apart, leaving a pillar of coal between each pit. Horizontal adits were also driven into a hillside to reach coal. In the case of such 'hill mines' tunnels known as watergates could be driven to provide horizontal drainage (Freese, 2005, p.54).

The standard method of accessing deeper level coal in the seventeenth century and later was via a vertical shaft. The word shaft in this sense is believed to come from Low German *Schacht*, and the techniques involved derived from earlier mining experience in Germany, Belgium, Bohemia, etc.

There were two basic challenges when sinking – to shore up the sides of the shaft while excavating; and to overcome the excess water feeding into the shaft as excavation reached water-bearing sands and similar pervious layers.

Supporting the walls of a shaft was achieved by a wooden lining of buntins; brick might be used where no natural hard rock formed the permanent wall. In the seventeenth century shafts were square at the surface and lined with closely fitted staves of fir or oak (hence the word tubbing), then changed to octagonal at a lower level.

> For framing back our Shaft Feeders [intruding water], we make use of Wood, but chiefly *Firr*, because it being a soft sort of, or spungy Wood, we think it swells with the Water lying against it, and wedges best by reason of its yielding Quality of Softness, so that the least Thread, or Leak of Water, which may proceed from the least Chinks, or openess of the Wood, are best stop'd, and wedged back by Firr Timber.
>
> (*Compleat Collier*, 1707, p.26)

Where the shaft went below the water table, and where it crossed any water-bearing strata an impervious lining was needed. Intense pumping would be needed until effective tubbing was in place. Sometimes an auxiliary shaft was dug for the express purpose of draining the main shaft and pumping the water out during construction. An 'endless chain' of buckets worked by a 'horse gin' on the surface was a standard method of raising water during sinking.

> And now as to Drawing of Water, we generally Draw it by Tubs or Buckets... if the Pit be Sunk more than thirty Fathom, then we use the Horse Engine, which Engine being wrought with one or two Horses at a time, as the Water requires, serves also, after we have Coaled the Pit, to draw up the Wrought Coals.
>
> (*Compleat Collier*, 1707, p.28)

The maximum width of a shaft was then 6 foot across; the maximum depth (by about 1700) 300–400 feet. In the nineteenth century iron rings were used as tubbing (e.g. at Wallsend, 1762 and Percy Main, 1790), later reinforced concete. (Other notable pits from this time were Walker, 1762; Hebburn, 1792–4; early deeper level pits were Monkwearmouth, 1831; Haswell, 1835; Murton, 1838; Shotton, 1841; Castle Eden, 1842 and Trimdon, 1843.)

Murton proved a difficult sinking, begun 1837 – "in addition to passing through a considrable thickness of magnesium limestone full of waterbearing fissures and 417ft thick, a sand bed occurred at the base of this formation 28 ft thick; the total feeders of water per minute at one time amounted to 9,306 gallons, and this water was dealt with by 27 sets of lifting buckets pumps operating with steam supplied by 39 boilers" (*HRCM*, ch.3).

The caisson system was useful in soft waterbearing ground near the surface: "This consisted of the employment of a cutting shoe, upon which brickwork was built up…the weight…driving the whole cylinder of brickwork down through the water-bearing measures to the rock head" (*HRCM*, ch.3).

At Washington 1901 and Dawdon 1903 time was taken to freeze the ground in the zone of the intended shaft before excavation. "…a number of holes are bored round the site of each shaft to be sunk and a freezing solution circulated through tubes inserted in the boreholes. The freezing solution is maintained at a sufficiently low temperature and circulated over the the necessary period to effect a solid wall of ice round the shaft in process of being sunk. Freezing is maintained until the necessary tubbing cribs and tubbing have been inserted in shafts and the joints wedged" (*HRCM*, ch.3).

From 1911 on cementation was also used to block off the water bearing strata round the shaft.

Sinking was highly skilled, arduous and dangerous work, undertaken by hand in the seventeenth to nineteenth centuries; the poet Alexander Barrass was a sinker.

back casting – "a wall or lining of dry bricks used when sinking through soft ground, permanent walling being built within it. In the North of England and Scotland timber cribs and planking were used" (Tootle 1995) re early nineteenth century.

crab – "a winch used in sinking operations" (Wade, South Moor, 1966); "a windlass for lifting heavy weights" (Brockett, Newc, 1820s).

kibble – "a large iron bucket used in sinking operations, also a small low tub with open end" (Wade, South Moor, 1966); "kibble – a wooden tub. The early ones were usually barrelled shaped to prevent it tipping while being wound in the shaft. In later years they were of a square box shape, with a capacity of about 20 gallons. Used in conveying 'waste'. Carried on a 'tram', it was fitted with a hinged bow, similar to a 'corf-bow' for lifting purposes. Used in 'shaft sinking'" (Tootle, 1995); "kibble or hoppit – a bucket for use in the shaft during sinking. (At some collieries a kibble is the name for a small tram)" (Temple, 1994, pp.19–20) [Gm Kuebel].

Master Sinker – in charge (Tootle, 1995).

tubbing – "the practice of lining a shaft with a waterprrof lining to prevent the ingress of water" (Temple, 1994, pp.19–20); "tubbing – curved segments of cast iron used to hold back water from the strata in shafts" (Sharkey).

Maintenance

The shaft needed constant maintenance, to check it remained in good working fettle. This work needed to be done when the shaft was not otherwise in use. In general, maintenance could be carried out by workers standing on the 'roof' of the cage, which was lowered to the appropriate position.

> There were two shaft-men who rode on top of the cage each night shift to inspect the shaft. They also loaded oversized material which would not go in the cages, these would be fastened with chains and slung underneath the cage.
>
> (Wilson, Walbottle)

Other methods:

arse flap or **arse loop** – "a loop attached to the winding rope in which a man sat when carrying out repair work in the shaft. If it was fitted board to sit on it was known as an 'arse flap'." (Tootle, 1995, Yorks, N.East) [an early option].

cradle – "a suspended scaffold used in the shaft when repairs where being carried out" (Tootle, 1995); "used in sinking of shafts before cages are installed [and] used in a mine shaft when cages are out of action, owing to an accident. Used to enable someone to be lowered to point of stoppage in the shaft" (McBurnie,Washington, 1970s).

It was **shaftsmen** – "maintained the shaft" (Barnett, Seaham).

Auxiliary shafts might sometimes be needed:

Jack pit – "a shallow pit shaft in a mine connecting with an 'overcast' or at a fault. Also called a 'Jackey pit'" (Tootle, 1995, NE).

stappil – "shaft with steps to next coal seam" (Dodd, Tanfield Lea) C20/2; "stapel / stapple / stapel – a well, a small pit-shaft, an underground pit or a shaft within a pit" (Heslop, N'd, 1880s); "staple shaft – a shaft sunk between seams underground" (Temple, 1994, pp.19–20).

...and a terminology for stopping stations within the shaft:

inset – "an opening made in the side of a shaft to gain access to a seam of coal and to allow coal to be drawn up the shaft" (Temple, 1994, pp.19–20); "an inset was any opening in a shaft between the surface and the shaft bottom. Usually they were formed in a coal seam and sometimes coal was wound from there but it was inefficient because unless a clutch winder was used (a much later development and one I do not remember being used in the northeastern coalfield) the operation of unloading and loading the cage could not be done simultaneously. Furthermore it was forbidden by law to have keps anywhere in the shaft other than at the top and the bottom so positioning the cage accurately at the inset was critical for good loading" (Sharkey).

landing – "a stopping point for the cage in a shaft where various seams are being worked, to load and offload" (Tootle, 1995).

lift – "the vertical height travelled by the 'cage' in the shaft" (Tootle, 1995).

meetings – "where the cages pass each other in the shaft, or where the full and empty sets pass each other on a self-acting incline" (Nicholson, 1888); "meeting – the point in the shaft where 'creels' or 'corves' passed when winding coal" (Tootle, 1995).

As wider shafts became practicable, it was standard to divide them into two or four sections with a vertical brattice or partition. Specific sections of the shaft could then be devoted to man-riding and coal-raising, but the main purpose was to establish a route for ventilation where the pit had only one shaft.

brattish – "a wooden partition (a brattice), used for purpose of ventilation in coal mines... also... any slight partition dividing rooms" (Brockett, Newc, 1820s); "heavy woven material onetime impregnated with tar to make it airtight" http://www.therhondda.co.uk/; "brattice – a partition, generally of deal, placed in the shaft of a pit, or in a drift or other working of a colliery, for the purpose of ventilation. Its use is to divide the place in which it is fixed into two avenues, the current of air entering by the one and returning by the other" (Nicholson, 1888); "bratticing from brattice meaning a shaft lining or a wooden partition used underground in mines" (Davidson, Ashington) [OFr breteske].

main brattice – "a partition dividing a pit into two shafts, as a drawing and a pumping-shaft, or air-shaft" (Nicholson, 1888).

mudds – "small nails used for pinning brattice cloth" (Tootle, 1995, NE).

Such brattices were vulnerable in the case of explosion: "The gravity of explosions was increased in many cases by the destruction of the brattice partitions in the shafts, which blocked the pits and thus prevented the escape of possible survivors" (*HRCM*, ch.8). After the diasaster at Hartley Colliery, a law was passed requiring each pit to have two distinct shafts. The aim was to ensure an escape route if one shaft became blocked; also the two shafts served a more efficient role in ventilating the pit. One shaft was usually dedicated to raising coal, the other to carry the workers and materials.

> The Seaham Colliery pit was sunk about forty years ago. It was worked during about half that time with a single shaft for sending down the men and ventilating the pit. That old system of working was abolished by the Mines Regulation Act of 1862, which made it compulsory to have two separate and distinct shafts some distance apart for ventilation and

> taking the men up and down the pit. This colliery still preserved the old arrangement of a shaft with a brattice separating it, but this is now entirely worked as a downcast shaft, where men go down and come up, and it is called No.1 and No.2 shafts, but is really one shaft with a brattice up the centre. The upcast shaft is about 150 yards distant, and is the outlet by which all the foul air comes from the pit.
>
> (*Illustrated London News,* 18 September, 1880)

Kibble and cage

Access to and egress from the working mine was originally by means of a large bucket (kibble) on a rope:

> At Monkwearmouth Colliery a large iron tub, weighing 13 cwt, 3 qrs, was used for drawing coals and human beings. The dimensions of the tub (into which I descended by a ladder) were in perpendicular depth 6 foot 3 inches; the top diameter was 3 foot 8 inches; the middle 3 foot 2 inches; and the bottom diameter 3 foot 10 inches. Seven or eight men descended with me in this tub.
>
> (*PP*,1842, C.R. xvi, p.545)

The experience of a young lad descending for the first time, is more graphically described by Thomas Wilson:

Aw star'd at ev'ry thing aw saw,
For ev'ry thing was new to me;
And when wor turn to gan belaw
Was come, aw went on deddy's knee.

They popp'd us in a jiffy down,
Through smoke and styth and swelt'ren heat, — bad air
And often spinnen roun' and roun',
Just like a geuss upon a speet. — goose

We'd past the meetings aw've ne doubt; — half-way
Indeed, aw think, we'd reach'd the bottom,
After they'd bumm'd us round about — spun
For a' the warld like a tetotum.

(*The Pitman's Pay,* Part 2)

Once larger shafts were introduced (1830s), a cage fitting the dimension of the shaft and runing on skeets became realistic, with (from the 1840s) wire ropes connecting it to the winding engine. This also meant tubs of coal could be wheeled directly into the shaft at the bottom and wheeled off at bank (*HRCM*, ch.7). This basically remained the mode of operation, with safety features happily introduced, should the wire holding cage ever break...

Th' Raw between th' Caiges

(at Brockwell Pit)

One mornen wen Aw went ta wark,	
Th' seet wis most exsiten,	sight
Aw ard a noise, en luckt eroond,	heard
En we de ye think wis fiten?	who
Aw stud amais'd en at thim gaisd,	
Te see thim in such raiges;	
For Aw nivor seed e row like that	saw
Between th' Brockwil caiges.	
Wor aud caig sais, "Cum ower th' gaits,	
Becaws it's mei intenshin	
Te let th' see wethor thoo or me	
Is th' best invenshin."	
Th' neuin been rais'd, teuk off hes clais	new-one/clothes
Then at it thae went dabin;	dabbing
Th' blud wis runen doon th' skeets,	guide-timbers
En past th' weimin's cabin.	weighman's
Wor aud caige sais,"Let's heh me clais,	have/clothes
Thoo thowt thit thoo cud flae me;	scare
But if Aw'd been is young is thoo	as
Aw's certain Aw cud pae th'."	beat thee
Th' paitint nockt hees ankel off,	patent cage

En th' buaith ad cutten fuaices;	had/faces
Th' shifters rapt three for te ride,	i.e. signalled
So th' buaith went to thor plaices.	their
Wen gannen up en doon th' shaft,	
Th' paitint caige did threetin	
For te tuaik wor audin's life	our old one's
If thae stopt it meeten;	at halfway
Wor aud cage bauld oot is thae pas't;	bawled…as
"Thoo nasty, dorty paitint,	
Rub thee ies eguain th' skeets –	eyes/runners
Aw think thoo's ardly wakinit."	wakened
Th' paitint te wor aud caige sais:	
"Altho' Aw be e strangor,	a stranger
Aw kin work me wark is weel is thoo,	can
An free th' men freh daingor;	from
Noo, if th' rope shud brick we me,	with
Aud skinny jaws, just watch us,	
Thoo'l see me clag on te th' skeets,	stick
For Aw's full e springs en catches.	of
Wor aud caige te th' paitint sais:	
"Aw warnd thoo think thoo's clivor,	warrant
Becaws thi'v polished thoo we paint,	with
But thoo'l not last for ivvor;	
Th' paint on thoo 'ill weer awae,	
En then thoo' lost thei beuty;	you'll lose your
Th' nivor painted me at awl,	
En still Aw've deun me deuty."	

Th' braiksmin browt thim buaith te bank,
Th' mischeef for te sattil; — settle
Thae fit freh five o'clock te six, — fought
En th' paitint won th' battle.
It teuk th' braiksmin half e shift
Te clag thim up we plaistors;
Wor aud caige sent hees noatese in, — notice to quit
But just te vext th' maistors. — owners

SPOAKEN: Thor matcht to fite eguain, but not under Queensbury Rools. Wor aud caige fancies fiten we th' bare fist Aw'll let ye knaw wen it comes off. It 'ill heh [have] to be kept quiet; if the bobby gets to naw, thae'll be buaith teun [taken, arrested], becaws th' winit aloo bare fist fitein noo. Keep on lucken in th' Christian Arald [!], en yil see wen it comes off, en ware [where]. Thor's six to fower on the auden [old one] noo. Bet nowt te that dae [day], en Aw'll see ye in the field; it's a cheet [?fixed].

(Tommy Armstrong)

Operation

The winding tower, containing the large pulley wheels over which the steel rope to the cage ran, is one of the most recognisable features of a pit. Left as a bare frame, or enclosed in cladding, the winding tower gave the pit its identity; along the coast, by day or night (when they were lit up) they formed sure landmarks to boats at sea.

But such structures were not only symbolically important; they were the crucial working centre of the pit, in effect controlling shifts and production rates. The engine that powered the winding gear was therefore a main concern. From around 1650 a simple cog and rung device was introduced: "This contrivance conisted of a drum placed immediately over the pit; a horiztonal wheel fixed on a vertical axis was turned by the horse which was yoked underneath it, and cogs set in this wheel engaged in the cogs on a small vertical wheel attached to the drum shaft" (*HRCM*, ch.11). Later in the seventeenth century the Whim Gin (a sort of capstan) was prefered, in which horses and drum were placed away from the pit head, power being conveyed over pulleys.

Although Newcomen atmospheric engines were available in North East pits from 1760, their low power and the problem of changing vertical stroke to rotary action meant they were of most use for pumping. It was at Walker Colliery on 1784 the first use of Watts' rotative engine was made, in combination with an endless chain winding system. After 1800 higher power steam engines came into general use for winding, and gins were discontinued (*HRCM*, ch.11).

The standard power base would come to be a bank of boilers fed with coal and generating steam for driving turbines which in turn generated electricity. In addition to the turbines there would be compressors also powered by the steam which would generate compressed air for numerous jobs on the surface and for underground (windy picks, rams, door controls, shaft bottom tub controllers, etc.) Diesel based turbines were sometimes introduced, and in general the pit would generate its own DC electricty for the winding motors.

in the bell – "a device to stop overwinding – a detaching hook combined with the bell – released the rope in case of an overwind" (Hill, Harrington).

buntons – "beams of wood or steel placed horizontally across a rectangular shaft to support and secure the 'barring' and the 'cage guides'" (Tootle, 1995); "buntons – shaft supports to carry guides" (Dodd, Tanfield Lea).

cage – "in its modern form consists of 3 or 4 stories or stages, into each of which 2 tubs are run. The tubs are held in their places [in the cage] by the sneck" (Heslop, N'd, 1880s); "cage – the lift in a mine shaft for raising and lowering men and materials. First introduced by John Curr of Sheffield in about 1787" (Tootle, 1995).

cage shoes – "fittings bolted to the side of a cage which engaged with the 'rigid guides' in the shaft. Of various designs there were usually two shoes to each cage, one at the top and the other at the bottom of the cage. The shoes were kept well greased to provide smooth running. In theory if the rope broke and the cage tilted the shoes would dig into the guides and stop the cage from falling to the bottom of the shaft" (Tootle, 1995).

drum – "The drum of a 'winding engine' upon which the 'winding rope' is coiled or wound" (Tootle, 1995).

keps or **keeps** – "movable frames or supports of iron, which, if left free, project about $1^1/_2$ inches into the shaft top at each side, immediately beneath the level of the settle boards. Their use is to support the cage containing the tubs of coals when drawn to the surface, the cage rising between the keeps and forcing them back; but when the cage is drawn above the keeps they fall forward to their places, forming a rest for the cage until the full tubs are replaced by empty ones. The keeps are then drawn back by a lever by the banksman or shover-in and the cage allowed to return down the shaft" (Nicholson 1888); "keps – the upcoming (full) cage would be drawn higher than the keps and then dropped back on to them. When the chummens had taken the place of the fullens and the cage had been rapped away the winder man would lift the cage off the keps, the banksman would pull a lever to move the keps back into a vertical position and the cage would be sent on its way. The keps were also used when men were being loaded and unloaded from the cage" (Sharkey); "working on raps, the winder man would lift the cage slightly to free the butterfly wings, and the banksman would use the special handle to close the wings allowing the keps to come back down through the hang-up hole." (Darby, Seaham); "keps – props on which the cage rests at bank while the tubs are being changed" (Wade, South Moor, 1966); "dropping of at the keps" (nodding off, feeling tired. After a shift maybe.) (McGee re Brandon) ['catches'].

Koepe winder – "a system where the winding drum is replaced by a large wheel or sheave. Both cages are connected to the same rope, which passes around some 200 degrees of the sheave in a groove of friction material. The Koepe sheave may be mounted on the ground adjacent to the headgear or in a tower over the shaft. The drive to the rope is the frictional resistance between the rope and the sheave. It requires the use of a balance rope. It is often used for hoisting heavy loads from deep shafts and has the advantage that the large inertia of the ordinary winding drum is avoided" (Johnson, Dawdon).

pit rope – "the winding rope" (Tootle, 1995).

pulleys – "the wheels on top of the framework above the shaft over which the winding rope passed from the winding engine to the top of the cages" (Tootle, 1995).

rowla – "roller supporting and guiding haulage rope" (Dodd, Tanfield Lea).

skip – "a large metal container for raising coal up a shaft" (Temple, 1994, pp.19–20).

skeets – "guides for the cages in a pit shaft" (Wade, South Moor, 1966); "now in other pits they had what they called the skeets – and a skeet was boards with flat plates down – down the shaft you see, and as the cage went down you were sliding down these plates three inches wide to half and inch thick; you were sliding down there and that kept the cage steady; but that was invented long before the guide ropes; and the guide ropes were a costly item because they were expensive ropes to buy you know; and it saved a lot of accidents though: it was a wonderful invention. But the skeets – we had some at the Lintz with like a wood plank – these long pieces of iron were screwed on you know – and that was the guide in some of the shafts you see; and they kept the cages nice and steady. And they had to be examined to make sure that none of the screws came loose, or bolts came loose – as they would automatically hit the cage, stop the cage and mebees break a link of the chain or anything like that – so, so many times – I don't know what – perhaps once a week – Sundays or something like that – the banksman and one of the other men, the engineer, would be going down on top of the cage and they would go down this side slowly and up the other and they would examine the guide ropes and examine the skeets, see, to make sure there was no bolts loose, no screws loose or anything like that; and that's how they kept the pits working smoothly. But for all they were so careful to avoid accidents there was always something happened that they hadn't expected. And it was the unexpected thing that caused a lot of accidents in the pits you see" (Jackon, Beamish,1984/259).

snecks – "the stops used in the cage and in the track leading into the cage whereby the tubs could be restrained. Throwing a lever usually released both sets and allowed to tub or tubs to run in or out of the cage" (Sharkey); **cage sneck** – "a movable part of the cage by which the tubs are kept in the cage during their passage in the shaft" (Nicholson, 1888).

steel rohp – "for hauling pit cage or tub set" (Dodd, Tanfield Lea); "cage rope" or simply the "rope" (Sharkey).

whimsey – "a turntable from which a rope is uncoiled" (Wade, South Moor, 1966).

How the Engine was Extracted

The Engine was a Gardner underground diesel loco engine, approx. 5' high, 20" wide, 6' long. A stationary engine, at the time, 70–100 h.p. Standing on timbers in a siding underground, Dawdon Colliery. Not much used. Would probably have been buried alive when the pit shut. But someone went to the trouble of providing a low-loader chassis on wheels, the engine was lifted, placed onto the wheels, fastened and secured, transported to the shaft, brought up the shaft, transported from shaft to stockyard where it was unloaded from its wheels onto a waiting lorry by forklift – I guess. It then disappeared. This was Friday night, after nightshift had left the stockyard. The tricky bit is to get aught up and down a shaft: to do this, chitties need to be given out, etc. for it is a bottleneck in the transport system – you can wait weeks.

To be more exact it would have to be lifted, below, onto a low-loader using chain blocks. It would be in a stowage siding or loco shed near the bottom of shaft (which are cathedral-like spaces) – it might have been used, had it been spared, to go into an actual loco to carry men or materials through the pit. Anyway, it would have been less than a quarter mile to the shaft from where it was, and once on tracks, those tracks carry on into the cage. The cage itself is only about 8' by 6'. At bank, too, there would be rails to go out to the turntable, and it would have to pass over 2 turntables to reach the stockyard (these are all switched from the banksman's cabin). There must have been an awful lot of suspects.

When the theft came to light a few days later, all hell broke loose. The Manager of the Colliery learned of it from the Traffic Manager, and said (I quote) "I want this man found and when he's found he gets your job." A few days later it was the Manager's bad luck to have to attend a Colliery Conference on security. He entered the room and received a standing ovation from the rest of the Colliery Managers, which did not please him.

Meanwhile police were quite active in Seaham and district, visiting suspicious characters all to no avail. The warrant they used must have made interesting reading. They searched back gardens and fishing boats and everything. The engine would have been ideal for running either a trawler, or farm machinery, or anything. It could have fetched a canny sum. To this day its fate has not been discovered.

(after T.C.)

The operator

Associated with working the engine itself are:

brakesman – "the engineman who attends to the winding machine" (Nicholson, 1888); "brakesman – the man in charge of the winding engine at a pit" (Heslop, N'd, 1880s).

drawer – "a man who raised the coal up the shaft and 'banked' it." (Raby, Co Durham, 1460, *V.C.H. Durham*, ii. 342 qu. Tootle, 1995) [compare verb, 'draw', below].

engineman – "a man having charge of an engine and boilers" (Nicholson, 1888); "engine-man or fireman: the term 'fireman' meant the man who kept the engine's fire alive" (Freese, 2005, p.59, re C18); injinryt – "engine-wright" plus "wyndin injinman" (Dodd, Tanfield Lea).

whimsey man – "he finds a whimsey man at the engine who lets him down the shaft" (*PP*, 1842, C.R. xvi, p.134) [from whim, a capstan].

winderman: "The winderman or the winding-engineman, or the engineman were one and the same. This was the man who controlled the machine (steam or electrically powered) that moved the cages in the shafts. The machine was known as the winder or the winding engine and it was housed in a building known as the **engine house** or the winder" (Tony Sharkey); "winding engineman – very responsible post – signals from top to bottom of shaft by 'rapping' – no longer a physcial knock but an electric signal via button" (Barnett, Seaham).

These are all one person. However it was a banksman who had control of operations at the top of the shaft and who gave directions to the winderman:

banksman – "a higher order of pitmen who take care of the pit heaps or mouth of the coal pit" (*Bell MS*); "banksman – a man employed in taking the coals from the mouth of the shaft...to the skreen" (Brockett); "bankman – a man who stands at the mouth of a pit to receive the coals as they ascend – James Carre, then bankeman of the said cole pitts" (Houghton-le-spring, 1604, qu. Raine from *Egerton MS*); "banksman – collects tokens, raps cage down" (Barnett, Seaham).

> The banksman is the man who stands at the gates where the cage stops at its highest point. He has contact with the winder man by means of electric bells – banksman has the buttons, winder man has a board full of electirc bells. One rap is one press of the button.
>
> (Geordie Darby)

> The Banksman was the person at the surface (at bank!) who was in charge of loading and unloading the cages and was responsible for giving the last signal to the winderman that it was OK to move the cages. He used a rapper for this purpose. His opposite number at the shaft bottom (or an inset if one was used) was known as the Onsetter. He signalled to the Banksman when the cages were clear to move and the banksman gave the final signal to the engineman.
>
> (Tony Sharkey)

He might be assisted by a **shover-in** (Nicholson, 1888) who loaded the empty tubs into the cage at bank.

Corresponding to the banksman, at the bottom of the shaft, was the onsetter:

onsetter – "the person who attaches the corf to the pit-rope at the bottom of the shaft" (Brockett); "onsetters – men who put the full tubs in and take the empty ones out of the cage at the shaft bottom" (Nicholson, 1888); "onsetta – underground shaft attendant" (Dodd, Tanfield Lea); "onsetter – the man in charge of the cage at the shaft bottom" (Wade, South Moor, 1966); "the onsetter tyeuk the tubs outa the cage and put Jonty [a sick worker] in" (Hay, Ushaw Moor, C20/1); "onsetter – at bottom of shaft – loaded the cage esp. when people ascending" (Barnett, Seaham).

Or **hanger-on** – "Another name for the 'onsetter'. Possibly derived from hanging baskets on the winding rope" (Tootle, 1995).

Verbs:

braking – "The action of operating a winding engine" (Tootle, 1995, NE).

draw –"to wind. The act of hoisting or winding. To haul" (Tootle, 1995).

Signalling

Clearly, the onsetter, at the bottom of the shaft, had to be able to communicate with the banksman and egineman, at the top – to tell him when the cage was ready to be drawn up. Equally the banksman had to be able to contact the onsetter and engineman when a load was ready to descend. Early on, a simple percussive signal did the job; later this was replaced by a system of electric bells, and supplemented by telephone:

bells – "THE BANKSMAN is the man who stands at the gates where the cage stops at its highest point. HE'S THE MAN in contact with THE WINDER MAN !!! This contact is BY MEANS OF ELECTRIC BELLS ! Banksman has the buttons, WINDER MAN has A BOARD FULL OF ELECTRIC BELLS" (Darby, Seaham).

bend-up – "a signal to draw away in a coal mine: 'Bend up the **crab**'" (Brockett, Newc, 1820s); "bend-away or bend-up – a signal in a pit, given to raise up, or set away" (Heslop, N'd, 1880s).

hing-on or **hang-on** – "a call from the banksman to the onsetter after any stop (the cause of which has been at bank), meaning recommence coal work" (Nicholson, 1888).

howway – "a call to lower the 'cage' down'" (Tootle, 1995, NE); "howay – a call to the brakesmen if the engine is standing to put it in motion, and if in motion the signal means move quicker" (Nicholson, 1888).

to rap – "to signal – "the' rapped the cage ter bank" (Hay, Ushaw Moor, C20/1); 'rap 'er away!' Signal to the winder man that it was OK to move the cages" (Sharkey); "the gates closed with a clang, the cage was rapped away" (Grice, 1960, ch.14).

rapper – "signalling on these systems was long effected by a simple rapper, consisting of a hammer pivoted at one end and attached to a long wire. By pulling and releasing the wire, the hammer would rap on a steel plate, [at the other end] giving instructions to the engineman" (Temple, 1994, p.18); "rapper – a clapper of steel" (G. Patrickson, Dawdon); "a lever placed at the top of a shaft or inclined plane, to one end of which a hammer is attached, and to the other a line, communicating with the bottom of the shaft or incline. Its use is to give signals when everything is ready at the bottom for drawing away" (Nicholson, 1888); "signals from the onsetter and banksman were heard by each other and also by the winding engineman" (Sharkey) ["rappers were implements used for scraping the sweat from the pit ponies' backs" www.rapper.org.uk]

> The original rappers as far as I know were gongs which were simply struck with a hammer. I saw gongs at one of the older mines (I cannot remember which) that were a little more sophisticated in as much as the hammer was caused to strike the gong by pulling a lever that was connected to it by a chain. A light chain running through the shaft connected to a similar arrangement at the surface.
>
> But the universal method was electrical and the 'rapper' was a handle (on a metal box about 6 inches in all dimensions) that had to be turned through 90 degrees before it could be depressed.
>
> (Tony Sharkey)

raps – "3 raps meant man-riding, 2 meant start, 1 meant stop" (G. Patrickson, Dawdon).

> Raps were definitely 3 for manriding but the signals 1 and 2 were used when the onsetter and the banksman gave permission for the cage to be moved. When the cage was moving, "1" definitely meant STOP but not otherwise. Other signals were developed for individual mines, usually for the insets to which the cage was to be sent. And one very important one which had to be agreed with the winderman was the signal that the person who was entering the cage was the same one who was giving the signal, in which case the winderman waited for a period of time to ensure that the person was indeed in the cage and that the gates were closed. Before actually moving away, the winderman would move the cage slightly to indicate that final movement was imminent.
>
> (Tony Sharkey)

There were aids for the unsighted engine man to work out where to stop the cage:

indicator – "a mechanical device in the winding engine house which shows the position of the cage in the shaft" (Tootle, 1995).

mark – "a band of hemp, etc. wrapped around the winding rope, to indicate to the engine man the position of the load in the shaft" (Tootle, 1995).

seams – "winding drum marked for different levels of seams" (G. Patrickson, Dawdon).

A special set of terms related to the use of the cage for carrying workers:

hunkers – "the men entered the cage... they sat down on their 'hunkers'; they believed they could better take the shock of any unexpected bump or jolt if they were crouching" (Grice, 1960, ch.14).

men on – "Everybody's favourite signal at the end of a shift was 'three' which meant 'Men On' and they could be loaded into the cage to go to bank...One of my favourite stories concerns a man who was leaving the mine early and he was asked by the onsetter if he was coming back. His reply was 'Aye, if the rope breaks'" (Sharkey).

ride – "to ascend or be drawn up the shaft; does not apply to going down" (Nicholson, 1888).

tak had – "you might say 'tak had' (take hold) as in steady yourself (in the cage) or use the handrail to take care of yourself" (McGee, Sherburn Hill).

Unloading the Cage

At bank, the process was to unload the tubs full of coal, and load in their place empty tubs for the use of the hewers below. Originally a manual job, gravity was made to help, for once cages were made in several stories, the tubs arrived on bank well above surface level. The process of unloading was made as speedy as possible: "when the cage is landed it is in line win the rails either side on the cage so the tubs were loaded, unloaded" (Darby, Seaham).

> We longed to start work at the pit after hearing tales from the older boys about the workings and having a pony to work with. Father took us to the office to get fixed up to start work down the mine. We were excited at going to work. The first job you got in the pit was letting out. The full tubs used to come out of the pit on an endless hauler. A chap used to send so many down the hill and you had to put a wooden drag in the wheel to stop them. Then you would louse off [release the tub] and set it down to the onsetter to put in the cage to send to bank. The bottom of the shaft was big – it was white-washed and had electric lights. They used to make their own electricity at the pit: they had a big dynamo which never stopped
>
> (Mr Cawson, Kibblesworth, Beamish 1993/5)

> Right the coal tubs, by the way all this is above ground, thirty feet above ground, when you're at ground level you see these cages coming out of the hole and away up to the top, the proper heap as they called it, the level where all the tubs are taken out and what have you. These tubs now go down the incline and in doing so they have to have a pretty reasonable steep incline to make them go because the mine was very automatic, you understand, and instead of having horses drawing or men pushing, [they used] inclines, but they had to be inclines so that the stiffest tub would run, which means that the easiest tub would run too fast... so before they come to the bottom of the creeper as we called it the tubs ran through what was called a retarder which was really just two wooden planks, the planks were renewed every now and again, which were held at about a metre from the ground level and parallel with the railway line and they are brought together by a compressed air cylinder and the space between them was just slightly narrower than the width of the tub, and as the tub came along it would get squeezed and held back a little bit. Quite obviously it didn't want to be stopped there you just want to reduce its speed and so a young fella would be there with a lever easing these two planks apart or bringing them together as required so that he didn't knock them off the way but kept them right.
>
> [Having controlled the speed, a new incline took the tubs up toward the washery ...]
>
> Right when it got to the end of this incline going down it come to a bottom of a very, very steep incline upwards, with a creeper, ah, you don't know what a creeper is now, it's a chain running between the railway lines up, around the sprocket at the top, its going round and round, it would be about thirty yards long, this incline, on this huge mechanical chain at about two and a half metre intervals, yards if you like, there was these big hooks as it were on the chain which got a hold of the axle of the tubs and they took these tubs up this incline which no horse, no man, no one could take even an empty tub up that incline.
>
> (Mr Cheesman, Beamish, 1998/6)

Chapter 4: Undergound

Areas

The main organisational/geographical division of a mine was the district:

> The pit was divided into districts and in each district the officials had so many places to hew in.
>
> (Cawson, Kibblesworth, Beamish, 1993/5)

> A district was a section of a mine controlled by a deputy (usually with a series of 'owermen') per shift over the Deputy, with a district or number of districts. Districts were often named as bord position from shaft/azimuth/then seam ...for example:
>
> 18 North Maudlin
>
> 1st South Middle Five Quarter
>
> 26 South East Low Main
>
> 18 South Main Coal
>
> (Dawdon) ...all of these were Districts in my time of the early sixties...
>
> (Ken Johnson)

Also mentioned, but not perhaps in regular use were:

flats – "flats were split up into districts – 2nd South, or 1st North and so on" (qu. Douglass, 1973, re Wardley).

panel system – "a system of working the coal, which came into use in the North of England, in about 1810, in an attempt to improve the ventilation. The colliery was divided into large squares or 'panels'..." (Tootle, 1995); "He [Buddle], therefore, divided the workings into districts or panels, separated from each other by ribs or barriers of solid coal, and ventilated by distinct currents of air" (*MC*, April 1889).

way – "a working district underground" (Nicholson, 1888).

Directions

Pitmen held by two cardinal points – towards or away from the shaft. Even this may not have been easy to calculate where the workings were complex, and impossible when lights were extinguished by clumsiness or some accident. Stories are telled of pitmen being led safely to the shaft by their ponies – the earliest of pit songs, *The Collier's Rant*, gives the sound advice of "Follow the ponies, Johnny me lad-oh!"

back-by – "behind, a little way distant" (Brockett); "bakby – away from coal face" (Dodd, Tanfield Lea); "back-bye, i.e. away from the face" (Johnson, Dawdon).

boardways – at right angles to the cleat (main vertical fracture line of coal).

headways – in line with the cleat.

in-bye – "in the workings, or in any direction away from the shaft" (Nicholson, 1888); "To gan inbye – to go from the shaft bottom into the workings" (Wade, South Moor, 1966); "to travel into a mine is to go in-bye" (Tootle, 1995); "I knew what in-bye meant. It signified in or approaching the working area" (Hitchin, 1962, p.66). [Inbye therefore has the sense of 'away from the shaft, towards the interior', outbye 'towards the shaft, and the outside' and were used similarly of the two rooms downstairs in a standard miner's house.] [OE, inbutan.]

ny hand gannin – "nearby working place [in pit]" (Dodd, Tamfield Lea); "nigh-hand-gannen – a shorter way" (Wade, South Moor, 1966).

oot-bye – "at the shaft or bottom of the pit" (Wilson, G'head, 1820s); "the direction in any part of a mine towards the shaft" (Nicholson, 1888); "technical, of a miner coming towards the shaft in order to get to bank. The corresponding term is 'inbye,' i.e. further along underground, towards one's cavil" (Palgrave, Hetton, 1896); "outbye – travelling from the face to the shaft" (Wade, South Moor, 1966); "ootby – away from coal face" (Dodd, Tanfield Lea).

The Collier's Rant

As me and my marrow was ganning to wark,	work-mate
We met with the devil, it was in the dark;	
I up with my pick, it being in the neit,	
I knock'd off his horns, likewise his club feet.	
chorus:	
Follow the horses, Johnny my lad oh!	
Follow them through, my canny lad oh!	
Follow the horses, Johnny my lad oh!	
Oh lad ly away, canny lad oh!	
As me and my marrow was putting the tram,	pushing
The low it went out, and my marrow went wrang;	light
You would have laugh'd had you seen the gam,	sport
The deil gat my marrow, but I gat the tram...	devil

Oh! marrow, oh! marrow, what dost thou think?	
I've broken my bottle, and spilt a' my drink;	
I lost a' my shin-splints among the great stanes,	
Draw me t' the shaft, it's time to gan hame…	
Oh! marrow, oh! marrow, where hast thou been?	
Driving the drift from the low seam,	tunnel through stone
Driving the drift from the low seam,	
Had up the low, lad, deil stop oot thy een!…	hold… eyes
Oh! marrow, oh! marrow, this is wor pay week,	
We'll get penny loaves and drink to our beek;	i.e. fill
And we'll fill up our bumper, and round it shall go,	
Follow the horses, Johnny lad oh!…	
There is my horse, and there is my tram –	
Twee horns full of grease will make her to gang!	two
There is my hoggars, likewise my half shoon,	shin-guards
And smash my heart, marrow, my putting's a' done	

(Ritson, *The Northumberland Garland*, 1809, item XIII)

Passages and places

Each passage must serve a purpose: for winning coal, for transporting coal, for ventilation, for access… but only needed to be large enough for the function they fulfilled. Thin seams of coal, as they were mined, would only warrant low passages!

Following the coal strata, such passages can dip and rise, narrow in height or expand; and involve costly tunnelling through stone where hitches dislocated the strata. Once the coal had been removed, much of the 'waste' or 'goaf' was left to collapse, with only special roadways kept open for ventilation.

The older method ('board and pillar') was to hew two-thirds or three-quarters of the coal, leaving the remainder to support the roof. The work would advance to the end of the colliery's territory (or sometimes a little beyond!) and then come back, freeing as much of the remaining coal as possible – thus 'whole working' and 'brokken working'. In this case, the passages tended to form a grid.

> The seams in this county [Durham] are not one in a hundred less than three feet in depth, and then when it does so happen there is part cut away at the top or bottom to make the working 3 feet thick, which is the lowest we have. Our horse-way is 5 foot or 5 foot 6 inches. Four foot is far more usual, and sometimes it is a little more." [re Little Town & Sherburn]
>
> (*PP*, 1842, CR xvi, p.56)

In longwall working, a wider coalface was tackled, a pair of passages being maintained either side for access. The terminology differs slightly from that of 'board and pillar' working.

> ...mothergates were always about 10 feet high [to start with ...although crushed much lower after weight came on] tailgates about 7 feet. Both had stone packing on the goaf side...just like dry stone walling... to act as a permanent 'prop' to support that side of the gate where goaf collapse would degrade the strength of the arches.
>
> (Ken Johnson, Dawdon)

And inevitably, the map of the mine would change rapidly as work progressed...

adit – "a more or less horizontal entrance to a mine usually such that water will run out of it" (Tootle, 1995); "an adit is an entry into a coal seam from the surface, either level or gently inclining. In the North East we would more likely call anything from the surface to access a seam a 'drift'" (Sharkey). [Latin aditus, 'approach', used 1602.]

boards – "the principal excavations in a coal mine, made at right-angles to the winning head-ways" (Brockett); "bords" (Sharkey); "often used as almost equivalent to an open passage, e.g. 'mothergate board'" (*PP*, 1842); "bord – a working place in the pit" (Wade, South Moor, 1966). [Originally a passage with a board or boards laid down to assist wheelbarrows? – but see next entry.]

bord – "Similarly, a 'bord', meaning a gallery, owes its origins to the lead miner. Most Pennines lead seams were near vertical and to reach the ore, boards were wedged above the workings, to provide a platform from which the miners could work. As the exploitation of the seam progressed the next bite at the seam was described as 'the next bord'" (Temple, 1994, pp.11–12).

brow edge – "the rock face that accompanied a change of height in a roadway" (Sharkey).

cabins – "these are occupied by the overmen and fitters. They are generally places hewn out of the stone and white-washed. Long tables and benches will be in these along with desks for the overmen's plans, books and deployment tables" (Douglass, 1973).

Charlston bunker – "a gallery where coal is stored undergound" (Temple, 1994, pp.19–20).

crosscuts – "are entries or roadways driven at an angle to the bords and headways" (Sharkey).

crut – "underground incline" (Briscoe, 2003); "short cut or narrow track?" (Sharkey).

dip – "a working roadway which leads downhill" (McBurnie, Washington, 1970s); "'down dip' simply meant 'down hill'. Could refer to an undulation in a roadway" (Sharkey).

drift – "in coal, an exploring place; usually a pair of drifts are driven simultaneously for the purpose of ventilation. In stone, sometimes for the purpose of exploring, but more frequently rendered necessary by the occurrence of dislocations in the, strata" (Nicholson, 1888); "only know of 'drift' being used to describe a roadway driven in rock. Could be entry from surface to give access to a seam, could be connection between two different seams, or it could be the roadway driven through a fault to connect with the displaced seam" (Sharkey); "the driving of the roadway was known as 'drifting'" (Tootle, 1995). [From 'drive'.]

floor – see strata.

drive – "to excavate; to carry forward, as driving a drift, &c." (Nicholson, 1888).

ganibil – "passage or use possible" (Dodd, Tanfield Lea).

gate – "a roadway in a mine. Adapted from the old Norse 'gata' meaning a road" (Tootle, 1995); "'gate' is a word meaning entry roadway and I have never heard it used except in connection with longwall mining. In the very early days of [advancing] longwall the gates were formed in the waste (goaf) after the coal had been extracted and provided access to each section of the face which was worked by individual hewers. When longwall was developed using conveyors, the gates were usually one at each end of the face on a single unit face, and one gate in the middle and one at each end on a double unit face" (Sharkey). See also 'maingate'.

going bord or **gannen bord** – "a 'bord' down which coal was trammed, or one along which the production from several working places was transported into the main wagon-way" (Tootle, 1995, N.E.).

Thor's a hitch an' then a swally	dislocation...dip (in strata)
Filled wi' wetter like a ford,	water
An' a lot o' way aal twisted	i.e.rails
I' the clarty gannin bord	muddy

(Alexander Barrass)

headways – "excavations in a coal pit at right angles to the boards, for the purposes of ventilating and exploring the mine" (Brockett, Newc, 1820s); "**heedwis-end** – headway, passages that lead to the crane or shaft" (Wilson, G'head, 1820s); **head-ways course** – "when a set of 'headings', shortwall or longwall faces, extend from side to side from a set of bords they were said to be driven head-ways course" (Tootle 1995, N.E.); "headways were driven in the line of cleat or 'on the end' and were chiefly driven for ventilative purposes" (Sharkey).

holeing – "a communication passage between two places" (Colls, 1987).

incline – "where a road falls as little as 2 ins in 1 yard it is said to be an incline. It was then possible to use a 'self-acting' or 'balance' system of haulage. The weight of the full tubs going down the incline is used to pull the empties up the incline" (Tootle, 1995); "The word 'incline' is a posh word for 'dip' when used underground. On the surface it is a rail track which is on a gradient" (Sharkey).

kip – "a level or gently sloping roadway running outbye at the end of a haulage road. Here the full tubs would stand, so that they could be run down to the shaft bottom under gravity to be loaded into the cage" (Tootle, 1995); "kips were used to marshall tubs, to run them using gravity past loading points and on shaft sidings. Kips were constructed with bricks and mortar in a roadway that had been considerably enlarged vertically" (Sharkey).

lines – "directional aids for driving roadways straight or in a given direction. The lines were painted on the roof by surveyors using whitewash. 'Strings' were a more sophisticated method of doing the same thing and usually consisted of three vertical weighted strings suspended from nails embedded in the roof which were also put there by surveyors. The nails were commonly horse shoe nails with a horizontal hole drilled in them through which to thread the string" (Sharkey).

loco level – "the main level going inbye from the shaft along which the locomotive hauls the coal, men and materials" (Tootle, 1995); "a term used in 'horizon mining' where a roadway is driven to a gradient suitable for locomotive haulage, without regard to whether the roadway coincided with a coal seam. The loco level was the place in the shaft where such a roadway would be located" (Sharkey).

maingate – "the maingate or mothergate was the roadway in which the haulage was situated and the tailgate(s) were usually the return airway for the face, the second means of egress (required by law) and the roadway along which supplies (chiefly timber) were brought to the face. To describe the difference between a conveyor face and the early longwalls the early longwalls were called 'gateway longwalls'" (Sharkey).

mothergate – "in the workings of a colliery are the way by which the workmen first proceed" (*Bell MS*); "the principal road of a coal-pit" (Brockett, Newc, 1820s); "mutha git/tail git – mothergate, tailgate, ends of [coal] face" (Dodd, Tanfield Lea); "mothergate – especially the main haulage roadway from a longwall face. The tailgate was the other entry to the face which provided for a ventilation circuit and a secondary means of egress. Mothergate and tailgate are inseparable from longwall working" (Sharkey); "mothergate – route for air in – term used at inland collieries, more usual on coast was maingate" (Hill, Harrington).

retarder drift – the retarder drift was used to take coal down to a lower level for most efficient single level coal-drawing up-shaft; it linked the faces in the Main Coal to the loco level. It had a huge armoured conveyor with paddle-like flights to slow down (retard) coal when dropping down the conveyor to the Loco Drift loading point (after Johnson, Dawdon).

scours – "roadways driven through the gob or goaf" (Sharkey); "equals off-gates; 'gob-' or 'goaf-roads' in longwall working, usually about 150yds apart" (Tootle 1995, N.E.).

snicket – "short connection road in a mine" (Briscoe, 2003); "Snicket/Snicket Gate – a short connection road" (Riley, Blyth).

staple – "its purpose was to lower full tubs to another level" (Hitchin, 1962, p.69); "staples were simply vertical connections between seams, often used for ventilation purposes. Problem was that unless there was provision for men to travel via the staple another means of egress from the district or seam had to be provided" (Sharkey); "this staple, which was a footway down to underground workings…" (Grice, 1960, ch.3).

stenton – "interconnecting draft between main road-ways" (Temple, 1994, pp.19–20).

thirling – drilling or penetrating: "thirling was used for 'holing' or connecting and could be used in connection with a chocking back but not necessarily. In bord and pillar operations the mere action of connecting the places in the coal could be described as 'thirling'. On the other hand '**chocking back**' usually meant two headings being driven towards each other on a bearing that would ensure a continuous straight roadway when they 'holed' or 'thirled'. (By the way, we never used 'thirled' in south west Durham)" (Sharkey). [OE thyrlian 'to pierce'.]

winning – "'winning' in this sense describes the main roadway being driven as a development into the coal reserves. Sometimes it was called the 'main winning'" (Sharkey).

winning headway – "main passage from shaft inbye" (*PP*, 1842); "a 'main winning' would be the main intake airway and usually have an associated and mostly parallel 'back winning' – the main return airway. As a verb 'winning' is the act of extracting coal. Incidentally, winning is not a peculiarly Geordie word. It is widely used in mining" (Roxborough, swDm).

Maintenance of passages

Because of the pressure from overlying strata, passages did not maintain themselves: roof and floor were always liable to move together or the roof could simply collapse. The gap that constituted a passage had therefore to be shored up – by props, or if the roof seemed soft, cross-planks at the top, wedged in place by uprights (a sort of Stonehenge-like combination). Wooden props were traditional, imported from Sweden, and had the advantage that their straining and bending gave warning of strata starting to move. In the modern era, adjustable metal props or girder arches (for more permanent ways) became standard, giving the passage a more rounded profile.

Traditional mode:

balk – "a strong piece of timber for supporting the roof in a coal pit" (Brockett, Newc, 1820s); "a piece of strong timber, usually used in rolley-ways or permanent passages to support the roof" (Nicholson, 1888); "baaks (bawks) – heavy timber roof supports" (Wilson, North Walbottle); "baulk – a very large roof timber used to support roadways" (Sharkey).

breaking-off timber – "the roof supports that were set under the canch that defined the dimensions of the canch before it was fired down" (Sharkey).

cap piece – "block of wood: 'gis a cap piece to put over this prop end'" (Dawdon Pit).

chocks – "wooden pillars built up of oblong pieces of timber laid crosswise, two and two alternately" (Nicholson, 1888); "chock – a square pillar for supporting the roof of a pit, built up of short lengths of wood" (Heslop, Newc, 1880s).

castle – a construct of chocks, set cross-wise in a vertical tower, to give maximum roof support... "wooden castles of beechwood chocks" (Johnny Handle).

gallows timber – "a 'crown tree' with a prop placed under each end" (Tootle, 1995, N.E.).

head tree – "usually a piece of wood laid horizontally between a prop and a bar as the prop was hammered into place. As the roof subsequently lowered the head tree was squeezed before the prop was subjected to a (possible) breaking load" (Sharkey).

plangk – "wooden roof support held by props" (Dodd, Tanfield Lea).

lagging – "the material that was placed between supports and the roof or sides" (Sharkey).

pack – "a stone wall built near the face to help take the weight of the earth. A pack is built like a dry stone wall..." (Douglass, 1973).

splets – "thin wooden chocks used to tighten up supports where the props were a little short" (Wilson, North Walbottle). [But "spletter" glossed as 'air splitter, pit ventilation worker' by Dave Harker, Bell-Harker, p.124, ca.1812.]

stook – "removable roof support" (Dodd, Tanfield Lea).

timber leader – someone who pushed/drove timber round on a tram; "originally used when they moved trams of timber to the workface; when things became more mechanised, the term was still used at Vane Tempest for someone moving any supplies" (Brown, Ryhope).

Modern mode:

arch girder – "a length of H rolled steel joist, bent to a semi-circular shape. Two or more sections would be fitted together by using bolts and 'fishplates' to make up an arched shaped roof support for the roadways in a mine" (Tootle, 1995).

chock – "A hydraulic powered roof support with up to six 'legs'" (Tootle, 1995).

Dowty prop – "The first British made hydraulic prop developed by Dowty Mining Equipment in 1946" (Tootle, 1995); hydraulic prop, raised by pump action from a rod, and oil pressure. Developed originally by Sir George Dowty for use in aircraft undercarriages, it had a pressure release valve in case of sudden shock. Though expensive at £10 per prop (1950s), it could be reused in a way wooden props could not; however this also meant the loss of any in the goaf was the more regretted! known as 'milkbottles'" (Sharkey, re Randholph Pit, Evenwood).

powered roof supports – or shield – dramatically reduced fatal accidents from roof falls at the coal face, 1950s to 1980s.

rings – "the word used for steel arches" (Sharkey).

stickleback – "type of steel arch-girder normally with an almost flat top" (McBurnie, Washington, 1970s).

stilts – "pieces of wood or metal attached to the bottom of the legs of an arched girder which also took the first weight by sliding up the girder legs as the roof pressure came on" (Sharkey).

Maintenance:

bargain work – "work such as stone or coal drifting, i.e. tunnelling. Let by tender, amongst the workmen at a colliery, the work going to the lowest tender" (Tootle, 1995, N.E.).

bating – "excavating the floor of a roadway to make more 'headroom'" (Tootle, 1995, N.E.).

bigging – "the building of 'packs' in a working place or heading to support the roof, e.g. 'bigging the gob'. The building of 'packs' to support the roadways through the 'waste' using waste materials, i.e. poor coal and stone" (Tootle, 1995, N.E., Scots). [ON byggja 'to build'.]

brig – "a small section of 'uncaunched' (still in the 'law') roadway usually 'back-bye', i.e. away from the face" (Johnson, Dawdon).

canch or **caunch** — "a part of the roof or thill to be removed for the purpose of making height" (Nicholson, 1888); "caunch – section of roof taken down, or section of floor taken up, to make height to travel along" (McBurnie, Washington, 1970s); "cansh (proper word caunch or 'ripping') – making mine road higher by removal of stone above or below: 'borrum cansh coal seam'; also at side to maintain or widen roadway [gate]; stone rendered by caunch used to create intricate dry stone 'packing' at sides to supplement support of arches or 'sets of gears'" (Johnson, Dawdon); "mak'n canch ower th' pans – clearing stone, etc. to create headroom over conveyor belts (pans) which carried coal away from coal face" (Trelogan, New Herrington).

cast (as in hoy!) – "this expression was used to describe the activity of two or more men with shovels moving the same dirt or coal from its source to its destination when the distance was too much for one man to accomplish. It was used regularly in the building of packs" (Sharkey).

ta dint – to remove part of the mine floor which has lifted (Briscoe, 2003); "dinting or bate – to 'rip' the floor, in order to gain headroom or to mine the fire-clay after the coal has been removed" (Tootle, 1995); "in most cases and ALWAYS dependant on floor and roof strata, a bottom [borrum] caunch is carried out in the mothergate stall known as the DINT, as well as a top kansh just back from the face. By the removal of twelve or eighteen inches of floor, first of all the face conveyor is able to discharge onto the gate conveyor where increased height differential is necessary... secondly, in the maingate increased overall height is gained beyond seam depth, at both floor and ceiling positions, so that the major activities of power transformer/conveyor installation and latterly man-riding conveyors are facilitated" (Johnson, Dawdon).

Dowty fitter – "a name for a chock maintenance man on a longwall face" (Tootle, 1995).

fettling – "cleaning up and tidying an underground roadway" (Tootle, 1995, N.E.).

redding.— "clearing away the stones produced by blasting, falls, &c." (Nicholson, 1888); rid – clean up loose mine stone (Dodd, C20/2); "rid – clean up loose stone. Usually used to describe progress through a fall" (Sharkey). [ON rythja.]

shifters – "underground workmen employed at miscellaneous work, such as timbering rolleyways, taking up bottom stone or taking down top to make height where necessary, setting doors, building stoppings, redding falls, &c." (Nicholson, 1888).

spalling – "can occur when the coal has been undercut and it can also occur at the sides of roadways driven parallel to the cleat (headways) and the wider the roadway the more likely the spalling. Spalling could, I suppose be described as the coal simply flopping over" (Sharkey).

spile – "a verb used to describe the process of presupporting very weak and broken roof prior to taking out the rock or other material under it. As a noun it simply described whatever was used for the spiling" (Sharkey). [?Du]

> Spiling is an operation carried out in severely broken ground and the whole idea is to make forward progress, while at the same time clearing away the minimum amount of broken material which would otherwise fall in front of the supports and have to be cleared. In the situation described, permanent roadway supports would be set closer together than normal and spiles would be driven into the broken roof material over the top of the last roof bar. Spiles could be pointed planks or even old steel rails. Sufficient space was left between adjacent spiles for the next lot of spiles to be driven after the next roof bar was set. This process would be repeated until competent ground was reached (often at the inbye side of a roof fall).
>
> (Tony Sharkey)

spiting – storing up loose stone after a place has closed to make a way through (Wade, South Moor, 1966). [OE spittan, to dig.]

stone-men – "men employed in driving stone drifts, taking up bottom, or taking down top stone to make height for horses, &c." (Nicholson, 1888).

stopping – "a brick wall sealing off a road-way" (Temple, 1994, pp.19–20).

stub and feathers – the stub is a wedge driven in between two tapered wedges in a bore hole to break down stone (Wade, South Moor, 1966).

Keeping a general eye on the condition of passage-ways was the job of the Deputy, who would make a tour of inspection on a Sunday, or come in early on the shift, to check conditions. Thus Alexander Barrass of the Deputy's job:

"Aw'm duty-bund inbye te be	down in the pit
An' oor before the men,	
For Aw've got ivory place te see	every work-place
Before they start; an' then	
Aw've chocks te set, or props te draw,	remove
Or turns te lead an' lay...	bends on the tram-way

Another art associated with checking the condition of the strata, and the relationship between passages was 'jowling':

jowl – "to tap wall/ceiling to check condition; to signal" (Roxborough, swDm); "jowl – pitmen ascertain, by jowling against the coal, the probable thickness and direction of two approaching workings. 'Gan and gie us a jowl to see if she's fair on'" (Brockett, Newc, 1820s); "jowl or jowell – the noise made when beating on the 'face' of the coal to test the thickness of the coal *between* two 'headings' which are about to meet" (Tootle, 1995, N.E.); "the main purpose of jowlin in the pit was to check how solid the roof was. A trained ear could assess the situation by this process" (Wilson, North Walbottle); "jowling could be done with any solid implement, e.g. a pick, a stick, a hammer. If the jowl resulted in a hollow sound then care an extra support was usually necessary" (Sharkey).

> Well... you always – you had either a pricker or a stick and you used to tap the top just to check – what the condition – the stone – was like. If it was – you used to get a nice ring if it was alright – if it was – you used get like a holla sound if conditions were poor. And you'd shove props in as soon as you possibly could if you had the holla sound.
>
> (Brian Muter, Bates Colliery, 1950s on)

Jowl and Listen

Chorus:
Jowl, Jowl and listen lad
Ye'll hear the coalface working
There's many a marrer missing lad
Because he wadn't listen lad.

Me Father always used to say
Pit work's more than hewing

You've got to coax the coal along	
And not be riving and chewing	ripping at/getting impatient

Chorus

The deputy crawls from flat to flat	
The putter rams the chummins	empty tubs
And the man at the face must kna his place	know
Like a mother kna's her young un.	

Chorus

Chapter 5: Ventilation

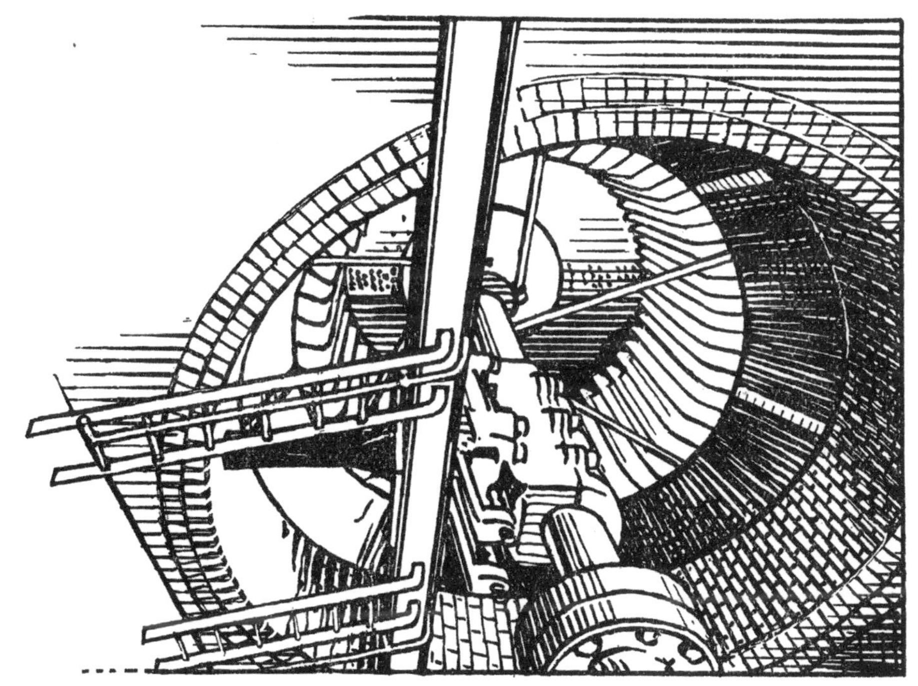

> If we as surveyors finished our work early we would have a sneak kip in the returns...probably near an 'owercast' ...a bricked structured/sealed crossover of intake versus return, access between both being through a set of three airtight doors...sometimes a huge booster fan would be located nearby in the return to assist ventilation.
>
> (Kenn Johnson, Dawdon)

> Despite some uncertainty and superstition over the nature of gases, "A system of ventilating a mine using the principle of hot air rising" was introduced in the seventeenth century, perhaps on the model of Belgian mining practices.
>
> This was achieved by hanging an iron basket containing burning coals in one of the two shafts or in a section of a bratticed shaft. The hot air rising in the shaft caused an updraft which drew the foul air out of the mine which was replaced by clean descending the other shaft or section. The first recorded use of this system was in a colliery at Cheadle, North Staffs in about the 1650s.
>
> (Tootle, 1995)

In 1708, after an explosion at Fatfield Colliery near Chester-le-Street, it was noted that, "…as the only remedy known here, the viewer of the works takes the best care he can to preserve a free current of air through all the works, and as the air goes down one pit [i.e. shaft] it should ascend another" (qu., *HRCM*, ch.8). The science was to dilute any dangerous gases and remove them from the mine in the current of air.

This became more difficult and more urgent as mines reached greater depths, where the greater pressures of overlying strata led to more frequent 'blows' of gas. To encourage a circulation of air, a furnace was put in place at Wallsend Pit in 1787 at the bottom of the upcast shaft, a system that continued throughout the nineteenth century, aided by the insistence in law on two separate shafts in 1862. By the mid-nineteenth century a 'dumb drift' was the ideal, a short tunnel by-passing the furnace itself, so that the rising air did not physically come in contact with the raw fire.

Other improvements were the subdivision of the air course: "A system of ventilation [was] introduced in about 1760 by James Spedding… in which the air current was directed through all the underground roads before going to the 'upcast' shaft" (Tootle, 1995). In the North East this was acted on by Buddle at Wallsend G Pit in 1810 – so that instead of one single route for the air, it was divided into a number of courses (panels), giving more effective coverage of a large area. This meant directing the air current through and round the underground workings by a system of doors, controlled by 'trapper lads'. The doors would be opened to let tubs pass, then closed again to resume the proper current of air.

Trapper Boy

I will be 15 on the 22nd May. I first went down at 8 to be a trapper in the tram-way, or barrow-way. I had six candles from my father to burn beside me; I liked it well at first, but afterwards I kept a horse-way door, and I had an accident; the tub broke my arm in two places. I got no smart money when I was ill. I was four months out of work from it. I had a coal fall on my forehead, and the mark still remains, and will always remain. The mark is on my arm where it is broke. I had 10d. a-day. I used to come down at three and go up at three; it was at South Hetton. I liked it very well. I thought about many things; I used to think if anything was to come how I should get out of its way. I used to catch mice, I did not catch many with my hands, I used to have a trap, which I baited with a bit of cheese, roasted first at the candle. I have caught two or three in an hour, and tied them together by the tails. I used to bring two or three home with me, and tie them to the cat's tail, to make her turn round and round. I would give the cat [the] other two for making so much sport. I used to give the other boys some: I have caught ten in a day. Sometimes there are black clocks [beetles] in the pit near Sunderland, and horse lice, which are like other lice, only much bigger. There are midges, which sometimes put out the candle.

(*PP,* 1842, CR xvi, pp.162–3)

brattice – "A division or partition in a shaft, 'heading' or other underground 'working place' to provide ventilation. It divides the place into two parts, one for the ingress of fresh air and the other for the egress of the used air. A brattice could be constructed of brick or stonework, or heavy-duty tightly woven cloth nailed to a timber frame or timber boarding" (Tootle, 1995); "a partition, generally of deal, placed in the shaft of a pit, or in a drift or other working of a colliery, for the purpose of ventilation. Its use is to divide the place in which it is fixed into two avenues, the current of air entering by the one and returning by the other" (Nicholson, 1888); "brattice – heavy woven material onetime impregnated with tar to make it airtight, later a lighter material used" (www.therhondda.co.uk); "brattice cloth was used instead of doors or stoppings near the face of bord and pillar workings. It was the most immediate ventilation device available to a deputy after a connection had been made inbye. The brattice was eventually replaced by a more permanent device such as a door or a stopping" (Sharkey); "The purpose being to redirect the air, sometimes to prevent it going round the pit too quickly, sometimes to prevent it going into a particular area and at other times to direct it into the roof where gas may be accumulating" (Douglass, 1973); "brattish" (Dodd, Tanfield Lea).

brattice-cloth – "cloth used for brattices or doors" (Tootle, 1995).

clacks – "flaps as ventilation control in the pit were sometimes referred to as clacks due to the sudden sharp noise when the heavy flap (often thick rubber sheet) returned to the closed positon" (Trelogan, New Herrington).

course – "a roadway used mainly for ventilation in a mine" (Tootle, 1995).

coursing – "a more efficient conducting of air through the mine by means of partitions and stoppings" (Colls, 1987).

downcast-shaft – "the shaft by which the air enters a coal pit, by which the men descend to their work, and by which the coals are drawn up" (Brockett, Newc, 1820s).

fire lamp – "a round iron cage supported on three legs or hung by chains. Sometimes placed at the bottom of a shaft to produce ventilation when opening out a colliery" (Tootle, 1995, N.East).

furnace – "a large fire placed near the bottom of the upcast shaft, which by rarefying the air contained in the upcast occasions a constant current of air to travel to and up the upcast shaft. This current is, by proper arrangements, employed to ventilate the workings" (Nicholson, 1888).

intake – "the fresh air airway going inbye from the bottom of the downcast" or "the fresh air descending into the mine" (Tootle, 1995.)

lum — "a chimney placed upon an upcast pit" (Nicholson, 1888).

panel – "separately ventilated district of a mine" (Colls, 1987).

panel system – "a system of working the coal, which came into use in the North of England, in about 1810, in an attempt to improve the ventilation. The colliery was divided into large squares or panels, separated and isolated by solid ribs of coal. Each panel would have its own boards and pillars fed by its own intake air supply and the return was carried straight to the upcast shaft" (Tootle, 1995).

reetawn – "tunnel carrying foul air to shaft" (Dodd, Tanfield Lea).

splitting – "division of the incoming current of air into the mine" (Colls, 1987); "prior to the use of splitting the air after leaving the downcast shaft was coursed continuously round all the working places and was returned to the upcast shaft. The result was that the air used in last place to be ventilated was polluted by all the impurities (gases, etc.) that had been picked up as it coursed around the mine. Splitting the air allowed each district to be fed with its own clean air supply" (Sharkey).

stopping — "a wall built in any excavation for the purpose of conducting air further into the mine" (Nicholson, 1888).

trapper – "a lad who the charge of a door in the mine, for preserving the circulation of the air" (Wilson, G'head, 1820s); "a boy whose business it is to attend to the trap-doors in a coal-mine [for ventilation]" (Brockett, Newc, 1820s); "a little boy, whose employment consists in opening and shutting a trap-door when required for the passage of tubs" (Nicholson, 1888); "youngest of mineworkers, employed to open trap-doors to allow passage of tubs and close them to aid current of air" (Colls, 1987); "a very old term describing a young child whose job it was to sit alone in the mine beside a ventilation door on the haulage track and open and close the door to allow a pony hauled set to pass through" (Sharkey).

an upcast (pronounced upkest) – "shaft in a coal-mine is one used to promote a circulation or upward draft of air" (Brockett, Newc, 1820s); "shaft by which the return air is discharged from the mine" (Nicholson, 1888).

waistman – "shifter attending airway" (Dodd, Tanfield Lea).

winning – "a 'main winning' would be the main intake airway and usually have an associated and mostly parallel 'back winning' – the main return airway". (Roxborough, swDm).

The major step forwards was the elimination of the furnace altogether, and the use of a giant fan to produce air circulation. In an early example in Wales, 1849, "The fan was placed horizontally over a culvert in communication with the upcast shaft which was closed by a cover" (*HRCM*, ch.8). During the twentieth century more powerful fans were introduced, incidentally lowering the working temperature throughout the mine.

The Trapper Boy Starts Work

Mi gran-fadder Tim, this is in 1860,
Startid wark as a trapper-boy in the pit (Aa think – at Elemore).

His Mam com waken'd him, pure dark still it woz aal aboot;
"The caller's been, seea get up, or thoo'll be late."

His Mam set him on the way, fer it woz pick-black thor,
Hand in hand, til the lit-up pit-shaft an' open cage.

"Leave him ti mi – he's Dick Platts' lad in-he?
His fadder's waitin' at the bottom," the man sed.

Forbye it woz aal wheest an' black. Wiv a whoosh — hushed
Th' cage shot doon; it made his ears pop.

His Dad was waitin' for him at the borrom:
"Here lad, tak this lamp. Howay, the owerman's waitin' fer us."

In the flickerin' shaddy an' lamp-leet they com tiv a door;
"Leave him with me, Dick," sed th' owerman, "thoo can see him later."

"You're ti stay here Tim," he sed, "an' mind the door.
Open the trap like this wi' this rope when thoo hears the coal-tub comin'."

Tim tried it oot, it was not ower-heavy for him,
An' he judged it nice when he heer'd the tub comin', yowked the door open.

Oot thru the gap com a fiery-eyed pony, pantin' and gleamin' i' the lowe, — light
An' the putter caal'd, "How, lad, new?" an' th' pony snorted.

Wick as owt, the little calvalcade hed passed, — quick, lively
An' oor Tim woz on his ahn agyen, on the listen.

An' roon' his bit cove, raws o' dottid e'en lit up,
Mouse-folk it woz, wadda et his bait if it wornit ina box.

There woz tubs and waits an' then his Dad com an' et bait wi' him.
Then, "Back ti wark. Noo be careful thoo dinnut faal asleep."

But ten hours is a dowly lang time; Tim dover'd ower — dozed off
But waken'd a'reet jus' in time fer the las' tub.

An' then they was oot, hyem agen in the dark, ti wesh an' eat. — home
His Da settled doon tiv a pipe. "Come an' sit doon lad.

"The morn, thoo'l collect thy ahn lamp; rimembor ti return it.
Second! Dinnot faal asleep agien."

"Aye (an' he laugh'd) – the owerman com by an' seed yi asleep
But it was near lowse, yi forst day, se yi got nae bunch. — end…kick

"But tak care it dizzent happen ye agien.

Them doors, they hev ti be shut for the air-flow an' open for the tubs."

"Aye, fadder, Ah'll mind," sed Tim. Then his big brother com in:

"How did thoo mak oot?" sed Sam, "Ah bet thoo's tired." "Aye, some."

At Dawdon in 1958 there was an oldish 'Dust-Sampler' called Lennie W. who told me of his bewilderment when first going underground, to be herded away from the shaft by a big fella with a stick [Owerman] shouting 'Get in bye the lot of yerr!' On that first day with only an oil lamp Lennie was given a trapper lad's job between air-doors, to open and close them in turn when he heard the putter coming. Nowt happened all day…no putter showed up and poor Lennie's lamp went out. After a shift in total darkness the next shift Deputy 'rescued' him and told him the putter had been sent to a different part of the District. Lennie always swore that your lamp had a better chance of staying on all shift if you gave a Lamp Cabin man a packet of 'tabs' each week.

(Kenn Johnson, Dawdon)

One last note. After the explosion of 1880 at Seaham Pit:

Coroner: Did you find that furnace [no.3] alight for any considerable time after the explosion?

Stratton [Colliery Manager]: It was alight at 7 o'clock on Friday morning.

Q. That is some fifty-four hours after the explosion?

A. Yes. It had been omitted to be examined so minutely, and it was found to be smouldering at that time, fifty-four hours after, 7 o'clock.

Q. That shows the explosion had been very severe at that furnace?

A. Well, it had not been severe at all. A lot of the things which the furnace-men had there were still there, these little windmills and things.

Q. Those little toys? [Presumably pointing to some examples].

A. Yes; they had a lot of little toys, and these toys are there still and are going at this moment I believe.

(*PP*, 1881, CR x, qq.5236–9)

Chapter 6: Drainage

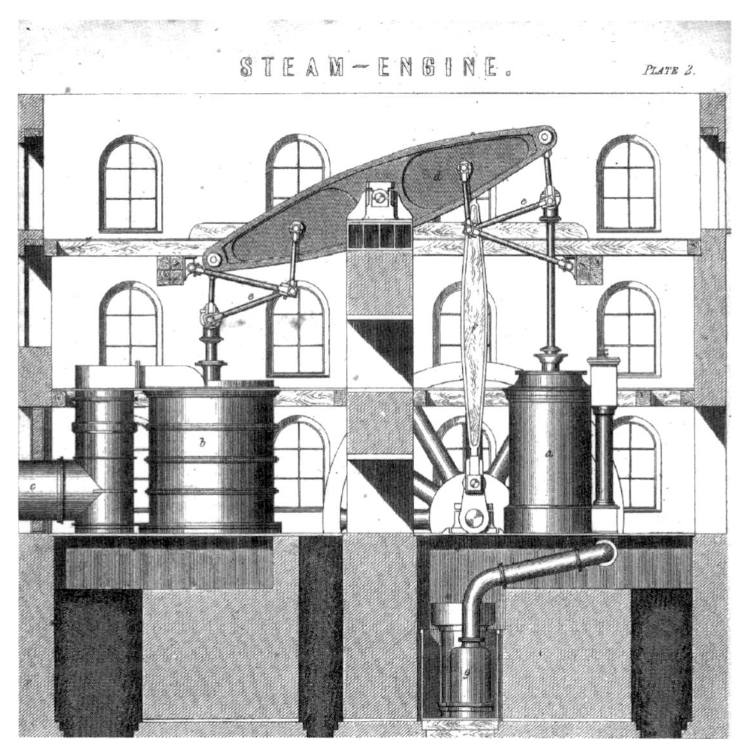

A major risk to mine working was the influx of water from porous, water-holding strata (especially layers of sand) above the coal seams. While this was most persistent during sinking (see section 3.1), it remained a hazard to everyday working. Early solutions included carrying the water "in raw hide vessels on men's backs up ladders" (*HRCM*, ch.3) or an endless chain of buckets worked by a horse gin – but these only sufficed shallow mines. The extraction of deeper coal depended on the development of efficient steam engines to pump the water out of the mine – the Newcomen (condensation) engine was first used for this purpose in 1712; the more efficient 'Cornish Engine' of Watts was used during sinking at Murton Colliery 1837–38. Electric pumps became standard in the twentieth century.

> Yes, it was hard times at the coal face. We were on piece work – the more coal you hewed the more money you made. It was a wet pit: in the north west, in the bell hole, it was up to your knees – terrible, terrible. You had the pumps going but still the water used to come out of the bottom and it used to drop all the time from the roof. We had to do this everyday – everyday taking a dry shirt to put on to come home. And that isn't all we had to cope with for there was the foul air which made us gasp for breath and many, many times your Davy lamp would burn down to just a small light – not enough to keep it burning.
>
> (Mr Cawson, Kibblesworth, Beamish 1993/5)

adit – horizontal tunnel with downward slope for draining water, e.g. 2 mile drainage adit from Old Kenton Colliery to Tyne in 1770.

atmospheric engine – "this was a sort of steam engine with a cylinder and piston; the power for driving the piston was derived from letting steam into the cylinder when the piston was raised and then condensing it to form a vacuum, bringing about the piston stroke (the 'vacuum' being less than the external atmospheric pressure). At the beginning of the eighteenth century Newcomen's atmospheric engine was first used at Griff Colliery, Warwickshire for pumping water from a depth of 50 yds. It was used extensively in the North of England. [It was not successful in use for winding coal] due to the difficulty in converting reciprocating into rotary motion" (Tootle, 1995).

blogged up – "a pipe stopped up with dirt" (Wade, South Moor, 1966).

cankery water – "impure, poisonous water, red in colour" (Wade, South Moor, 1966).

chain of dippers or **chain of buckets** – "an early device for pumping water from a mine… At regular intervals on the outside of the chain were attached oblong wooden buckets or oxhide dippers; they descended inverted and filled with water as they passed under the bar in the 'pool' and emptied into a flume as they passed over the drum at the top of the shaft" (Tootle, 1995).

clacks – "pump valves" (Wade, South Moor, 1966); "kep-clack – the foot valve in a pump suction pipe" (Wade, South Moor, 1966).

clog – "in mining, a sledge loaded with stones and dragged round by the gin, to which it acts as a brake" (Heslop, Newc, 1880s). [log]

cundy — "a culvert or drain" (Nicholson, 1888); "kundee – small tunnel, drain" (Dodd, Tanfield Lea).

day water – "water which penetrates into the mine through some direct opening from the surface" (Tootle, 1995, N.East).

grathe – "to put in order, to dress or replace a worn 'clack' or 'bucket' leather in a mine pump" (Tootle, 1995).

hogger — "a wide leather pipe used to deliver water into a cistern" (Nicholson, 1888); "a large leather pipe" (Tootle, 1995).

lift – "parallel columns of 'pumps' in a shaft... In multiple 'pumping systems' the lift was the distance from one 'pump' 'inset' in the shaft to the next" (Tootle, 1995).

pit pond – "a pond, on the surface, for the water pumped out of the mine. If the colliery had a steam winding engine, the water was used to feed the boilers" (Tootle, 1995).

plunger – "the piston in the water end of a pump" (Wade, South Moor, 1966).

pumping engine – "the engine used to raise water out of the pit. The first application of steam power in the mining industry was in pumping engines. At a later date some pumping engines served a dual purpose and were also adapted to wind coal and men" (Tootle, 1995).

pump house – "a building on the surface, or the place underground, where the main pumps for the colliery are situated" (Tootle, 1995).

pypman – "instals and extends pipes in mine" (Dodd, Tanfield Lea).

pypyahd – "for storing non-metalic pipes" (Dodd, Tanfield Lea).

rising main – "the pump delivery pipes in a shaft" (Wade, South Moor, 1966).

siping — "a very small feeder of water" (Nicholson, 1888).

snore holes – "holes in the strainer that make a snoring noise when the sump is drained" (Wade, South Moor, 1966); "on the snore – when a pump was drawing air and water, making a distinctive snoring sound" (Tootle, 1995).

spigot and faucet – "a type of pipe joint" (Wade, South Moor, 1966).

siphon – "a method of drainage that required no power. We had a massive one at Dean and Chapter" (Sharkey).

strum end – "the end of the suction pipe on a pump which was placed in the water. It was supposed to filter out the dirt and other foreign objects" (Sharkey); "strum – the strainer on the end of a pump suction pipe" (Wade, South Moor, 1966).

sump – "a dirty settleing of water" (*Bell MS*); "at the bottom of the shaft, a standage for water" (Wade, South Moor, 1966); "keep the sump away – leave plenty of space for drainage in a wet coal seam" (Briscoe, 2003); sump – "the sump is under the shaft – under the resting place of the cage" (Douglass, 1973).

watter-leading – "here an empty (usually metal) tub set was sent down to the lowest point of a flooded area known as a 'swalley'. Each tub had a hole in the bottom and soon filled with water up to the flood level. A man then entered the area and with arms under water, forced a wooden bung into the hole from the outside. The whole set was then hauled off by windy-engine or by pony and eventually un-bunged and emptied in an area where the water would not (hopefully) return to the original flooding" (Johnson, Dawdon).

yell watta – "excessive rain, water from top and bottom of miners' working place" (Dodd, Tanfield Lea).

Chapter 7: Coal

Coal is defined as "a black carbonaceous substance of vegetable origin, usually found beneath overlaying strata... mainly used as a fuel" (Tootle, 1995). What is most commonly encountered is indeed the familiar compact black type, but that belies the variety of forms coal occurs in, depending on the variable conditions that applied 250 million years ago in the Carboniferous forests. From the miners' and consumers' point of view, the coal is valued according to its carbon content: the grades, from lower to higher carbon, are known as 'lignite', 'bituminous' and 'anthracite'. The Great North East Coalfield is almost exclusively concerned with the bituminous coals.

> The Coal-Measures consist of a series of shales, grits, sandstones, and ironstones, characterlzed by the abundance of coal-seams and the general absence of limestones...
>
> Coal is not, strictly speaking, a mineral, being of organic origin; but it is nevertheless frequently classed as such amongst the Hydrocarbons. It is composed of vegetable matter, which through chemical change and pressure, as well as from original decomposition, has lost much of its structure. Amongst the conspicuous kinds of plants which helped to form it, are ferns, *Equisetacae*, Giant Club Mosses, and Conifers...
>
> (H.B.Woodward, *Geology of England & Wales*, London, 1876, ch.4)

Names for coal

anthracite – the 'best' coal, with the highest carbon content, and the type most used for domestic heating. It is mostly found in the Wales coalfield. "Anthracite steam coal...burns almost smokelessly and was greatly prized by the navies of the world" (Benson, 1989, p.7).

band – similar to splent, but in the middle of the seam, not at the bottom (John Kell, Leasingthorne).

bituminous coal – coloured brown to black, is mostly used for industrial purposes, including the production of coke; the type most typical of the Great North Coalfield, it was used for steam engines, coke production and domestic fuel.

black diamonds – "coal" (Heslop, N'd, 1880s); "dimond – coal" (Wilson, G'head, 1820s); "black diamonds – an expression used by politicians, poets and journalists when talking about the mineral wealth of Britain" (Sharkey).

brass thill – "a coal seam" (Dodd, Tanfield Lea).

brat – "a black inferior sort of coal" (Wade, South Moor, 1966); "a thin seam of coal with 'iron pyrites' and/or 'carbonate of lime'" (Tootle 1995, N.East).

brown coal – "woody or soft peaty looking coal, brown or black in colour" (Tootle, 1995); "Aw've bray'd for hours at woody coal" (Wilson, G'head, 1820s).

cannel coal — "a fine, compact description of coal, with a conchoidal fracture; burns with a bright flame like a candle, whence its name" (Nicholson, 1888); "cannel or sometimes 'candle' coal – in the collieries a thin piece of unmarketable [coal] at the top of the seam" (*Bell MS*); "cannel-coal – a hard, opaque, inflammable fossil coal, sufficiently solid to be cut and polished" (Brockett, Newc, 1820s). However this type is more typical of the Staffordshire and Lancashire coalfields than the N.E.

claggy coal – "a coalseam where a layer of coal has a tendency to stick to the roof or floor making it difficult to work" (Tootle, 1995, N.East).

crow coal – "a term sometimes used for 'anthracite', due to its shiny black appearance" (Tootle, 1995); "craa, craw – an outcrop or crop of strata, [hence] craw coal" (Heslop, N'd, 1880s).

dant – "soft sooty coal found at backs, and at the leaders of hitches and troubles" (Nicholson, 1888); "dunt – bad coal, mineral charcoal; any imperfection in the quality of a seam of coal" (Brockett, Newc, 1820s).

glede, gleed – "a coal in a state of strong heat" (Brockett, Newc, 1820s). [OE gled – any glowing hot substance.]

lignite – also called brown coal or steam coal. Its main use was as fuel for steam engines, today for steam powered electricity generators. Not mined in the N.E. though.

parrot coal – "A variety of 'cannel' coal. It was said to split and crack with a chattering noise, like a parrot talking" (Tootle, 1995 N.E./Scots).

pitcoal – "A general term for the 'bituminous' type of coal" (Tootle, 1995).

quolls – coals: "'ar'ye gawn t' th' quolls', are you going to the coal pit for coals?" (*Bell MS*).

rammel – "a thin piece of coarse cannel coal which lies at the top of the marketable coal" (*Bell MS*). [In this however, Bell is mistaken; see 'rammel' under 'stone'.]

sea coal – a term with many applications; see below.

splent – "a hard substance (almost coal, but stony – burns in fire but leaves a large mass). It is part of the seam in the Brockwell. It lies at the foot of the seam in some parts, therefore the seam is then kurved at the top... Band – similar to splent, but in the middle of the seam, not at the bottom" (John Kell, Leasingthorne).

swad – "impure shaly coal" (Nicholson, 1888).

Walls-End – "a name extensively used for Newcastle coals... The coals from this place being at one time of the most valuable description, other coalowners began to append to the name of their coals the favourite term of Walls-end, no matter from whence they came" (Brockett, Newc, 1820s); "Walls-end – quality coal from Dawdon pit" (G.Patrickson).

woody coal – see brown coal.

Sea Coal

The story of 'sea-coal' as a term is a complex one. It has been often assumed that the term 'sea-coal' reflects the ease with which coal may be gathered on the seashore in some places, giving a hint as to how coal in this island was first discovered and named. The *Oxford English Dictionary* says: "Possibly in early times the chief source of coal supply may have been the beds exposed by marine denudation on the coast of Northumberland and South Wales." [To which we can add the Fife coast.] The antiquary, Leland, visiting the north in 1769, used the word 'sea-coal' in a similar sense: "The vaynes of the se-coles be sometyme upon clives [cliffs] of the se, as round about Coket Island."

Sea-coal, as coal washed up by the sea and recovered on the shore, is current still in local usage, for the fragments collected off the beach into sacks and wheeled away on a bicycle (traditionally) for local use. The process was noted in the 1930s by J.B.Priestley: "Along the coast road between Sunderland and Seaham Harbour, we came upon quite a number of men riding or wheeling bicycles loaded with two or three small sacks of coal. I heard afterwards that these men descend very steep and dangerous cliffs near Seaham Harbour and pick up coal from the shore. They were now going to Sunderland to sell the coal." In more recent memory: "coal-line – marker scratched in the sand, in front of seacoal patch being left by the tide; it gives you sole rights to all seacoal left, in front of line towards the sea; many a battle fought over this line being moved further back or side by the oppos [enemy]" (Alf Sterling, H'pool). Plus 'nutter' – for "someone who collects small coal" (Newcastle, 2001).

Both 'coal' and 'sea-coal' go back to Anglo-Saxon usage. The Old English term *cōl* (pronounced 'kohl', much as today) applied in fact to any red-hot burning substance, not just coal as we know it, but charcoal, or even red-hot wood embers perhaps. This sense is preserved in Herbert's poem, *Vertue*, where "Onely a sweet and vertuous soul, / Like season'd timber, never gives; / But though the whole world turn to coal, / Then chiefly lives" – in which 'coal' is not some cold, fossilised state, but the fiery Christian end of the world. Compare Sir Thomas Browne's reference to 'the coals of juniper' ca.1682.

About 1050 AD mention occurs of *sæcol* (sea-coal), applied in fact to jet ('jet' itself is a later loan-word from Old French *jaiet*). As jet is a type of coal, found typically on the coast, e.g. at Whitby, the OE usage is reasonable, but confusing to us.

The situation is a little clearer by about 1200 AD, when 'sea-coal' (or its Latin equivalent, *carbo maris*), becomes the standard term for mineral coal, even when the coal is being found inland, as in references to 'sea-coal pits'. This may well reflect the earlier reality of coal as something found near the sea, but now extended to apply to the mineral anywhere, in order to distinguish that sort of 'coal' from the more general use of the word for a range of burning substances.

In the sixteenth to eighteenth centuries, as a commercial coal trade developed, the standard term for the mineral became 'coal' or 'pit-coale'. The older 'sea-coal' is still found, sometimes in contexts that relate to a coastal origin (e.g. early seventeenth century "the fore said sea-cole and pitt cole is become the general fewell of this Britaine Island" (qu., *HRCM*, ch.1), but sometimes implying 'coal shipped by sea'. Thus Daniel Defoe in his *Tour through the Whole Island of Great Britain* says: "The City of London, and Parts adjacent, as also all the South of England, are supplied with Coals, called therefore Sea-coal, from Newcastle upon Tyne, and from the coast of Durham and Northumberland."

Lastly, 'sea-coal' has also been used for those reserves of the mineral under the North Sea that pits like Easington, Dawdon and Monwearmouth accessed – until so recently. Thus, "coal worked from under the bed of the sea" in Nicholson's dictionary (1888).

Sizes of coal

The terms here have more to do with marketing than geology, but include many (formerly) familiar words.

beans – small coals of the size of beans: "beany coals" (Brockett, Newc, 1820s); "beans – small coals, so-called for their size" (Heslop, N'd, 1880s).

chinglees – "pieces of coal the size of a marble" (Wade, South Moor, 1966); "chinley coals, 'shingly' – a medium sized high grade of coal" (Tootle, 1995, C19, N.East).

dead small – "The smallest coal, which passed through the screens, almost as fine as dust" (Tootle, 1995, N.East).

dolly-wash – "coal dust from the beck" (Wheatley Hill).

duff – "the smallest coal, after separating the 'nuts, 'beans' and 'peas'" (Brockett, Newc, 1820s); "small coals, from which, by means of the apparatus, the nuts have been separated" (Nicholson, 1888); "small coals and fine dust" (Tootle, 1995); "a sandlike sediment" (Douglass, 1973) [esp. used in limekilns].

house, house-fire or **household coal** – "A good clean coal, which burnt away leaving little ash, suitable for household use" (Tootle, 1995); "household coal was a saleable product produced by screening, cleaning and sometimes blending" (Sharkey); "soft bituminous house coal" (Benson, 1989, p.7).

makings – "small coals made when 'kirving' or 'nicking'" (Tootle, 1995, N.East).

nickings – "the small coals made when 'nicking'" (Tootle, 1995, N.East).

> For what he gat was very sma'
> Frae out the kirvens and the nickens,
> The myest of whilk was left belaw,
> The rest like crums for feeden chickens.
>
> (Thomas Wilson, *Pitman's Pay*, Pt.2)

nuts – "coals that have passed through a half or three-quarter inch screen" (Brockett, Newc, 1820s).

nutty slack – "small coal with some slack" (Trelogan, New Herrington).

pan coal – "small coals, which used to be sold to salt makers, for the fires beneath the salt pans" (Tootle, 1995).

peas – "small coals from the duff that has been taken out by screening" (Nicholson, 1888); "A descriptive term for small coals. Smaller than 'beans' and also produced from 'duff'" (Tootle, 1995).

roondy (coal) – "roondee – large lump of coal" (Dodd, Tanfield Lea); "rundies – next quality to best" (Trelogan, New Herrington); "roondy (roondy coal) "lumps of coal 4 inches to 8 inches across" (Riley, Blyth); "Hoy a big roundy on the fire, son" (Alan Brown, Co.Dm).

run-of-the-mine coal – "unwashed coal" (Temple, 1994, pp.19–20).

sleck – "small pit-coal" (John Ray, 1674; Grose, 1787); "slack – burnable residue of coal dust" (Trelogan, New Herrington).

Associated products:

cat – "a ball made by mixing coal and clay together" (Heslop, N'd, 1880s).

coal-balles – "briquettes of coal and soil [intended to] make the smoke less problematical" ca.1603 (qu. Freese, 2005, p.34); "other recipes for coal balls included mixing seacoal with sawdust, chopped straw, tanner's bark, or even cow dung" (Tootle, 1995).

dough balls – "round cakes of coal dust made from slack" (Trelogan, New Herrington).

duff balls:

> I remember the out of work miners making duff balls. I was three years old and the country was in the throes of the 1926 General Strike. On the mineral railway the coal trucks had lumped their way down to the docks over the past fifty years leaving a thick bed of coal dust between the sleepers. The men would go at night and fill buckets with the dust, mix it with paraffin which cost one penny a pint and, with their hands, mould the mixture into balls. The balls were left to dry and harden and made excellent fuel. The coal dust had to be collected at night because, if caught, then men would have been charged with stealing the coal mine owner's property and would have received a month in jail from the magistrates who were also owned by the coal owner.
>
> (per Monica Halpins, Seaham 1930s)

> As for the coal dust, as carbonaceous as the other coal, and a ninth part of all that comes above the ground, it is woeful to see what becomes of it. A little of it is indeed sold to glasshouses, but if anyone will ascend a little eminence at night and look around him, he will see bright red fires in several directions pointing out to him the destruction that is going on... By the burning of these heaps is formed slag, which is drawn off for the common roads in the country, and is also sent down the shafts to repair the horse roads in the pits.
>
> (*PP*, 1842, CR xvi, p.147)

In the 1860s, a market was found for small coal:

> Meanwhile the agent [Mr Daglish] was working out a great colliery problem for the Londonderry Pits, the experiments

> showing that the coals mainly produced by Seaham and the other pits were very suitable for the production of gas, and larger customers were found in London, Beckton, and other places. Hitherto the Londonderry Collieries had suffered on account of the lack of demand for small coal, but when the gas trade was established, it was sent in bulk at good prices. It was one of the conditions of the Gas Companies that the coals were delivered to their wharf at an inclusive cost, the steamers, of course, being provided by the coalowners.
>
> (George Hardy, 'A Historical Account...', *Ant. Sunderland*,17 (1916), pp.34–35)

By the 1960s, coal was being sent to gas works in London, Portsmouth, Poole, Shoreham, Southampton and Exeter (see McCutcheon, *Seaham Urban District Official Handbook*, Seaham, 1963).

Stone and non-coal

band – "a layer of stone, or clay, in a coal seam" (Brockett, Newc, 1820s).

brasses – "pyrites" (Brockett, Newc, 1820s); "iron pyrites" (Tootle, 1995).

cauldron bottom – "the fossil root area of a tree or fern lying on the roof of a seam of coal. It derived its name from its resemblance to the bottom of a cauldron or pot. With little adhesion to the overlaying strata, and sometimes hard to detect in shale, they are prone to breaking away and falling without warning" (Tootle, 1995, N.East); "a 'cauldron bottom' but well known as 'carbonarse' – I've seen a number in Main Coal at top of 'retarder drift' and Maudlin 17 North" (Johnson, Dawdon); "caadron-arse (cauldron-arse) – a stone found in roof just above coal level. It is foreign to the normal roof strata and in all cases dangerous to leave without either supporting it with timber or removing it from the roof. Owing to it having a very smooth surface and having small coal piping around, it easily detaches itself from the roof. Cone shaped" (McBurnie, Washington, 1970s).

also –

carving arse – "fossil or stone in roof liable to fall" (J.Patrickson, Dawdon); "The material is mainly a metomorphosed tree stump surrounded by coally material. Potentially very dangerous. 'Kettle Bottoms' in other coalfields" (Sharkey). "I always thought the term was 'carbon arse' – carbon referring to the veneer of coal surrounding the stump, which spelled a hazard. The coal was comparatively weak and brittle and easily disintegrated when exposed" (Roxborough, swDm); "'carvinarce' – a smooth backed fossil easily dislodged" (Wade, South Moor, 1966); "'cattrinarse' – fossilised tree stump. If these happened to be located in the roof it was essential to support them as they suddenly dislodge under their own weight. They often had a very glossy outer surface and were also known as 'slippy-backs'" (Wilson, North Walbottle).

canch – "sometimes in posh circles spelt 'caunch'. The stone face of the roadway above the extracted seam which was blasted down and cleared away before roadway supports were set" (Sharkey); "canch – a rise like a step. In a thin seam of coal... coal and stone [i.e. canch] are worked away alternately" (Heslop, N'd, 1880s); "canch – the stone below the thill or floor of a narrow coal seam that has to be removed as coal-getting proceeds" (Wade, South Moor, 1966); "canch, or caunch – the part of the heading above the top of the seam, consisting of stone which has to be removed to allow arched supports to be put in for the roadways" (Shelley, Sth Hetton); "canch – the area of stone directly at the end of the mothergate or tailgate and directly above the coalface. This had to be removed to advance gateways" (Wilson, North Walbottle).

cat-heed – "an ironstone nodule" (Heslop, N'd, 1880s); "catheid – a nodule of iron ore found in coal seams" (Wade, South Moor, 1966); "a hard stone similar to a pebble, mostly in the strata forming the floor of the mine. Mostly ironstone in nature" (McBurnie, Washington, 1970s).

chalk or **pipe clay** – "A term used by sinkers and borers for gypsum" (Tootle, 1995, N.East).

clay – "A term used in mining for anything from soft clay to friable shales" (Tootle, 1995).

fossils – two main fossil plant/tree types: *lepidodendron* – with scaly bark; and *sigillaria* – with strap-like leaves (see Freese, 2005); "plus Stigmaria [fossil roots] and occasionally *Ammonites*" (Johnson, Dawdon).

ganister – a hard, fine-grained type of fireclay, used for making bricks to line blast-furnaces, etc.

girdle – "in mining a thin hard bed of slate clay on sandstone" (*Bell MS*).

mettal-post – "in mining, is slate clay" (*Bell MS*); "metal – shale of the lead mining districts" (Tootle, 1995, N.East).

plate – "in mining, is slate clay" (*Bell MS*).

post [in mining] – "is sandstone" (*Bell MS*), (Nicholson, 1888).

rammel – "a soft clay-like stone" (Temple, 1994, pp.19–20); "stone that gets mixed with the coal in the pit" (Wade, South Moor, 1966); "rammul – small stone from mine roof" (Dodd, Tanfield Lea); "a very incompetent rock sitting on top of the seam which fell away as the coal was mined" (Sharkey); "ramble – a thin stratum of shale, often found lying immediately above the seam of coal" (Nicholson, 1888). [rammel 'brushwood, rubbish'.]

segger's-clay – "a name given by miners in the county of Durham to a kind of clay lying immediately over a seam of coal. It...is used to make fire-bricks" (Brockett, Newc, 1820s); "seggar – segger's clay – used for fire bricks. It is the fireclay or seat earth under the seam. And it is the compressed material out of which the trees grew that ultimately became coal" (Sharkey).

shale – "a soft blue stone in the pits" (Wilson, North Walbottle).

spangles/sparkles – [specks of spar in situ in rock] (Heslop, N'd, 1880s).

thill – "in mining, clay" (*Bell MS*).

whynn – "hard stone – in mining" (*Bell MS*); "whin or whinstone – greenstone; an igneous rock; but the term is usually applied by borers and sinkers to any exceptionally hard rock that emits a sharp sound under the hammer or chisel; usually a greenstone or siliceous sandstone" (Nicholson, 1888).

Seams

The alternate seams of coal and stone represented the variation in climate and surface conditions when the strata were originally laid down, some 250 million years ago. Coal represents thick vegetation associated with shallow fresh water; but should a sea invade the site, then tree-less muds would be deposited, turning to shale. UK coal in fact occurs only as occasional bands, of varying depth, within the Carboniferous deposits.

As the seams vary within the coalfield, and can have different local names, there is insufficient space here to deal with the topic in detail, but note: "All seams had letter reference (e.g. High Main = E) but also had local names; and sometimes local names were not accurately correlated so, 'Main' in one pit may be something else next door...hence Coal Board letter ref" (Johnson, Dawdon). Fossils within the coal and adjacent beds are important evidence for correlating seams between collieries, and indeed coalfields.

> There is in some Collieries 7 or 8 sorts of Coal. There are the Pipe-Coal, which perhaps is not above 4 or 6 inches thick. The Crow-Coal about a Foot or less thick. The 3 Quarter Coal about 3 Quarters thick or more, all which are foul or bad Coals, and not worth much, tho' I have known the 3 Quarter Coals used in making Salt, and believe it is so yet at Shields or elsewhere... And there is the Half Yard Cole, which is so called, it being of about that thickness, but is generally good Coal, and better than the 3 Quarter Coal, yet being so low to work in, or but of that small Thickness, it is scarce worth while to work it, there is also the five Quarter Coal, which is of about that thickness of 5 Quarters, and this is in some Collieries very fine, and makes a hot quick Fire... But there is also the Main-Coal, which is in some Places thicker than in others, sometimes you have it 7 Quarters, sometimes 8 Quarters, and sometimes 8 Quarters and half thick, any of which indeed is thick enough and valuable; this is the Coal I would wish you to have, this is the thing I think may please all People for Use, for this in these Northern Parts is generally best, both for a good Fire, and a lasting Fire.
>
> (*Compleat Collier*, 1707, pp.16–7)
>
> [The quarter referred to above is a quarter of a yard, i.e. 9 inches.]

> ...In the Newcastle district, the best seam is the highest workable one – the High Main – and is five or six feet thick. The most consistent seam is probably the Low Main, which is an excellent house and coking coal, although northwards from Newcastle its nature changes and it becomes a good steam Coal.
>
> (Tonge, 1906, ch.2)

> There are five seams of coal worked [at Seaham]: the Main seam, 460 yards from the surface, the Maudlin seam, 490 yards deep, Nos.1,2 and 3, Hutton seams, which are broken up by a 'fault'; these are worked in three sections about twenty yards below the Main and Maudlin seams. There are two seams further down, the Harvey and Baskey, at a depth from the top of the shaft of 560 yards and 600 yards.
>
> (*The Illustrated London News*, 18 September 1880)

> The coal in the Hutton Seam was very soft in some districts and you could dig it out with a shovel. There was a band of stone about six inches in the middle of the Low Main seam. We used to curve underneath it, drop it down and throw it to one side. The conditions were terrible, terrible. You would be working in about eighteen inches in the Six Quarter Seam, about four foot in the Low Main and about four foot six inches in the Hutton Seam. The Hutton Seam was about eight foot high in places and that was where the gas was…
>
> (Mr Cawson, Kibblesworth, Beamish, 1993/5)

At Easington Colliery the main seams (from top descending, in feet and inches) were:

Ryhope Five–Quarter 1′9″

Ryhope Little 2-6″ and 1′10″

High Main & Metal (combined) 9″ and 6′2″ and 1′8″ and 1′8″

Five Quarter 3′

Main 1′10″ and 8″ and 4'3″

Low Main 4′3″

Hutton 5′4″

Harvey 3″

[After DCC leaflet, 'Geological Time Line – Easington Colliery', 2001.]

At Herrington Colliery:

Five Quarter 3′3″

Main Coal 7′4″

Maudlin 5′7″

Low Main 11″

Brass Thill 2′0″

Hutton 2′10″

Harvey 2′5″

Top Tilley 2′3″

Bottom Tilley 2′4″

Top Busty 2′6″

Bottom Busty 2′2″

[After *Herrington Colliery*, NCB, undated.]

At Ashington, the seams (in descending order) were:

Ashington D/E (alias Blackclose/Moorland) 2′

Main – 4′

Yard – 2′–4′

Low Main (alias Five Quarter) 4′

Brass Thill (alias Low Main) 3′

Plessey M (alias Bottom Plessey) 3′.

The Brockwell was named by Heslop as "the lowest workable seam of any district," but two lower seams were worked in southwest Durham – the Victoria and the Marshall Green. Below the coal measures was the Millstone Grit: "I have heard this referred to as the 'Farewell Rock' because no coal exited in it or below it" (Sharkey).

> You would find detailed descriptions in the coal geologists' bible – *The Nature & Origin of Coal Seams* by A. Raistrick and CE Marshall – I don't recall the publisher... Arthur Raistrick was long time Reader in Geology at King's College, Newcastle and Charles Marshall was a Geordie lad who was Professor of Geology at Sydney University.
>
> (Frank Roxborough, swDm)

Strata and cleavage

Coal seams occur in sedimentary layers, approximate to the ancient land surface on which they were laid down. Horizontal once, they now tilt significantly, being nearer the surface in the north and west of the coalfield, deeper in the east: accordingly the passages in a pit do not proceed on an even plane. With no horizon to compare it with, the incline of a seam and the roadway that follows it might not be immediately obvious – unless you were putting a tub of coal!

> But as well as the original bedding plane, there is a vertical jointing known as the 'cleat'. If this ran away from the hewer, his task could be difficult; if it lay across his path, then layer after layer of coal could be sliced away more easily. Hence 'heedwiss' and 'bordwiss'.

back – "in miner's language, a fissure in the coal" (Brockett, Newc, 1820s).

back or **knowe** – "partings in the coal" (Wilson, G'head, 1820s).

A 'back' or 'knowe' sometimes, 'tis true,	
Set doon maw top wi' ease enough;	aided extraction
But oftener far we had to tew	struggle
On wi' a nasty scabby reuf.	roof

(Thomas Wilson, 1820s)

band – "a layer of rock withing the coal seam section" (Sharkey).

back-cast – "in coal mines an impediment in the working" (Brockett, Newc, 1820s).

bawdwiss [board-wise] – "coal cleat easily worked" (Dodd, Tanfield Lea); "bordruss and headruss for bordwiss, etc." (Sharkey); Thus "bord or board – The main 'cleavage' or 'cleat' in coalseams. The direction of the 'cleat'" (Tootle, 1995).

bottom – "The floor beneath a coalseam. The 'seat-earth'" (Tootle, 1995). "Bottom or floor, e.g. the bottom's baukin'" (J.Patrickson, Dawdon).

cleat – a technical concept that needs some explanation. 'Cleat' is a potential line of fracture in the vertical plane, produced by pressure, as a horizontal plane of fracture is inherent in the original lines of bedding. There are two possible directions for such a vertical cleat – sometimes both are present, or both are indistinct, but usually there is one dominatant line of cleat, which affects the hewing.

Imagine you have a loaf of sliced bread and are holding it end on, with the flat crust vertical before you. That is the lie of a bordways cleat (flat in front of you). Alternately, imagine you are looking at the side of the loaf, showing a long row of ends of slices – that is the position of a headways cleat (edge on, as it were). Understandably, it is easier to access the bread, slice by slice from the crust onwards, rather than attempt to pull out a slice sideways!

On bordways, "The cleat is at right angles to the direction of drivage and hewing the coal down from the face is very much easier. Places could be driven wide and were the main production sources when coal was got by hand hewing" (Sharkey). Whereas headways is "Driving on end. Tough work and places usually driven narrow" (Sharkey.).

Also "cleat – line of cleavage in coal – if strong cleavage would help hand hewers lever off coal in large chunks – if little or poor cleat, could be difficult to hew" (Hill, Harrington).

dike – "a hedge or fence; in a coal mine, a large crack or breach of the solid strata" (Brockett, Newc, 1820s); "dyke – an intrusion of rock (usually igneous) which displaces the coal" (Sharkey); "in Northern England it is extended to mean a fault" (Tootle, 1995). [Origin: from dike meaning hedge or wall, i.e. a barrier.]

dip – "the declivity of a coal seam from a level line" (Brockett, Newc, 1820s); "declivity of the strata or coal seam" (Nicholson, 1888).

dipper, or **downcast** – "a dyke or dislocation of the strata" (Brockett, Newc, 1820s).

flats – "in mining, a swelling out of the vein" (*Bell MS*).

floor – "the name for the strata immediately beneath the coalseam, it usually consisted of 'fireclay' or 'seatearth'" or "the bottom surface of a roadway" (Tootle, 1995).

heedwiss [head-wise] – "difficult coal to hew" (Dodd, Tanfield Lea).

hitch – "a small 'trouble' or dyke, in coal-mines, generally limited to a few inches' dislocation" (Brockett, Newc, 1820s); "a sudden elevation or depression of the strata to the extent of from a few inches to the thickness of the working seam of coal. When of a larger size it is called a dyke" (Nicholson, 1888); "hitch – a fault in the strata" (Wade, South Moor, 1966).

jacks – "large fissures or cracks in the roof of a mine" (Heslop, N'd, 1880s).

metal ridge or **metal rig** – "the floor of a mine forced up by the action of creep" (Tootle, 1995, N.East).

nip – "when the strata comes together and meets, nipping-out the coalseam. A 'drift' would be driven forward though the 'nip-out' to find the coal on the other side" (Tootle, 1995).

siddle – "the inclination of a seam of coal" (Nicholson, 1888).

sill – (in mining) "the bed" (*Bell MS*).

slickenside – smoother face of a fault "where heat and force of nature sheared the seam" (Johnson, Dawdon).

slip – "same thing as hitch but usually less displacement" (Sharkey).

swalley – "a dip or hollow on a roadway" (Wade, South Moor, 1966); "swallee – dip in ground" (Dodd, Tanfield Lea); "swelly or swally – a small basin or dish in the strata produced by undulation" (Nicholson, 1888); "swally" (J.Patrickson, Dawdon); "Thor's a hitch an' then a swally / Filled wi' wetter like a ford" (Barrass, 1896).

thill – "the floor of a seam of coal" (Nicholson, 1888).

throw – "extent of the displacement" (Sharkey).

wrought out – "all the coal taken out – applied to a seam or pit where all the available coal has been exhausted" (Nicholson, 1888).

A serious dislocation or fault was encountered out under the sea, limiting the extent of mining for Vane Tempest and Dawdon collieries. Outside contractors were brought in to try to connect with coal beyond the fault, but politics in the 1990s overshadowed the outcome. (Monkwearmouth pit did not encounter the same fault problem, but was shut down anyway.)

The Dawdon Mole

Hush lads had thee gob ar'l tell yer arl an arful story
Hush lads had thee gob an' ar'l tell yer aboot the mole.

To Dawdon Colliery Thyssens came an' brung with 'em a mole
Its an arful fearsome lukin' thing wi' which to drive a hole
Thar's Jarmans, Welshmen, Yorkshire lads an' fella's off the dole
Thats drivin' this monster oot te sea, towards war cokin' coal.

Hush lad had thee gob ar'l tell yer arl an arful story
Hush lads had thee gob an' ar'l tell yer aboot the mole.

Noo Thyssens' men a' deem arl reet, they pay a lot o' tax
Still they divvent get owt for nowt they nivver can relax
An' if betimes they get oot o' line there's nee Depitation Agenda
Disputes for them just don't exist they're settled by the nose benda.

Hush lads had thee gob ar'l tell yer arl an arful story
Hush lads had thee gob an' ar'l tell yer aboot the mole.

Te these canny lads we'd like to give a wee bit o' advice
Watch yersels, an' dee whats reet an' divvent be pit mice
We waddent like te see any o' yer ivver cum te grief
There's ne carl at arl te smash yersels or Rarfie's perminent Relief.

Hush lad had thee gob ar'l tell yer an an arful story
Hush lads had thee gob an' ar'l tell yen aboot the mole.

Ye've a lang way to gan wi' that 12 foot span a churning oot that muck
An' arl the bonnie Dawdon lads wish ye's the best o' luck
Its up to ye's – but am warnin yer – ye'd better win the cup
Or wor 'Monster' at bank an' the one below 'ill turn an' gobble yer up.

Hush lads had thee gob ar'l tell yer arl an arful story
Hush lads had thee gob an' an'l tell yer aboot the mole.

(Ernie Taylor, Dawdon)

Measures for coal

The standard coal measure in the North East was the chauldron/chaldron/chalder (from French *chaldere*). In the Middle Ages this equalled 2,000 lbs (i.e. not far short of a ton), and a 'keel' carried two chaldrons. Since tax was levied per chaldron, the temptation was to increase the size of the measure. By the sixteenth century a chaldron had varnigh doubled in weight. In 1695 the Newcastle chaldron was fixed by weight at 53 cwt (i.e. about half a ton), and an Act of 1822 enforced sale of coal by weight [*HRCM*, ch.1].

In modern times, the ton – 2,240 pounds – was replaced 1971 by a metric tonne of 2,205 pounds or 1,000 kilograms. Used for measuring, e.g. coal reserves.

boll – coal measure: 6 bolls = 1 chaldron [*HRCM*, ch.21]; "the Newcastle chaldron is a measure of 24 bolls, containing 53 cwts of coals" (Nicholson, 1888); "boll – an old Scotch dry measure, still often used, varying according to locality and article measured, the potato, barley, oats, & c. boll, containing 6 bushels" (*Gresham Comprehensive Dictionary*, 1937). [A form of *bowl*, A.Sax. *bolla*, a bowl, cup, measure.]

canny-jagga-coal – "large lorry load, or barrow, of seacoal" (Sterling, H'pool).

chaldron (measure) – "from the Latin caldaria, a caldron, Middle French chaldere, a kettle or pot, Middle English chalder, chaldre. Originally pronounced chalder, later chaldron, although in some areas the older pronunciation was still used in the nineteenth century. A measure of capacity for coal, coke and grain which was used in England, Scotland and Wales… [In] Newcastle upon Tyne, the chaldron totalled 42 cwt and equalled $^{1}/_{8}$ of a keel" (Tootle, 1995). "101 chalder of grindstones" (Heworth, 1583, via Heslop, N'd, 1880s); "chalder – a chaldron. A Newcastle chaldron of coals weights fifty-three hundred weight. Eight of these chaldrons make one keel" (Brockett, Newc, 1820s); "chaldrun – obsolete horse–drawn coal-wagon" (Dodd, Tanfield Lea); "The old colliery wagon contains a chaldron, and is a called a chaldron wagon" (Heslop, N'd, 1880s).

corf, corfe or **corve** – "a measure of capacity for coal used throughout the British coalfields… about 4 $^{1}/_{2}$ cwt of coal" (Tootle, 1995); "the corf to hold 20 peck or 87.249 imperial gallons" (*Bell MS*).

fother or **futher** – “in Newcastle, as many coals as a two-horse cart can carry” (Brockett, Newc, 1820s); “fother – a measure of coal, being one-third of a chaldron, or 17 $^{2}/_{3}$ cwts” (Nicholson, 1888). [O.E. fother, a ‘cartload’.]

scope – ?scoop: “ilk pike (pick, i.e. workman) to wyn evere day sixty scopes” (D’m, 1447, via *HRCM*, ch.21) [Du schoep, bucket/basket.]

ten – [A ‘ten’ = 40 fothers] *HRCM*, ch.21.

Finally, in case that did not answer your questions…

HOW TO GROW YOUR OWN COAL

1. Spread some special earth (‘fireclay’) as widely as you can, add seeds of ferns, giant club mosses, conifers and others.

2. Keep moist and warm – almost swamp conditions – until a forest develops with trees over 100 foot high. Maintain supplies of water and warmth for half a million years.

3. Meanwhile admit some insects, not too many, and certainly no major leaf-eating animals (no dinosaurs! no mammals!). Unaffected by seasons, fire, or pests, your trees will grow to tremendous size before collapsing and yielding to replacement growth.

4. By the time you have tired of farming, the lower levels should already have turned to usable peat. For maximum effect, however, cover and leave for up to 300 million years.

5. You should now have prime coal not to mention possible gas and oil. According to its carbon content, your coals might be graded (low to high) – lignite, bituminous, anthracite (which has 90–95% carbon). The only problem now is getting it out....

Chapter 8: The officials

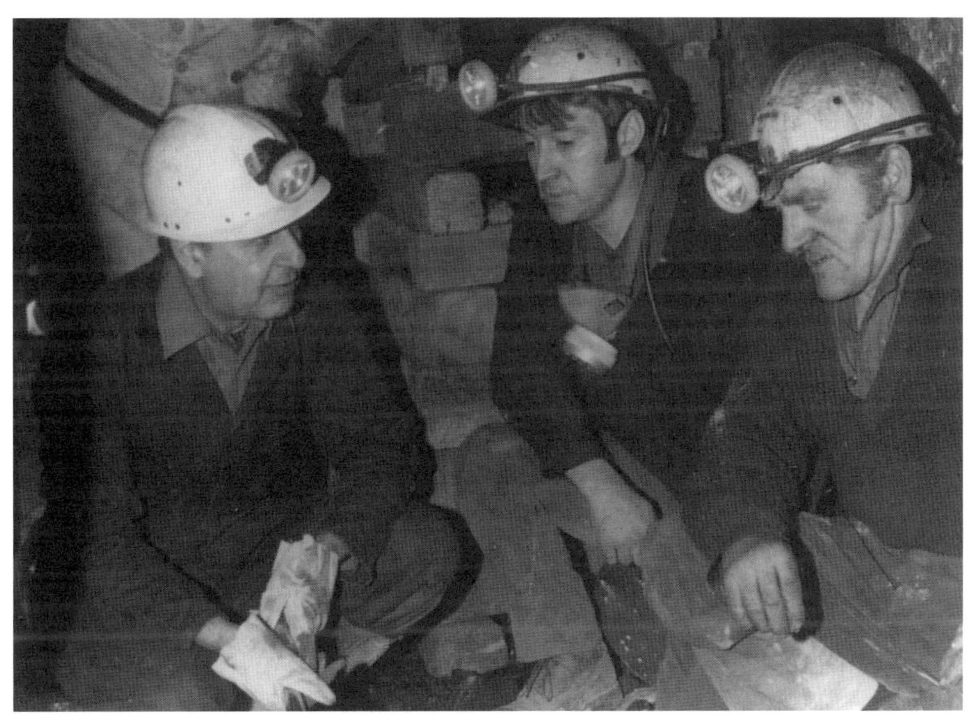

Owners

The role of organising and centralising the sale of coals is accredited to Newcastle. There a Society of Free Hosts had been founded in 1494 to entertain alien merchants coming to buy coal or grindstones. As 'Hostmen' or 'Oastmen' they came to dominate the trade after Newcastle secured the 'Grand Lease' from the Earl of Leicester and Queen Elizabeth I. This "comprised the manors of Gateshead and Whickham and afterwards had such a remarkable influence upon the coal trade of the Tyne as to be considered responsible for the real beginning of the coal trade in that district" (*HRCM*, ch.21). Though the Grand Lease expired in 1681, Newcastle was established as the commercial centre of the coal trade, and especially its export to Europe.

As to the extraction of coal, the land-owner has the mineral rights on his property, and could either start mining or issue a lease to someone to do the mining, in return for royalties. For coal under the sea-bed a royalty is due to the Crown. Not surprisingly, main players in the coal industry in Co. Durham in the nineteenth century were land-owners like the Lambton's (Earls of Durham), the Londonderry's and the Dean & Chapter of Durham Cathedral.

The owners of the colliery were known as:

Maistas – "coal owners" (Dodd, Tanfield Lea); "Maister – The owner of a pit or mine before nationalisation" (Tootle, 1995).

The manager of the day-to-day supervision of the mine technicalities was called the 'viewer':

Veiours – viewers (1367 lease from Bishop of Durham via *HRCM*, ch.21). "Viewer of the works" (1708, per *HRCM*, ch.8); "and now I must leave you to your Viewer, or Head Under-over Man, who is to take Charge of a Regular Working of the Colliery" (*Compleat Collier*, 1707, p.31). "Viewer – obsolete term for an underground official" (Wade, South Moor, 1966); "Viewer – the manager of a coal-mine. So, 'under-viewer' (under-manager)" (Palgrave, Hetton 1896);"Under-viewer – see under-manager" (Nicholson, 1888); "Vyoor – old word for mine manager" (Dodd, Tanfield Lea).

The term 'Viewer' persisted in the nineteenth century (see datable entries); legislation assisted in the change, e.g. the Coal Mines Act, 1887, established the certification of Managers and Under-managers The final break came with Nationalisation, when the Government replaced the 'Maisters' as effective owners of the coal mines… "Many miners believed that the owners were lucky to get away with their lives for the slaughter they had inflicted on the miners; instead they were paid £338 millions in compensation" (Douglass, 1973).

On the question of marketing, the operation of the 'vend' (literally 'sale' or 'selling') is mentioned in regard to Sunderland, also an important coal port, in 1707:

> First, you must have a good Stock of Coals provided against the time of Sale, which is chiefly in Summer by Reason of the Weather, which makes it hazardous for Ships to Sail in Winter on those Coasts... [Also] you get your Coals cheaper wrought in Winter time, th[a]n in Summer, or time of Trade, because Labourers or Miners are then more numerous thereabouts... [Thus] by having a good Stock aforehand, you have wherewith to Answer Demand, in time of Vend..."
>
> (*Compleat Collier*, 1707, pp.46–7)

More specifically, 'vend' came to refer to a "cartel of coalowners, formally from 1771; replaced in 1805 by Joint Durham and Northumberland Coal Owners' Association" (Colls, 1987). It reflected the growing cost of sinking deeper pits, and the consequent dominance of larger landowners and enterpreneurs: in the vend they co-operated to regulate or limit the production of coal in order to maintain an advantageous price. Thus the 'limitation of the vend' was "a compact into which the whole body of coal-owners entered to restrict the output of each coal-field to a certain agreed maximum, with the view to maintaining the price of coal at a figure sufficient high to recompense them for the restrictions under which they worked" (*HRCM*, ch.19). Its operation may not have been as effective as intended: "In 1805, the coal owners formalised the 'Limitation of the Vend' as the Joint Northumberland and Durham Coal Owners' Association... The longest period of regulation can be said to have been only two to three years up to the time of its collapse in 1844" (Tootle, 1995).

Moves towards free trade from 1845 on and the steep rise in the demand of coal in the nineteenth century made such protective caution unnecessary. Later associations of mine owners, e.g. the Steam Collieries Association (1852), Durham Coal Owners Association (1861) and Northumberland Coal Owners' Association (1871) were formed more to be able to respond formally to workers in their growing union organisations.

royalties – "rights of mineral ownership vested in the freehold, and rents accruing from exploitation of that mineral" (Colls, 1987).

restriction – "pitmen's collective strategy for regulating production in order to control hours and conditions" (Colls, 1987).

overs and shorts – "the over and under-production of collieries, relative to their issues" (Colls, 1987).

multipliers – "proportions of base allotted to coalfield districts for representation within the cartel" (Colls, 1987).

fighting trade – "periods of non or partial regulation of output by owners" (Colls, 1987).

fitter – "the agent of the shipping port who sells and loads the produce of a colliery [formerly, hostmen]" (Heslop, N'd, 1890s); "fitters – persons who vend and load coals" (Brockett, Newc, 1820s); "fitters – coal brokers who sold from colliery to shipper" (Colls, 1987).

issues – "collieries' fortnightly permitted output, decided by cartel, according to base multipliers and prevailing market conditions" (Colls, 1987).

base – "estimated limit of annual output, set by coalowners' cartel in order to regulate markets" (Colls, 1987).

vended – "coals sold" (Nicholson, 1888).

vends – "a limited sale of coal, as arranged by the 'trade': 'They were not hamper'd. then wi' vends'" (Wilson, G'head, 1820s).

Nationalisation in 1947 led to the formation of the National Coal Board, itself changed to British Coal in 1986.

Toward Vesting Day

Imagine for yourself a dowly winter-day, all road-slush and snaw on the bank, frizzin' and unusually quieted. Except fer us in oor lorry, takkin it easy alang the aud roads, an important enuf quest, Santy might say, but if we were not singin' exackly, ye may be certain we were hummin, an Bob's fing-ers woz tappin' on the wheel. His drivin' woz allus good-humoured; thissa day his extra lazy pace let us stop an let the odd cock-bird cross afore us – withoot any urge to twitch the horn.

Efter aal, thor's nae sense in hurryin' once the roadz iz icy, ye'd ony gerrinta a skid or ploo interra snaw-driff en hev ti be howked oot wi chains en a tractor. Nae gud that'd be. Nut wi the smart, weshed-ower truck we'd ti handle, today. An we've ti think ov us, forbye. Gan ower-fast an' the caad air rushed en' skittered aalways rund the cab. Nae gud at aal. "They'll wait," sez Bob, wi a grin.

Aa woz gerrin' on famous wi that tune o' the Tyne, and haaf day-dreamin o' being happy/hopeless ower-heed in luv, when we turned by the stane posts o Winyaad, the curly yrron gate-flaps tucked well back and the road aheed maist free o snaw, fer the early shift wudda bin oot wi thor sho'uls en brooms. The lodge was empty, but as we as drew up ti th'side o the hall, the game-keeper come up en Bob rowled his winder doon to pay his compl'ments. "How," siz the gadgie wi a canny feather in iz brim, "thor expecktin ye. Jes tyek them sacks ti the stable fost." "Reet," sez Bob sagely, and coins roon the back o the g'eat establishment.

The stables block woz brick en reek, where the hosses wos breethin i' th' caud air. An the man comes up en shews us where ti stow the coal. The varry best o coal, this woz, mind; fre the hardest seam o aal, Low Main it's caa'd, that wud burn langest wi the best low ower Krismus. Nice roondie coal. Fre Dawdon 'Wallsend'. Ye lifted it wi a gripe, that's a fork wi wide tines, se on'y the proper lumps is lifted en bagged. En i th' smartest bags we cud finnd. Drawn specially fre stores. Sixty bags; three tons ovit. "Aye, liv it bagged, will ye?" sez the man, affable like. "It'll help kip th snaw off," noted Bob, fer this coal-store hed nae door, nae glæss ti the winda.

Aa wiz about ti peg the flap back up, when he sez, "Thor's gear ti lade, ye knaw." Bob liuks impressed, like. Not expectin a treat, that's uz. "Jes pull in ower thor." An Aa leave the tail-board lowse en waak ower as Bob starts the motor an gessit berthed away at tuther side.

Na, Aa've heerd the windin-man tell of snaw, even in the shaft, on the man-riding side, where it woz open at th' top. He woz deeing a bit waak on the cage, it woz on the way up like, an it woz dry at th bottom aareet (we're taakin two thoosand foot ye knaw), an he travels up pass the three-quarter en the five-quarter, en then he kin start to feel the snaw driftin in, aal the way fre the top, but it nivvor gets ti the lowest level. (That woz what Aa thowt ov, as the snaw startid ti faa' once mare, en us stannin thor.)

Thor woz fower big trees ti be laded. One fer each coll'ry and a one fer the offices nex the Masons Palace i th seafrunt. Se it went ivry year. Nut that we wantid ti luik as if we woz expectin it, for aal that the wuds en plantshuns heoraboots cud spare us a canny bit deal for the home-fire if they wished. It's clear that, when ye luik back. Why the Haal issell woz the grandest, richest establishment i the total coonty. Them pit-owners, they cud weel spare a few trees en a few sovrins if they woz minded, but, o' corse, the lord hissell nivvor cam en shook wor hands. We wudna dream ovit. It woz mare ova mummers piece, to be laked [played] ower each year, an enjoyed fer what ye cud get. Seein as this woz the lasst occaziun. Ivvor. We waddent spoil it.

Egzackly, fower gran kersmas trees woz stowed on board. But thet wozna aal. Fre the back o' th hall, where the kitchins lay, they brought oot turkeys en goose, all ploted ready, for the managers o' the coll'ries, chickens fer the under-managers, rabbits fer ither ranks. In respeck o' thor offices en duties. It was a canny load. "Put them near the front," sez the man. "Ye can keep an eye on them better." En he nods ti me.

Rabbits woz a big thing in them days. Aa've seen them on the platforms, ready ti hoy on the trains, big blocks o' them, packed heed ti bob-tail, then anither layer cross-ways, en so forth, makkin a gross in toto en aal tied up wi wire. Likewise, az Aa weel knew, these woz gutted, and partly skinned, but some bits fur left decorative as well, being giffs as much as fud. Once the boards went up we woz a rare seet, wi the branches o' spruce wavin aal-ways en the gamburds neetly cownted inti bags stowed atween the crowns o the trees. We shudda hung bells on the back-board, Aa alwus sed.

Bob hed a quick tot, a waamer, as he caa'd it, en we set off fer to tour the pits, wi the trees an that. He woz thinkin o how they'd mebbe build a lot new cooncil hooses in the cummin years, that'd be bigger an waamer nor the coll'ry raas. "Aa fancy a big fam'ly," he sez. "Nae point being niggard. En jobs fer aal!" Thor woz nae doot ovit, this was a big year fer us. The prizzents we carried, weel, they wor both a token of th' menseful aud way, fer aal it woz a cruel, cussed sort o life, en a rainbow promise of a gud, worth-it world to be oors, fer the askin'.

We woz welcomed at the coll'ries, matter o course. Sum mare jolly then others. The union folk, partickler, woz stottin wi excitement, seein as they hed maist ti luik forward ti. They wud worship the tree aareet, counting the days till it cam doon. An i' th' dreams of yan or twee [one or two], ye might see th' knolledge o' fine new jobs ti cum, when they wud be promoted inti bosses, onti th' management side nae doot ovit; wi cheap coal-land ti build a fine new hyem on; extra brix en ciment en wud fer the axing; the power o' controllin aal th' owertime; en a salary that wud lift them oot th' clarts fer aal time. They nivver expected how the men wud tret them though: changin sides, sum wud caal it. Thor wud

> be sum canny flytin, en this en that'un wud be set on, mebbies, wi crakt ribs heor, en a brokken arm thor. Weel, ivry dream hez ti be paid fer.
>
> The trees woz handed ower for setting up; the goose en that was delivered ti the gaffors to deal oot. We got some bits siller fer oor troubles, en Aa set off hyem i' th gritty snaw, hardly believin, like many anuther, that things woz riddy ti move, it wud happen us that quick, it seemed. An the lasst day o fowrty-six wud pass, an the first day o fowrty-sivin wud arrive, wi a National Coal Board ti save wor pits en make safe wor futures. That woz sum New Year's Eve aareet. How! at the stroke o midnite, they fired the guns, that echoed rund en rund, en Aa kissed en clapped [patted] me lass (me hinny, me sweetheart, me Cushy), en promised hor this wud be a gud life fer us, az we'd warked fer, an' cud say we woz entitled ti.

Middle management

Like many a large institution in the nineteenth and twentieth centuries, the coal mine seemed caught in a Marxian dichotomy, with those in and under authority continually locked in a mutually supportive confrontation. Paradoxically, this did not stop the mines operating with profitable efficiency (which implies a concern for safety of the coal and men); and even more surprisingly, the divisiveness did not disappear with Nationalisation:

> It seems that in the hierarchy of the pit management that deputies and overmen and undermanagers came from the rank and file. Their attitudes changed once they actually became part of management – they kind of went over to the other side.
>
> (Mr Dawkin, Beamish, 1989/216)

Assistant Colliery Manager "…is usually appointed to manage each seam, thus allowing the 'under-manager' to carry on with his routine duties" (Tootle, 1995).

Back-Overman – "The overman in charge of the 'backshift'. His wages were about 21 shillings per week (£1·05p) in 1849" (Tootle, 1995, N.East).

Check-viewer – "one who checks the working of coal on behalf of the owner of the royalty" (Heslop, N'd, 1890s); "Checkweighman or Checkweigher. First legalised by the Act of 1860" (Tootle, 1995); "keeker – this was the owners' 'checkweighman'" (Douglass, 1973).

Clerk of works – "the clerk of works was responsible for all the clerical work at a colliery and for paying the wages of the surface labourers" (Tootle, 1995, re seventeenth century).

Deputy – "pit foreman" (J.Moreland, Dawdon, 1980); "deputy – an underground official" (Wade, South Moor, 1966); "depitee – deputy overman" (Dodd, Tanfield Lea).

Deputy Overman (usually shortened to Deputy – see above): "the deputy overman...wrote reports, rendered first aid, fired the explosive charges, and maintained discipline by example or sheer cussing" (Hitchin, 1962, p.69); "the deputy overman had charge of a 'district' in a mine. He would also lay the 'tub rails', 'landing plates' and be responsible for the 'timbering'" (Tootle, 1995, N.East).

Deppities – "deputies (mine officials)" (Hay, Ushaw Moor, C20/2); "deputies – a set of men employed in setting timber for the safety of the workmen; also in putting in brattice and brattice stoppings. They also draw the props from places where they are not required for further use" (Nicholson, 1888); "Deputies – set of pitmen employed to set timber and draw props, gradually becoming responsible for safety supervision underground" (Colls, 1987).

Gaffer – "a masterman or foreman" (Palgrave, Hetton, 1896); "gaffor – foreman" (Dodd, Tanfield Lea); "Pit Gaffer – the foreman in charge of the day workers on the surface at the colliery" (Tootle, 1995). [Godfather.]

This is a flexible term, used of anyone in authority; in the following it refers seemingly to the pit owners:

But really aal things reckon'd up,	
Ar' ye much warse off than yor gaffors?	masters
If ye mun toil, they hae thor care,	must...have
Thor chaffs an' bullyins just as mony:	humiliations?
Yor station's here, an' thor's is there,	theirs
aal the difference if thor's ony.	

(Alexander Barrass)

Keeker – "in Northumberland and Durham Collieries it is a sort of overlooker, or spy, on the pit heap of the Colliery" (*Bell MS*); "keeker – inspector" (Nicholson, 1888); "an inspector at the pit top who examined the coal coming out of the pit" (Tootle, 1995, N.East); "keeker: surface foreman who deals with the coal" (Wade, South Moor, 1966); "keeka – pit surface foreman" (Dodd, Tanfield Lea); "the guy in charge of the surface activities, surface superintendent" (Sharkey); "the man in charge of the screen was the keeker" (Wilson, Walbottle). [From 'keek' to look, to peep.]

Manishment – "Mispronunciation of 'management" (Palgrave, Hetton, 1896).

Master-shifter – "a person who has responsible charge of the mine during the night" (Nicholson, 1888); "mahsta shifta – in charge of night shift" (Dodd, Tanfield Lea); "Master shifter – name given to the night shift overman" (Wilson, North Walbottle); "He was the guy who had charge of the overnight shift when repairs and preparations for coal work were carried on" (Sharkey)... "Yes – he would start at 7 or 8 pm and work until the fore-shift came on" (Roxborough, swDm).

Overman – "overman – the person who has the daily supervision and responsible charge of the mine, under the direction of the manager or under-manager" (Nicholson, 1888); "supervisory grade beneath the viewer or underviewer responsible for underground workings" (Colls, 1987); "Overman – man in charge" (Barnett, Seaham); "above the deputy and below the under manager" (J. Moreland, Dawdon, 1980); "owa man – overman (underground official)" (Dodd, Tanfield Lea); "Overman or Oversman – the person who, beneath the 'viewer', had the charge of the working of the colliery. He would set the pit to work each morning. …the overman held a rank between that of a 'fireman' and the 'undermanager'. He would be responsible for a particular section of the work in a mine, e.g. haulage, salvage or the production of several districts, etc." (Tooootle, 1995); "The overman is the official immediately above the deputy and immediately below the under managers" (Douglass, 1973).

Puffler – "standard word for deputy" (Sacriston). [But reported by Tootle as a Warwickshire word for 'a man in charge of a longwall face' or Lancs for 'a senior haulage man'.]

Under-manager – "a person holding a second-class certificate, and who is responsible for the management and control of the mine in the absence of the manager" (Nicholson, 1888).

Skeeker – "in coal mining, a person employed to see that the coals are sent to bank in a proper state" (Brockett, Newc, 1820s). [Var. of keeker?]

If accountability and hierarchy appear muddled in the above list, here are two summaries of the system:

> …in my time of the early sixties, the mine was run by an Agent Manager then a series of Under-Managers then fore-overmen/back overmen, night/tubloading overmen…then Deputies …then Shotfirers."
>
> (Kenn Johnson, Dawdon)

> **Colliery Manager** – had clerk and secretary to help – own office – but not just desk job – would go underground a couple of times a month – formal inspection, or if a problem or if new roads being driven – he had distinctive white overalls.
>
> **Under-managers** – number depended on size of colliery – at Seaham 2 sharing same job, worked daytime only, 1 per shift. Their job to shout at people. 'Motivators'. In charge of overmen, above and below. Based in an office, latterly he would tend to stay in the control room and talk to overmen from there via the ?DAK (Radio) system.
>
> **Overmen** – 1 per shift underground and 1 per shift on surface. The surface overman was also known as a 'keeker'. Immediate superviser – hands on – available – practical as well as organisational. Ensured deputies had full teams – if shortfall, he would rearrange working parties – responsible for achieving targets, methods of operation – basic trouble-shooting role and in charge of deploying craftsmen.
>
> **Deputy** – a team-leader – responsible for labourers (daytal workers) and power-loaders (face men) – to see all set up right, care for safety – also special tasks like shot-firing – in charge of team av. 12 men. Could be quite young, e.g. early 30s. Recognisable as carried yard stick.
>
> **Fitters** – problem solvers. The Mechanical Engineer would get a report of difficulties – tells his fitting foreman what

needs doing, a matter of prioritising – he sends a fitter on a specific task, e.g. fixing machinery, roof supports (powered), belts. Similarly electricians under Electrical Engineer.

The pit was essentially a meritocracy – everyone had to be familiar with the work they were set to do."

(Steve Barnett, Seaham Pit)

The Deppity

(Tune: "Push ahead, show yor speed")

Maw workin' gear's the axe an' saw,	equipment
An' pockets myed for nails;	made
For its maw bus'ness doon belaw	
Te timmor an' lay the rails.	timber
Te watch an' keep the wark away,	underway
To order lads aboot,	
Or, when they stop te joke or play,	
Te dash thor rags an' shoot:	i.e. shake them up…shout

Chorus:

Noo up ye get, and load the set,	a train of tubs
It's time ye had yor lark oot,	
For de ye not see they'll blame aal me,	do
An' the men 'ill want thor wark oot:	
But idle away the whole o' the day,	
An' Aw'll tell the powers thit be;	
For, de ye not knaw thit Aw carry the saw,	
An' thit Aw'm the deppity.	

Aw'm duty-bund inbye te be	down in the pit
An' oor before the men,	
For Aw've got ivory place te see	every work-place
Before they start; an' then	
Aw've chocks te set, or props te draw,	remove
Or turns te lead an' lay,	bends on the tram-way
Before aw've time te get me blaw,	blow/breath
Or even time te say:...	
When throo the bordes an' walls Aw've gyen,	hewing area...gone
An' got them nicely deun,	done
Aw'm off oot bye te meet the men	toward the shaft
As hard as Aw can run.	
Bae they get yoked, the lads ar' in,	By the time
An' seun's thor stript te start,	soon as they're
Aw gar the daily row begin,	make
An' roar wi' aal my heart...	
Thor's sometimes stops throo bits o' falls,	
Let man de what he may;	do
Or some bit anxious putter calls –	
"O, Clark, Aw'm off the way!"	i.e. de-railed
Thor's doors torn doon, an' plates knock'd wrang,	rails
An' props sent reelin' oot:	
Thor's elwiz somethin' lads amang	always
That gars a man te shoot...	causes...shout

Thus kick'd aboot frae place te place,	from
Aw play me daily gam',	game
As roond the flats Aw wheel apace	
Atop o' the law flat tram:	(1)
But mark, an' mind the word is 'mum',	
Maw pays ar' pretty fair;	
An' seun Aw hope the time 'ill come	
When Aw need bawl ne mair...	

Noo up ye get, and load the set,
It's time ye had yor lark oot... etc.

(Alexander Barrass)

(1) The deputy had a special flat-bed tram, for moving wood, etc., with retaining posts in each corner.

What characteristics made a good deputy?

One thing, if he gave an instruction, he had to see that it was carried out. More or less, although he didn't have to do it himself, it was good if a Deputy were able to do it himself, then the workmen couldn't turn around and say you're telling me to do something that you cannot do yourself, so that by and large when a man becomes a Deputy, he usually he had been a good worker, because then he was able to tell other men things he had done himself.

(Mr Sherwood, Beamish, 1984/250)

Problem with a Deputy

"Why" he says, "they"re waiting on down here – Get away down there with that big pony."

Aa says, "This big pony hasn't to go down there" Aa says, "It'll never get out again if it gets underneath that stone"– Aa says, "It's low. This big pony here –" but I says, "If the other lad comes up with his load I'll swap him tubs so he could get away down there."

He says, "That'll not do for me." He says, "Get yer bloody self down there." He says, – they used to go – wi' yard sticks carrying – these deputies carrying a stick about with them, a yard long. He says, "I'll shove this bloody stick down your throat if you don't go down."

That's what he said to me – this man. So I made on I was going out to me pony and I just went away straight out on to the bank head where these two wagonweighmen was lighting lamps and such like: I said, "Aa've come over to see you two."

They said, "What for?"

I said, "The deputy up there he says he's going to make me go down that place with that big pony – and I says I'd swap loads and the other pony come down."

He says, "What?"

I said, "He's told me, – he says he's going to shove the stick down me throat if I don't go down."

He says, "Howay in with me."

The both of them come in and he's sitting – and he says, "Have you threatened this lad to shove the stick down his throat?"

He said, "Yes."

He said, "I've a good mind to knock you off that bloody kist lad."

By he was a good fighter an' all this fella – wagonweighman – he could have knocked his head off him. He says, "Threatening this lad: He's told what he has to do – just swap loads if a big pony comes up."

He says, "You threatened to shove the stick down his throat?"

He said, "Yes."

At the finish he says, "We'll go and see the undermanager us two and you've got the boy of the witness what's just – you've heard him say."

He says, "That's all we want."

Twenty years after I saw him and said, "Can you remember when you were going to shove the stick down my throat?"

He said, "Yes."

I said, "I wish you'd try and shove the stick down my throat now." I was bigger than him then.

(Mr Dawkin, Beamish 1989/216)

Inseparable from the Deputy (except here) was the Deputy's wand...

yard-wand – "deputy's stick measuring one yard" (Wade, South Moor, 1966); "yard-wand or yard-stick – a hazel stick 3 ft. in length, carried by overmen for measuring yard-work, maintaining discipline amongst the boys &c." (Nicholson, 1888); "yard stick – all officials from the deputy up to the gaffer carry one of these heavy walking sticks. Today used partially as a measuring instrument, in part as a hoist to put an oil lamp into high areas of the roof [to test for gas]" (Douglass, 1973).

The Deputy's kist ('chest'):

"The kist was a wooden chest in which the deputy kept consumables like cutter picks, nails, wedges, lumps of chalk and his report book, water bottle and bait" (Roxborough, swDm); "kist – a chest; the deputies' kist is used to keep their tools, plate and brattice nails, &c., in" (Nicholson, 1888).

"Deputy's kist – contained shot-firing cables, all suck details needed for work; no one could go the work at the face without reporting first to the deputy; kist also contained first-aid-kit, brought down each shift by the deputy" (Hill, Harrington).

"deputy's kist – the box in which he keeps his tools" (Wade, South Moor, 1966).

"Depitee's kist – holds tools and papers" (Dodd, Tanfield Lea).

"kist – wooden chest: in the mines, the deputy had a meeting station where he kept his report books in a large wooden chest called a kist" (Brown, Ryhope).

"The Deputy…assembled his workmen at the kist, to check attendance and delegate work areas. In this chest he kept tools and first aid equipment" (Tweedy, Shilbottle).

"On entering a District such as a face/set of faces in a seam (usually named as; 21 North Maudlin; 26 South Low Main; 18 South Hutton; 2nd South Five Quarter, etc., etc) workers/visitors must check in to the (Deputy's) kist. Here your lamp was 'checked'... duties/reason for visit, etc... sometimes arrival/departure chalked on board at kist" (Johnson, Dawdon).

"kist – tool chest (underground): The kist is at the bottom of the shaft, where you meet your marrers before going in-bye" (Shelley, Sth Hetton).

"The 'kist' was the deputy's chest where he kept his gear. It was located at the meeting station which was at the entrance to a district and where the miners congregated after travelling inbye at the start of the shift and where the deputy gave them orders or information about their working places. Also where all visitors to a District must report" (Sharkey).

"Kist – box or large wood chest which has lid and locks. Used for keeping any special tools in, also report and time books for all accounts of work in a district of the mine. Always placed at a meeting station where the deputy places workmen to their daily jobs" (McBurnie, Washington, 1970s).

"Crack at the Kist – talk at the Deputy's kist (assembly point)" (Roxborough, swDm).

"Wey ye see, wor Lizzy got it from the lad she gans with, and he was telt it by his marra' that hord it at the deputy's kist from a man whaat got the story in the train on a Setorda' neet. Se ye see, it's hed to be true" (*Ashington Col Mag*, March 1935).

"See you at the kist" (Johnson, Dawdon).

The Kist

"Aw noa!"

The lid o me kist wor wide-open, dust frev ivry airt o the pit free tiv enter – jes wipe yor feet on ma saw en settle any pliace ye pleese.

"Ha ye bin at ma kist?"

I spun arund en gollered at the putter that was bannagin his knee.

"Me? Na, man," he sez, puttin on a canny convincin wince.

"Weel, whe's left the lid up? Aa'd like te knaa that."

"Aw thot ye did."

"Ye what?"

"Theer Aa wor, hippin alang, en Aa thot Aa did see thee the'sell, hovrin ower the thing… but itz ower-easy ti gan off-track i' the mirk."

This lasst bit he added on, seein Aa was aboot to clag him one.

"It wos summun short, anygates," he finished, nut makkin' me eny better pleesed. Aa'm stocky, Aa admit, but dinnot c'are ti be m'ade gam ov. Like when Aa raised the lid yance, en a fox lowpt oot.

Se Aa lent him a hand tie up his knee, but aal he cud say woz he thot he gliffed a short gadjee – or a youth, mebbe – stannin reet nex the kist as he cum up, but then the so-caa'd fella musta ta'en his skite. Vanisht.

Weel, thor's nut that menny yung'uns doon the pit th'day; thor at skiul, larnin ti be menseful en industrious, Aa whope. Wheerfore Aa cudna help but doot sum sconse or ither. En dangerous that cud be, when Aa need me gear ti see ti the safety ov aal in heeraboots. Hammers, saws, mells, drills, chizzels, box-pl'anes – thor aal kept in the deppity's kist, that's god's truth. Let alane the bannages en siklike safety gear. Borrowin – why thet's maist as bad as leavin the lid open, fer the dust ti gerrin – bluntin en fowlin the edges, mixin en messin th' wh'ole box o' tricks an endin up lossin the gear, like as not. Then thor's an emergency, en ye cannut finnd the reet t'ool, or itz jammed, or the heft's aal clarty n slippy.

Fer itz ma job to owersee the runnin o this part o th' pit, ti test thet th chocks en props is stannin', ti keep a watch on the flo-or en th' roof, if the yan heaves or tother lowers. Ti warn folk away fre the brokken mine, the goaf, thats riddy ti collapse on itsell. Fer pits are nut st'able endurin st'ates ov affairs, like a city or a mountain, but iz mainly access – get the co-al oot en then gerraway. The road-ways are used, then maist abandoned, en let faa', as we move on ti new zones fer co-al. On'y a varry few permanent ways are left in good fettle, fer ventilashun or roon' th' shaft itsell, and that's wheer the deppity's kist is allus kept, shud ye ivvor need it.

Or – likelier – need me. Why, thor like bairns some o these, ivvor wantin advice en a bit sympathy. Sum job mine is.

"Maw workin gear's the axe an saw
An pockits myed fer nails;
Fer its maw bisness doon belaw
Te timmor an lay the rails"

That's the sang, ye knaw. Forbye Aa serve as dominee [schoolman], en check thor work tallies, en dee a manager's task fer free:

"Te watch an keep the wark away
To order lads aboot..."

Aye, en sum o thim'ld challenge me tiv a fight if they could wi'out riskin thor jobs. Ignorant bairns, them sum.

"Aw'm duty-bound inbye te be
An oor before the men
For Aw've got ivory place te see
Before they start..."

En its true, Aa've ti be in early each shift en check th' gannin-bords en th' props. Lay a bit roadway or fettle an aad bit o rails. It can be eerie, Aa knaw it, waakin roon i' th dark on a non-coalin shift, or a Sunda l'ate, when its varnigh desertid doon here, wiv on'y yer ahn lamp ti gie a low en illuminate th' workins. En then ye hev ti prog yor lamp intiv some hole, whiles, ti check th' air's nut changin', or squeeze thru a hitch ti test fer heave outbye, or fer gas. Sumtimes Aa bring th'bairn wi me, for company, like, but Aa nivvor did thet this nex time Aa'se gan ti tell aboot. Aa mean, when the kist was left wopen en naeboddy but me i' the pit.

It happend me like this. Aa'd diun ma roond, en fettled a few rails that wor oot o kilter, en woz returnin a clutch o tools ti th' kist missell. When Aa keeked [saw] it: sum sort o figger, a bairn like as nut, glowerin ower the contents o th' kist, as tho huntin' fer summat, like. Aa thot it wor sum thief, sum lowp-heed up te nae gud, en Aa thot o me gear, that he wor set to plote [steal], en Aa gollered oot: How! Ye're ti leave that!

The figger musta heered, for it turned roon, cast a pleadin, greetin' l'ook toward me, desp'rate en tearfu' it wor, en plain vanisht. Aa mean it. Yan second thor, ennither – he'd went. Naw, th'illumination i' pits is nut brilliant, Aa admit, but Aa cudnut be mista'en. Thet wor nae eorthly body, up ti sum eorthly evil. It was – weel – a mazer, a boggle, a phantom o sum kinnd; en itz nut offens ye heer aboot such, i' the hugger-mugger o pit life. Its genrally ower busy en loud ti be spirituel, Aa finnd.

Exackly, Aa didnut panic – thet's fatal as like as nut, inna pit. But Aa went up, giv th'gear a quick inpsecshun, shut th' lid – en then it struck me, this woz th'second occasion Aa'd been obleeged ti shut th'lid fer sum person unknawn. The putter lad, afore, he'd sed aboot a short'un, at th' kist. Aa mind that. Noo, Aa'd hev thot it aal in the coorse o Nature – summun fishin in th'kist fer a lark or ti fetch a wrench or a mell to fettle sum jam or even rescue sum marra – but then the way he clean vanished! (En Aa nivvor tiuk me een [eyes] off him.) Yet if he wor actin oot sum passt tragedy, he wor a gay ineffective ghostie, fer nowt was moved, nut a brush tip shifted, on'y th' fost specks o dust cummin ti settle unner the lid.

Aa picked up th'saw, en set to wipin it. In auden days, ye knaw, th' saw wor the on'y handy writin surface i-the pit, en men used it ti figgor thor wark-pl'aces, cavvels, they caal them. Thors nae polished flo-or, nae whitewash waa's, nae b'ooks nor sl'ates liggin aboot; nowt as gud as the smooth lenth o a saw en a bit chawk. That's gannin back a bit, but then this was nigh th'auder part o th'pit, Aa weel knaa'd. Wheer roads was kep wopen fer th sake o ventilashun, we caa'd the 'returns'. But Aa nivvor heered o a tragedy jes here, tho thor wos sum terruble trubble lang since, i'the aad workins, noo bricked up. That wor when the stithe killed sum, en ithers wor trapped; then thor was need fer t'ools aareet; but what possible use woz a sho'ul or an adze noo, fer an axident lang passt?

It woz a puzzle Aa cud nut reetly wark oot, se Aa finished ma inspeckshun double-sharp en rang ti ride ti bank. Aa didnut say owt aboot it then. Aa didnut c'are ti. It woz ma ahn problem, en Aa dinnut say that Aa wazzint a tadge sh'akey for sum oors. But mi lad wanted me ti tak him te th' dance at Whoreden, en Aa cudnut refuse. Aa needed a bit relief, ti be honest. En them dances wor summat like what it shud be, fer Aa s'oon gormed whee was whee, en finnt a lass ti play wi behint th haa'. Me son was inbye, courtin th' mensefu' way, Aa reckon. Gud luck tiv im. A wifey's fine, but love ootside o th' st'ale pairin's a wonder. Different as chaak n cheese. En chance-gi'en, wi'oot calculashun or obligashun.

Fer if ivvor Aa needed a bit cheeryin, then wor it. Aa even went fer th' lasst bus, ti keep fre waakin h'ame i' th dark. Draggin th' lad wi me. He'll nut m'ake a bonny pitman, mind; he's ower-big o th' b'ane, uncomfortish in th' rat-runs en gr'ave-tunnels ov a pit-way. En slaa he is. Nut the sort at aa'.

Nor de ye ushully gerra gentleman, or eny but a mine offishal, cummin doon ti l'ook rund. But Lord Lop, he hez these pals, en yan is keen as radish ti see inti th' workins. Nowt'll dee but doon he rides, wi this en that under-manager en owerman ti set him reet, en entertain him on his to-or. Th' men is warned ti keep thor sarks o thor backs, en nivvor to sweer an oath throo-oot the day. Mesell Aa hed a clean sark en a neck-chief, but Aa noaticed he nivvor sh'ook ma hand. He wazzint smilin much when he cam doon, en eftor he'd bin on th' stravage, he wor e'en less cheery. Pits can hev that effeck, en sum folk will nivvor mak pitmen, ye knaa. They gen'rally enlist as sailors, in thet c'ase. But this chep woz a grandee, en nut inclined to fash hissell wi toil Aa doot, bar a lal bit observashun, like. He sat doon, nut hunkered, but sat – if ye pleese – on ma kist, as tho it wor a handy sort of sofa, en mops his forr'ed. It can get reet maftin on a warkshiff like his'n. Aa offerred a pot o watter, but he nivvor e'en replied. Thet sort o Aa'm-speshul gob-tightness.

His smart marras tactfully suggested it meit be time to resurface, en should they ring fer the cage? Aa t'ook the hint, en went ti mak certin the c'age woz still thor, which of course it woz, for that naebody else wor likely to barley it when the gentry wor in need ov it. Lork! when Aa stepped the few p'aces back ower, Aa fand a reet dirdum [row]. The lord wor liggin o th grund, caa'in fer hilp, en th'lid o the kist (that wor his seat afore) wor thrust up, en t'ools jiggin aboot as if they cud nut quite lift thorsells free. Aa wor ower-freet ti laff, en stood like a fondy as the gentlemen handed th' lord tiv is feet, efter he'd cowped his creels.

"The lid – the lid," yan o'them tellt me: "it flew wopen." Aa saw strite off it wor that kelpie fella, seein th' way me gear wor stottin aboot i' th' kist. It wor a stiff ghost, this, it seemed, and ettled ti get summat done. But noo aal them things wor still for a bit. Aa clicked up the breetest lamp i' me hand, ti guard it, less we wor suddenly hoyed inti darkness by sum new sconce o th' ghost-lad. Tho he did nut seem a perilous mak o spirit, jes fashful [troublesome] – as ony warkman meit be (Aa recognised) if yan o his men woz sairly hurt. An hilp wor needed urgent, like.

They wor aal upreet noo, en makkin oot it wor purely an axident ("but someone pushed me!"), en bein soothin aboot it, milld aza humblick, en him bletherin on, when a sho-ul, stacked i'th corner, lifted ov itsell, en travelled a f'oot or twee, staggerin-like, ettlin to gan in-bye. Aa m'ade sure the lamp shone on th' miracle, se thet they cudnot miss it. Sumhoo Aa kenned it hed aal happened them on purpose: they wor to witness it whether they wor willin or noa. They musta bin sair flayed, fer yan turns cruelly on me en spits oot, "Is this sum sort of trick?" Aa did nut answer. Aa felt Aa did nut need to come atwix them en thor psychic f'ate, az Aa dooted it wud prove ti be.

In less than a minnit, the sho'ul dropped, ov its ahn accord, ye meit say, en lay still. En then the sh'ape of a lad began ti form, jes wheer th' shiul had fa'en, stannin' quite as a body wud, if he hed getten haad o th' heft. Frev invisible ti visible, in the time it t'ook ti tell yor fingers yance ower. Th'under-manager wud a run then, but the ithers restrained him. The lord he gav a quick howl ov amazement, as if it wor sum new treat, a speshul unnergroon entertainment, common (mebbies) in mining sorcles.

The lad wor formed, like Aa'd noated im afore. En he spoke, summat like "Help me, help me!" en pointed en run a lal way to a coinin o th ways, en waited like fer us ti foller.

Noo th' leet wor i' me hand, but move Aa didnut.

The lord it wor speaks up. "Come on, fellow," he says, "there is someone needs our help!" As tho it wor a mortal advencher in a weekly joornal. En off he moves. Then the maistors mak ti follow; en then Aa hev ti follow them, seein as how them's the gaffors. At the twinnin o th' ro-ads, the lord gets a new sytin o th' phantom, en "There!" he gollers, en maks off again, tho Aa knaa en th' ithers jaloose, that this is nut a path much in use. Bits dust rise wi th' lord's fleetie footin it, that hed nivvor m'ade a stour when the kelpie streak'd aheed. En then we aal saw the lad agyen, this time fornenst a stoppin, as we caa' it – a brickin up ov a former access, that is. En then the lad that woz not a real un passt thru it en inti the waa' [wall]. Bit by bit he disappeared, as if thor had been nae bricks in pl'ace at aa'.

En the lord – God bless im – call'd oot: "Quick! A pickaxe, some tools. We must break through. It is a sign! There is someone needs our help! Hurry yourselves."

Th' ithers stand en dinnut answer. They knaa, as Aa dee, that the waa' o' bricks hes stood thor fer yors en yors, ivvor sin the terruble explosion o th' lasst cent'ry. En that ivry body that cud, hez been recovered en gi'en decent burial; en the brix put in ti guard against eny fiery influence dwellin beyont.

"God help us" – he exclaims – "you cannot leave a fellow-workman to perish! Look lively! Break the tools out!"

En they leave it ti me tiv explain.

"Ma lord," Aa sez, "thet waa' hes nut bin touched for fowerty or feefty year. Nae person livin can be fand behint that waa'. What ye hev seen, is a poor speerit. He dizzent seem ti ettle us ony harm. Mebbe he yance was liukin fer help ti reach an injured marra, but that emergency – if sae – hes lang sine passt. If ye want ti help him, when ye're nex in church, wi th' rich-dressed vicar fornenst th' shiny altar, en the ither lords en ladies in th' foremaist raas, en th' managers en thor lasses i' th' pews ahint, en then the sarvants en thor families at the back, then kneel ye doon, en pray fer the lad, fer that's aal that ye or eny o' us can dee."

En God help me, forbye.

Chapter 9: Work practices

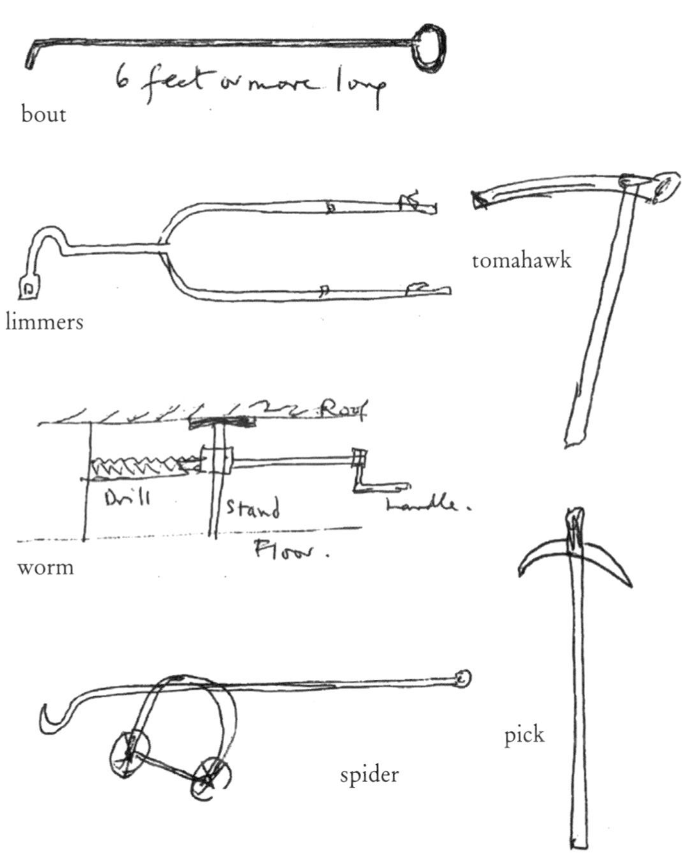

Although women working underground as a practice ceased in the North East in the late eighteenth century, it was the Mines & Collieries Act of 1844 that legally forbad woman, and girls and boys under 10 from working underground. A local agreement of 1863 reduced the hours worked by boys under 14 to 8 hours a day [*HRCM*, ch.22]. A series of Acts in 1850, 1855 and 1860 began to deal with safety issues and mines inspections, and raised the minimum age working age to 12 [*HRCM*, ch.19]. Further improvements in working hours and conditions were the concern of Unions as well as Parliament...

Yearly bonds

The 'yearly bond' was a system of contract that bound the miner to his employer for a year, with the reality of deductions from wages, eviction from housing and/or imprisonment for the miner if he erred or defaulted. It was resented as a system that both kept the miner in strict subservience, yet offered no security of long-term employment. Common procedure in mines in the seventeenth century, the yearly bond was based on an agricultural model:

> The annual bond in Northumberland and Durham had its origins in the traditional method of binding farm servants and labourers and the signing ceremony was in many areas, accompanied by a feast day comparable to the hiring fairs in rural districts. Reflecting its agricultural origins, the colliers' bond ran originally from autumn to autumn, but as this caused a hitch in production at a time of peak sales of coal, the term was altered in 1812 to run from April to April.
>
> www.durham-miner.org.uk

The change meant that any disputes were likely to occur in the summer, a period of low demand for coal, when the pit owners could better stand the effects of any industrial action. In practice the fairness or otherwise of the rates of pay it laid down were governed by the demand for coal and the supply of labour, but the wide scope of the bond was in itself a point of grievance.

> In the county of Durham the hiring of the hewers, putters, and generally of the drivers, is by the year. There is a bond signed by them specifying the conditions, the substance being that they are to do the work of the pit, and be subject to certain forfeitures or penalties for their neglect of duty; the chief of which is a penalty of 2s 6d for being a day absent without leave. The masters on the other hand are bound to pay a certain fixed price for the work performed; also if the hewers be not employed at all, or only partially employed, the masters are bound to advance them at the end of every fortnight the sum of 30s for their maintenance. This is in addition to the house and coals. But when the hewer comes into employment which yields more than 30s in the fortnight, the surplus above 30s is detained to pay off the sum advanced to him in slack time; which sum, therefore, is to be considered as simply a loan, and not a payment of money due. By this system the miner is always sure of the means of support, with 15s a-week, his house, and firing. The trappers and other young children in the pit do not sign the bond, neither do the people employed in screening, or in

other work on the bank. The wages are paid once a fortnight, on the Friday afternoon, the reckoning being made up to the end of the preceding week.

(*PP*, 1842, CR xvi, p.141)

The apparent security offered was illusory, for while the work to be undertaken was specified in great detail, the employers could release themselves from obligation at any time:

PROVIDED ALWAYS, that in case of accident to the shaft, machinery, or pit, or the appurtenances belonging thereto, or strike of workmen, or interruption from any cause to the safe and efficient working of the colliery, or to the drawing, leading, or shipping of the coals, the said owner, may, at his option, either pay the average rate of wages aforesaid, and continue the workman under this contract, or release the said workman from this contract and discharge the same by giving fourteen days' notice to the workman of such intention, and in case of such discharge, all matters and things herein contained (except as regards any previous breach) shall absolutely cease and determine.

(D/Lo/B/265)

Nor does the careful legal language in which the Bond was constructed convey the confusion that in practice could attend its signing:

On a Saturday near to the of March the whole of the workmen were called to the colliery office, and there the manager would read over nearly always in tones inaudible to all except those who were close to him the conditions of labour for the next twelve months. There was usually a balancing of the prices. As an inducement to the men there was, say, a sovereign given to the first man bound, ten shillings to the second, five shillings to the third, and then two shillings and six pence to every man after. The crush to secure the first place was generally so great that the manager was fortunate if he were not carried off his feet. As a preparation for this rush certain men would be bribed to incite, and thus induce men to act an unthinking manner.

(Wilson, 1907, p.49)

Just like wor maisters when we're bun, — bound, contracted
If men and lads be varra scant,
They wheedle us wi' yell and fun, — ale
And coax us into what they want.

(Thomas Wilson, *Pitman's Pay*, pt.1)

It is not surprising that the yearly bond became a symbol of the oppositive stances of masters and men.

> The masters have sometimes a great deal of trouble in enforcing the condition of the bond, and preserving good order. In the years 1839 and 1840 no less than 66 pit-men were committed for short periods to gaol as vagrants; that is, for leaving their usual places of work; and 106 were committed for disobedience of orders, and other matters subject to summary jurisdiction.
>
> (*PP*, 1842, CR xvi, p.141)

Strikes of 1831 and 1844 failed to defeat the bond system. At a meeting of Northumberland and Durham miners on 5 April 1844, Mark Dent addressed the crowd in impassioned terms:

> Fellow men, we have long been divided, but I hope this day is the uniting of the miners of the Tees, Wear and Tyne for the purpose of having our grievances adjusted, for they are manifold and severe. We have long sought for redress, we have been treated with scorn, but now we are resolved to be free. We are an insulted, oppressed, and degraded body of men. If the masters had made anything like reasonable proposals we would have accepted them; but they have brought forward a miserable proposition, an infamous bond, under which men have been working for a mere pretence; but we will do so no longer. We will stand together till we obtain our rights. We are determined to be free, and I hope that the time is not far distant when we will not have to use such means as we have had to resort to on the present occasion; but that the time of reasoning between master and man will take place the place of strikes, and the working man will get a fair day's wage for a fair day's work. Miners as a class are not looked on with respect by the public, and the great majority of the press seems against us. Our employers use every means to oppress us, and this is not wondered at, for we have had not respect for ourselves. But now that there is an understanding amongst us, are we any longer to continue to drag the chains of slavery, to bear the yoked of bondage and toil in the bowels of the earth, as we have done?
>
> www.mymarras.co.uk

The turning point came in the early 1870s, after a lawyer, W.P. Roberts, mounted a successful legal challenge to the yearly bond; in 1869 the Durham Miners Association was founded; in 1872 the Coal Mine's Regulation Act was passed, signalling the end of the Yearly Bond:

> By 1872, Durham coal had everything going for it – high prices and rising demand. Following this improvement in the coal industry the coal owners formed themselves into a new organisation called the North of England United Coal Trades Association and decided to give reason a chance. The new association invited the DMA to the negotiating table in February 1872 to discuss wages and conditions. It was at this meeting that the hated yearly bond was abolished and the Durham miner was now a free man to sell his labour where he chose.
>
> www.family-learning.org.uk

Cavils

cavilling – "pitmen's quarterly lottery to allocate working places" (Colls, 1987); "cavilling-day – the day the draw takes place" (Wade, 1966).

cavils – "lots; a periodical allotment of working places to the hewers and putters of a colliery, usually quarterly; each person having assigned to him, by lot, that place in which he is to work during the ensuing three months" (Nicholson, 1888); "cavels – lots; casting cavels – casting lots" (Grose, 1787, re N'd); "cavel or kavel – a lot, a share. Cavil is the place allotted to a hewer in a coal mine, by ballot. 'I've getten a canny cavil for this quarter, however.' It means also an allotment of ground in a common field" (Brockett, Newc, 1820s); "cavel, cavil – the lots cast by pitmen at stated periods for the different working places. Each collier draws his cavel and the number on this ticket is the number of the 'bord' at which he must hew" (Heslop, N'd, 1890s); "kyevil – hewers' working places for which they draw lots periodically" (Dodd, Tanfield Lea); "quarterly cavil – every three months the names of 'marras' would be drawn out of a hat to determine their cavil and the shift they would work for the next three months" (Temple, 1994, p.12); "kyevil – hewers' working places for which they draw lots periodically" (Dodd, Tanfield Lea); "piece-workers changed their working area every three months...The moves were based on a lottery, called 'cavils'" (Hitchin, 1962, p.105).

> Every quarter at the mine teams of men who were marras used to draw 'cavils', which was like drawing lots for their working place for the next 3 months. In the old bord and pillar days the teams of hewers would be contesting for cavils or working places. A team would consist of one or two individuals who would work in the same place on different shifts, i.e., fore shift, back shift and night shift. In the part of Durham where I came from the working places were numbered clockwise from the farthest left to the farthest right on the mine map or in the district. Longwall mining reduced the numbers of cavils but the principle was the same and in both cases there were good cyavils and bad cyavils and depending on your luck, you and yer marras' financial status for the next 3 months was settled on cyavillen day.
>
> (Tony Sharkey)

> Next you became a hewer and I remember that I used a 22 lb pick all the time I was in the pit. The pit was divided into districts and in each district the officials had so many places to hew in. The names of all the hewers were put into a basin and they were drawn out and you would go to the part of the pit where you had been drawn. You stayed there until the next cavils went in – in three months, sometimes six months time. If you got a bad cavil well you got a bad cavil: if you got a good one well you got a good one. A good cavil was where the coals were soft you know and you could fill a lot.
>
> (Mr Cawson, Kibblesworth, Beamish 1993/5)

Perhaps the results were written up on the deputy's saw – as smooth a writing surface as you could wish for:

But dash me, somehoo or other,
  Hoo it comes Aw divn't knaw; — don't know
But as sure's Aw rub me kyevel, — (1)
  It's the warst one o' the saw... — worst...

(Alexander Barrass)

1. "To equalise all the chances the putters would rub for places. This was by the deputy placing numbers on his saw or a piece of wood. They were written down in this fashion 2, 5, 1, 4, 3; of course the putters didn't know in which order the numbers had been placed. No. l would rub first, then the others follow. The next day it was the turn of no.2, to rub first so that by the end of the week, each putter had had a first rub..." (Douglass, 1973).

coup — "an exchange of cavils" (Nicholson, 1888); "coup or cowp – an exchange of 'cavil' or working place. To be valid the coup had to have the consent of the overman" (Tootle, 1995, N.East).

cross-marras – "The men who shared the same work-place but in a different shift, were known as 'cross-marras'. At the change of shift, the path of the two sets of men would cross. Here they would pause to give the on-coming shift a report of 'how their cavil was standing'" (Benson, 1989, p.12).

dowly – miserable: "ma dowly cavel" (Wilson, G'head, 1820s).

marras – "In the Durham mines men who shared the same place of work were called 'marras'... their earnings were pooled, and shared out equally" (Benson, 1989, p.12).

Pay systems

Details of pay systems are complex, comprising both 'piece workers' (paid by productivity) and 'shift workers' and 'day workers' paid on a time basis.

In the yearly bonds, considerable detail was given to each type of work, the payment of hewers standing first in the list. The following extracts relate to Seaham Colliery, 1869 (from D/Lo/B/265).

> And to each Hewer for every score of coals wrought (hewing end filling) in the Hutton Seam in the No.2 Pit each score consisting of 21 Tubs and the Standard Weight of the Tub to be 7 and three-quarters cwt. of one hundred and twelve pounds to the hundredweight the Sum of 7/6 per Score in the West District and 6/3 per Score in the East District in the Whole Mine and 5/10 per score in the West District 5/6 per Score in the East District in the Broken or Long Wall Mine And for Overweight in the same proportions and further the sum of 1/0 per Score when the places

are driven in a North and South direction in the West District in the whole Mine 4 Yards wide.

The above prices to include a full compensation for either Filling up or Casting back all the Small or Refuse Coals as may be required from time to time by the Viewer of the Colliery for the time being.

The hewers to be paid 4 [shillings] per Score in the No.1 & 2 Pits for taking up Bottom and casting back or filling up as required the Coal or Stone 4 feet wide so as to leave each place 4 feet high from the top of the Bridge rails.

Yard Work. In the No. l & 2 Pits Mining Headway, 8 feet wide 1/4 per Yard Holling Walls 8 feet wide 1/2 per Yard Crosscutts 8 feet Wide 1/4 per Yard 10ft boards 6d per Yard. Holling Walls in Pillars 8d per Yard Sides [Siding?] over 4d per Score Holling Stooks (paid after the first half Yard) 4d per Yard. For Double Working in the Whole Mine only, two following two 6d per Score. Wet place 4d per Score. And Ramble the whole width of the place 4d per score...

However...

The Hewer shall work the Coal so as to produce the greatest quantity of Rounded Merchantable Coal, that the nature of the mine will permit, and when the Coal will stand and when they are requested so to do, shall Kirve, Nick and Make proper Vantage of not less than 3 feet, and the Kirving and Nicking shall not exceed 15 inches [?height] at the foreside – And shall keep the filled Coals free from Stone, Band and Grey top, or foul Coal. And in case any Stone, Band, and Grey top or foul Coal, shall be found in any tub out of the Hutton Seam, at the No I + 2 Pits to the Amount of 17 $^1/_2$ Pounds the Hewer thereof shall forfeit and pay onto the said Owner 3d, for 40 pounds 6d and for 60 pounds 1/0 And out of the Hutton Seam in the No.3 Pit for 20 pounds the Hewer thereof shall forfeit and pay unto the said owner 3d, and for 25 pounds 6d and for 30 pounds 9d and for 40 pounds 1/0.

And out of the Main Coal, Low Main and Maudlin Seams, all over the Colliery for 14 pounds 3d, 25 pounds 6d, 30 pounds 9d, and for 40 pounds 1/0.

And if the whole quantity of Stone, Band, and Grey Stone or Foul Coal, found in any one tub out of any Score shall exceed 84 pounds, the Hewer thereof shall forfeit and pay 2/6d but such hewer shall notwithstanding receive the agreed price (less the forfeiture and payment aforesaid) for hewing the actual quantity of Clean Coal.

Putters and hewers were paid by a count of the number of tokens attached to tubs:

Each hewer and each putter shall attach a token to each several tub that they may severally hew or put.

Though paid by results, the hewers and putters were nonetheless set a minimum work shift along with other workers; elsewhere in the coafield putters and drivers could be paid by the shift.

The workmen hereby hired shall, where required, except where prevented by absolute inability from sickness or other physical incapacity, do and perform a full day's work, on each and every working day, and shall not leave their work

> until such day's work has been fully performed. The duration of the hewers' day's work to be in accordance with the regulations of the owner, his viewers or agents, but not to exceed eight hours, or be less than six hours working 'in the face'. The duration of the putters' day's work shall be not less than twelve hours, to commence half-an-hour after they shall have gone down the pit. And the drivers shall daily drive and lead away such a number of tubs or coals as shall be a reasonable and fair day's work of not less than twelve hours, to commence from the drawing of the first coals, or half-an-hour after they shall have gone down the pit...

And an important clause dealt with the issue of colliery housing:

> Each person for whom the said owner may provide a dwelling-house and premises, shall occupy the same as part of his wages and in the character of a workman of the said owner; and shall keep in good repair the glass in the windows thereof, or pay for the repairs of the same, and shall not injure any part thereof further than the ordinary and necessary wear and tear; and during possession, or on leaving, shall not remove, take down, or injure any spoutings, pigstyes, or other erections, the property of the said owner; and on expiration of the said hiring, or on the non-performance of any of the stipulations herein contained, shall quit such dwelling-house or dwelling-house and premises. And in case of neglect or refusal the said owner shall be at liberty, and he and they his agent and servants are hereby authorised and enpowered, without any previous demand or the adoption of any legal proceedings, to enter into and upon such dwelling-house and premises, and to remove and turn out of possession such workman, and all his and their families' furniture and effects.

Free housing was especially likely for married hewers with children to raise (Benson, 1989, p.73), making the risk of eviction more painful to bear. Yet such evictions were often enforced; for example in the 1844 strike, the 3rd Marquis of Londonderry told his workers:

> I have been amongst you – I have reasoned, – I have pointed out to you the folly, the misery, the destruction awaiting you, by your stupid and most insane Union. I gave you two weeks to consider whether you would return to your work, before I proceeded to eject you from your houses. I returned to Penshor, and I found you dogged, obstinate, and determined – indifferent to my really paternal advice and kind feelings...

The reality of the situation was painted rather well by Tommy Armstrong, at the end of the nineteenth century:

Oakey's Strike

(Tune: "Th' Pride of Petticote Lane")

It wis in November en aw nivor well forget
Th' polises en th' candymen it Oakey's hooses met;
Johny th' bellmin, he wis thare, squinten roond eboot;
En he plaic'd three men it ivory hoose te torn th' pitmen oot.

Chorus:
Oh wat wad aw dee if ad th' poower me sel,   do…I'd
Aw wid hang th' twenty candymen en Johny thit carry's th' bell.

Thare th' went freh hoose to hoose te put things on th' road,
But mind th' didn't hort thorsels we liften hevy loads;
Sum wid carry th' poker oot, th' fender, or th' rake,
If th' lifted two it once i[t] wis a greet mistake.

Sum e theese dandy-candy men wis drest up like e cloon:
Sum ad hats wivoot e flipe, en sum wivoot e croon;   brim
Sum ad nee laps ipon thor cotes but thare wis one chep warse: ?lapels
Ivory time he ad te stoop it was e laffable farse.

Thare wis one chep ad nee sleeves nor buttins ipon hes cote;
Enuthor ad e bairns hippin lapt eroond his throte.   nappy i.e. as scarf
One chep wore e pair e breeks thit belang tiv e boi,
One leg wis e sort is e tweed, th' tuthor wis cordyroi.

Next thare cums th' maistor's, aw think thae shud think shem   be ashamed
Depriven wives en familys of a comfortible yem.   home
But wen thae shift freh ware thae liv, aw hope thail gan te th' well,   they'll
Elang we th' twenty candy men, en Johny thit carry's th' bell.

(Tommy Armstrong)

[Note: the lines ending 'farse' and 'well' are surely tidied up versions of the original!]

Terminology of pay

The era of the yearly bond was replaced in the 1870s in the North East by the era of trade unionism. Unionism arose in the North East, we learn, "because of the sheer reaction of the workmen in given areas against the tyranny and selfishness of the employers" (*HRCM*, ch.22).

addlins – "a term not often heard any more, to describe earnings or wages" (Tootle, 1995, Lancs, N.East and Yorks.); "somebody's got to addle a few pence" (Grice, 1960, ch.14).

allowance coal – "coal allowed to married workmen at the colliery. In some areas the allowance was restricted to underground workers only or to the 'collier' or 'coal getter'" (Tootle, 1995); also known as 'concessionary coal'.

arles or **earles** – "money to bind a bargain... Also known as 'earnest money'. Prior to 1804 it was the custom to pay 2 to 3 guineas per hewer as 'binding' or 'bounty' money. From 1804 onwards, due to the shortage of manpower, the amount rose to 12 to 14 guineas along the Tyne, and up to 18 guineas along the River Wear. Arles was also paid to putters, drivers and irregular workmen. The custom was discontinued after the strike of 1844" (Tootle, 1995).

baff week – "baff – blank: baff-week – the week in which the pitmen receive no pay; a card not a trump is a baff one" (Brockett, Newc, 1820s); "baff means blank. The second week following payday when wages were paid fortnightly" (Tootle, 1995, N.East); "baff week – in the 19th. and 20th. century men were paid fortnightly – such a week was when they worked for 'nowt'"(Brian Davidson, Ashington); "it was 'baff' Friday, a day on which the pay was not to be collected" (Grice, 1960, ch,7); "baff Saturday – the day on which the pay or fortnight ends, and when the men's work is made up, the wages being paid on the succeeding Friday" (Nicholson, 1888); "baff weekend – when fortnightly pays were the custom, the baff week was when there was no pay" (Wade, South Moor, 1966).

bond — "an agreement by which the men were formerly bound to work under stated conditions for twelve months" (Nicholson, 1888). See above.

binding or **bindin** – "the contract or hiring for the year; the colliery bond" (Brockett, Newc, 1820s); "bindings – the time at which the yearly bond used to be signed, which was on the Saturday previous to March 22nd" (Nicholson, 1888).

chalking deal – "a flat, wooden, board on which the 'crane-man' or 'flat-boy' apportioned, and kept account of the work done by the putters, in the district of which he had charge" (Tootle, 1995, C19, N.East).

chalker on – "at every flat there was a boy or man who was known as the 'chalker on', whose duty it was to keep an account... When a putter came out with a tub he shouted 'chalk on'. The question was put, 'Whe's the been at?' The reply was the name of the hewer. The initials of the hewer who had filled the tub were marked on the outside of the tub [and on a board]" (qu. Benson, 1989, p.70, re Durham).

consideration money – "extra money paid to a hewer for working in adverse conditions" (Tootle, 1995, N.East).

darg – "a fixed quantity of coal to be worked for a certain price. This word is seldom heard in the Newcastle mines, but is the general term in use about Berwick. It is equivalent to the hewing or score price of the Newcastle collieries" (Nicholson, 1888). [Also 'darroc', i.e. a day's work.]

daytaleman – "a day labourer, chiefly in husbandry... a man whose labour is... reckoned by the day, not by the week or year. Daytalemen, about coal pits, are those who are not employed in working the coal" (Brockett, Newc, 1820s); "daital wark – work paid by day or shift" (Dodd, Tanfield Lea). [*OED* day + reckoning, 1530.]

hand money – "extra money paid at binding to encourage and consolidate agreements" (Colls, 1987).

minnee – "short for minimum wage" (Dodd, Tanfield Lea); "Clearly, for this day's work he was only to get the minimum wage" (Hitchin, 1962, p.106, re 1926). [Minimum Wage Act, Coal Mines, 1912.]

offtaks – "deductions form wages" (Roxborough, swDm).

renk – "the distance of the face of the workings in a coal pit from the crane, determining the wages paid to the putters. The places are balloted for by the putters each day" (Brockett, Newc, 1820s).

score – "a standard number of tubs of coals at each colliery, upon which the hewers' and putters' prices for working are paid. It varies in different localities from 20 to 26 tubs" (Nicholson, 1888); " 'scoreprice' – pitmen's wages, the price current for filling a 'score,' i.e. 21 (or, in some places, 25) tubs" (Palgrave, Hetton, 1896).

smart money – "negotiated payments made by employers to those injured while unable to work" (Colls, 1987).

token – "a piece of metal, tin, or leather, having stamped into it some distinguishing mark by which the owner may be known. It is from 1 $^1/_2$ to 2 inches long by 1 to 1 $^1/_4$ inches broad, and either oval, round, or oblong. Each set of hewers and each putter is supplied with a set, the hewers and putter of each tub placing a token thereon, which is taken off at bank" (Nicholson, 1888); "leather or tin discs on cord which were attached to a hook inside the tubs of coal, to identify the producer of the coal. Each disc had identifying letter or number" (Tootle, 1995); "Bill – if you haven't got a bit in about 'tokens' you need it. This was the way miners on piece (or bargain) work got paid... by burying a token thro' a hole at the bottom inside of a tub. Each token was identifiable to a man/team... no token means the value of that tub went into the overall 'pot'. So hewers jealously guarded their reserve of tokens. One man well known in Seaham, having lost his lower arm; he had hidden his tokens in a stationary massive booster fan... when he returned to get his tokens the fan was moving hence his arm!" (Johnson, Dawdon).

tommy ticket – "the pay ticket, otherwise the ticket denoting the deduction for 'tommy'; 'tommy' being one of the names for 'truck' [i.e. goods, food from employers' stores]" (*Mbro Weekly News*, 21 April 1860); "some miners received binding money, free housing, rent allowances, concessionary coal, cheap firewood, free beer and gifts on special occasions. Many, on the other hand, were made to shop in a company store, subscribe to a pit insurance fund or pay fines for 'unsatisfactory' work" (Benson, 1989, pp.64–5).

yahds – "basis of payment for stonework" (Dodd, Tanfield Lea).

Jack's Reckoning

A few years ago a man I knew well, a Joiner to trade, commenced to hew coals at East Tanfield Colliery. He was in the fore shift after he had been on a while. When his marrow came in on the back shift he said to Jack,"be sure and go to the reckoning to-night. The overman will tell you how many yards and scores you have, and think him on about the dip hitch, and helping up." At that time it was fortnightly pays. Miners had to go to the overman's house or office and he would tell you what the pay was for you to draw on the following night. Jack says, "Alright, good morning."

When Jack got home he says to his wife, Meg, "call me up at three o'clock, I am going to the reckoning to night."

"The reckoning," says Meg. "What's that, it will likely be at the Store Hall. Who is it for, what time does it go in, I will go with you." Meg though the reckoning was a concert.

"Get away," says Jack, "you don't understand it. I will get to know to-night what I will have to take for my pay to-morrow night."

"Oh I see," says Meg; "how much do you think you will have to take for pay?"

Jack says, "I cannot say exactly, but I should have three pound six or seven. I would like to have a pair of pit shoes this time, but I'll go and see."

When Jack got to the office he was bet how to introduce hiimself to the overman. He had never been at the reckoning before, in he goes and says, "Well master what fettle to-night? I have never seen you this week, I thought perhaps you had got the influenza. Just before I came from home I saw two men with a cab to take Bessie Brown to the asylum, but they got the wrong house and took Mary Cooper, and nothing ails her. Poor soul. Bob Watson's wife fell into the gutter to-day and broke her leg, but she's not much worse. Is this the reckoning night, Master?"

The Master says "Listen to me awhile, you have six score six of coal, and nine tubs of overweights that makes six score fifteen. One tub set out, four tubs laid out, that leaves six score ten, at seven shillings a score, makes thy money for coals, two pound five and seven pence. Sixpence a score for helping up, two shillings a score for working wet. Four yards of narrow board at tenpence a yard. Two yards of winning headways at one and fivepence a yard. Five yards of wall at one an twopence a yard. Ten yards of side coal at sixpence a yard. Half a crown for dip hitch, I forgot the rent but I will put it in next time. That makes the money three pounds ten and threepence."

"Thank you, master, I have a better pay than I thought – my wife Meg will be pleased, don't forget the rent next time, good night, Master."

"Stop," wsays the master, "until you get the offtakes."

"Offtakes," says Jack, "never mind them, I can get them next time. I am quite content."

"Listen to me," says the master, "there's seven shillings for powder and candles. Twopence for the pick sharper, and sixpence for house and coal. Ninepence for the doctor. Sixpence for water. Ninepence for the weighman. Half a crown you got over much last time. Two shillings for the hospital. Two shillings for picks and shafts and four shillings for stricking [sc.striking] at a putter. That leaves two pounds ten and twopence for you to draw for your pay to-morrow night."

Jack says, "If I had known you were going to treat me like this I would not have come. If you had another try it will be all offtakes."

When he got home he says to his wife, "Meg, I will never go to the reckoning again."

"What for?" says Meg.

"I had three pounds ten and threepence at first and when I came away I had two pounds ten and twopence, he left one pound and a penny off for what he called off-takes."

Meg says, "The dirty scoundrel, I'll go to the reckoning myself next time, and if he starts with his off takes I'll take his nose off his face. Let us see if we can pay our way: there's one pouind six and a penny for groceries. Fifteen and twopence for the butcher. two and sixpence for the sewing machine man. One shilling for milk. Ninepence for the union, one and sixpence for insurance. Two shillings for the tailor, and fourpence for yeast. That leave tenpence to get a pair of pit shoes. What a shame – it's a blessing you are teetotal."

(Tommy Armstrong)

The totalling up was more of an office skill in the twentieth century:

The Clerks used to come along to me and call off the summary of each of their seams totals such as the Harvey seam etc., etc., including the deductions and all that, and then I had it all to total up, deduct petty cash from it – get the total for the pay cheque. When the Chief Clerk had to go to a Manager's Meeting, I was left with the keys for the cash box control so that I could pay the men their coal allowance.

I was just a Bill Clerk. I had a splendid reference from Mr. Howson who was Manager at the time and he said about me being honest and trustworthy and all that sort of thing. I used to feel a bit embarrassed thinking there were older people there: I absolutely love figures, and it became a mania with me.

(Miss D. Turner, Beamish 1983/235)

The need for accuracy can be judged from the following:

The wages came on Friday and were in big trays; these trays were divided into squares and each square contained a small open-topped round tin which contained the money. Each square was numbered to correspond with the payment slip number of the particular employee. The money was counted out to you at the pay window and handed over loose.

(Norman Wilson, North Walbottle Colliery)

The importance of pay week and baff week in the pitman's almanac can be judged from the following:

> Aitcheson shifted to Gordon Terrace on Wed, after the pay, April 21st.
>
> Henry Winter, 19 yrs of age, of No. 3 John Street West, Ayre's Quay, was picking coals at Ryhope, when he had his leg crushed between two waggons, he was taken to the Sunderland Infirmary, where his leg had to be amputated.
>
> Mr W. Tweddle, land steward to the Ryhope Coal Co. Ltd. was reported dead same day namely Baff Fri. April 23rd.
>
> Fred Williams was at the South Pit Haul Rope, on Baff Sat. April 24th and had his first trip down the pit, and finished at six oclock on the Sun. morning...
>
> (J.C. Walshaw's diary, Ryhope, 1908)

Shifts

A coal mine is open 24 hours a day, if only because it needs constant checks and maintenance. How much of that 24 hours was spent 'winning coal' depended on the technology of hewing, hauling and winding. In the early nineteenth century, a shift of hewers went in before daylight to bring down a first load of coal; putters and drivers (and more hewers) were needed a few hours later – in the morning – and counted as a separate shift. These two shifts were called 'fore' and 'back':

fore shift – "The first shift of hewers into the pit, 2 to 3 hours before the boys and day workers" (Tootle, 1995, N.East); "in fawst – morning shift" (Dodd, Tanfield Lea, C20/2); "the fore shift... meant going to work at 4 a.m. and returning at noon" (Hitchin, 1962, p.62).

back shift – "the second shift of hewers in each day. It commences about four hours after the pit begins to draw coals" (Nicholson, 1888); "in the back shift one worked from 9 a.m. until 5 p.m." (Hitchin, 1962, p.62).

Night-time accordingly became a time for maintenance work: "It was the night shift, when as necessary, the stone men cleared any obstructions to the seam of coal" (Trelogan, New Herrington).

With improved capacity for handling coal, a three shift system was introduced in 1870 and helped provoke the strike of 1871. The new system still left a space of time overnight for maintenance. Thus at Seaham Pit:

> Q. [Coroner] How many shifts have you got in the mine?
>
> A. [Colliery Manager]: Three shifts.
>
> Q. From when to when?
>
> A. From 4.30 am to 11.30 pm. That is the whole time embracing the three shifts.
>
> Q. What are they?
>
> A. The first is 4 o'clock am to 11.30 am.

Q. What is the second?
A. From 10 am to 5.30 pm.

Q. And what is the third?
A. From 4 pm to 11.30 pm.

Q. What is the name of these shifts?
A. The fore shift, the back shift, and the night shift.

Q. The fore shift is that beginning at 4.30 am?
A. Yes.

Q. In all parts of the mine?
A. In all parts of the mine in question. The No. 2 pit is not a double shift; No. 2 pit has only two shifts of men.

Q. At the time of the explosion there were no shifts down?
A. No, not a regular order of shift.

Q. What was there doing at the time of the explosions? [2am]
A. The shifters.

Q. Would that be what is called in some placed a repairing shift?
A. Yes.

Q. When do they go down?
A. Ten o'clock.

Q. Ten o'clock pm?
A. Yes.

Q. When do they come up?
A. Six am.

Q. Is there a separate gang of shifters for each of these four districts?
A. Yes.

(*PP*, 1881, CR x, p.17)

Three shifts of hewers overlapping with two of haulage was implicit in this system and confirmed in the Coal Mines Regulation Act of 1908 which both limited the work-day to 8 hours and encouraged the imposition of the three-shift system (see W. R. Garside, *The Durham Miner*, 1919–1960, London 1971, pp.20–21; John Wilson, *A History of the Durham Miners' Association* 1870–1904, Durham 1907, pp.55–58 and Benson, *British Coalminers in the nineteenth century*, 1989, pp.115–6).

While such legislation was perceived as benefiting the pitman, in fact by sub-dividing the work-force further, it left the worker little initiative in what he was doing, and proved (it may be) a significant factor in moving his status towards that of purely directable labour. Issues arising became the reserve of the Union meeting.

With automation, there was no reason coal getting could not be maintained 24 hours out of 24, so that three evenly spaced 8-hour shifts were introduced, with a short break for maintenance at the weekend. Confusingly, the old terminology was retained, so that the back shift tended to start in the afternoon. Thus at Wallbottle Colliery the shifts were 8 am till 4 pm ("also called dayshift"), 4 pm till midnight, and midnight till 8 am (Wilson, North Walbottle) and "in bakk" became the "afternoon shift" (Dodd, Tanfield Lea). Elsewhere the "tub-loading shift [was] still used to distinguish overnight shift, originally a maintenance shift, but now coal-producing" (McGee, Sherburn Hill). In effect, some collieries thought in terms of four shifts: "first shift starting 4.30 am, back shift 10.30 am, night shift 4.30 pm, tub-loading shift 10.30 pm – in fact all shifts coal-producing shifts; with surface shifts 7–3, 3–11, 11–7 (for washer, fitters, etc.)" (Barnett, Seaham).

At Dawdon

For surface workers there was a three-shift system, 7am–3pm, 3pm–11pm, and 11pm–7am. This arrangement had a tendency to merge into a single convenient day shift of 8am–4pm, but that was never officially approved. Underground the shift system depended on the pit and the needs at any particular time. At Dawdon, tub-loading started at 12 midnight, the foreshift started at 4.30am, the dayshift at 8 or 8.30am, the backshift at 10.30am, and the nightshift at 3.30pm. They would be about seven and three-quarters hours each. Dayshift was the one most favoured. Generally you would work a shift one week, then change, but men on supplies, for example, could work a permanent nightshift if they asked to. Or if there was a special job to finish, you would stay with that shift till it was done. Every shift was a coaling shift (except for maintenance periods, which were Friday night to Sunday night). But when it was slacker, they wouldn't get coal at night – the overnight shift (4pm–4am) would become the maintenance shift. Or similarly, they would lay one face off, and coal 24 hours a day on some other faces during refitting the idle one. It depended a lot on the Manager.

(Trevor Charlton)

Johnny Fry the Putter

Either confused by the shift system or seduced by the idea of a minimum wage, Johnny Fry is the original ideal bad worker. Fred Wade attributes the song to Tommy Armstrong in his typescript *Story of West Stanley* (pp.372–3), but it is not in the official list of his works. Note the banksmen's revenge for Johnny's aggression.

At a quarter to six in the morning	
Not feeling very fit,	hung over?
Aa went across the Sheel Raw fields	
As far as the Margaret Pit.	
When Aa got to the pit-heap	
The banksman was closing the gate	
"Noo Johnny," sez he, "this'll not dee	do
Thouse varney ten minits late."	very nearly
At this Aa got me monkey up,	temper
Aa sez "Whaats thou got to dee wid?	with it
Wheese thee think thou's taaking te,	
A bloomin little kid?"	
We had a few hot words	
But at last, after a bloomin' age	
He rapped 'Men On' to the brakesman	
And away Aa went in the cage.	
At forst we went quite canny	
But all at once came a bump	
And then she went that hard	
Aa thout she wiz away for the sump.	bottom

When Aa got te the bottom
Somebody shouted, "Here's Johnny Fry"
An the owerman said after blawing me lamp,
"Get theesell in-bye." — to the work-face

Aa says, "Aal reet" and away Aa went
As fast as Aw cud gan
And efter yolkin me gallower — pony
Went strite in te the man. — hewer

Efter being off the way fifteen times — derailed
Aa got in te the hewer
He sez, "Where the hang he ye been,
Ye bloomin' little stewer?"

Aa says, "Divint get excited
Aa've had to wait for the cage;
Besides it disint matter much:
Thou's on the minimum wage."

Aa was kinda hungry at half past ten
Sa Aa sat doon and had me bait
And to my surprise Aa fell asleep
And started kinda late.

Aa lifted tubs on till Aa was sick
An me back woz that bloomin saor
That efter putting the men three fives
Aa thout Aa wad gan back nee maor.

So Aa sat a bit till me marrow came in
And efter heving a bit taak
Aa says, "It's varney two o'clock,
Aa think Aa'l hev a waak." — walk

At two o'clock exackly
Aa wis waaking off the heap — premises
And eftor getting cannily weshed
Aa went en had some sleep.

Start work

The early start of work (for those in the fore shift) has proved, paradoxically, a poetic subject and the 'caller' is a prominent figure in the mythology of the coalfield.

calling course – "the time at which the 'caller' made his rounds from house to house to wake the early shift men. He would then make a later call to wake the boys and day workers. In early days he would knock on the door and call 'Wake up and go to work, in the name of God!'" (Tootle, 1995, C19, N.East),

The neet before aw went to wark
A warld of wonders cross'd ma brain,
Through whilk they did se skelp and yark, — slap… hit
As if ma wits had run amain. — out of control

Aw thought th' time wad ne'er be gyen,
That callen-course wad never come;
And when the caller call'd at yen, — 1 a.m.
Aw'd getten neither sleep nor slum.

Aw lap up nimmel as a flea –
Or lop, amang war blankets spangen; — flea
And i' the twinklen of an e'e
Was fairly ower the bedstock bangen.

(Thomas Wilson, *The Pitman's Pay*, pt.2)

caaler – "an official at a colliery engaged to call up the men for work. He makes his first round at half-past 12 a.m., and knocks at all the doors with D chalked on them. These are the deputies' houses; they go to work an hour before the hewers. Every man of the fore-shift marks 1 on his door – that is the sign for the caller to wake him at that hour. The hewer fills his tubs, and continues alternately hewing and filling. Meanwhile, the caller having roused the putters, drivers, and off-handed man, the pit 'hings on', that is, starts work at 5 o'clock" (R. Wilson, 'Coal mines of Durham and Northumberland,' *Trans. of Tyneside Naturalists' Field Club*, vol. 6, pp.203–4).

put-on – "to over sleep or lie in. A term used by the miners in the North East" (Tootle, 1995),

sleep the carrler – "How yer makin out Bill, thinkin the other day a nuther couple of sayins came to mind, afore the waar the pits used a carrler to get the fist shift outa beed, he used ta come round and tap on the beedroom winda win a pole it deed out but the sayin staid (as in if yer slept in/ or were late deeing summit yud slept the carrler)" (Geordie Darby); "sleep thi kaala – sleep in" (Dodd, Tanfield Lea).

Knocker and the Ghosts

The other day, me marra was late for work, so I says, "Hey, what's the matter wit ye the day?"

He says, "Oh, man, Ned... I slept the caller!"

Why, I knew what he meant... that he'd slept in... but it took me mind back to the time when every pit village really did have a Caller. Ye know, a sort of human alarm clock, somebody that went round the rows in the night, gettin' folks out o' bed in time for work.

The one I remember best was the one they had when I was a bairn, Old Knocker Jordan. There used to be a lot o' talk about how he got his name, an' some folks said they called him Knocker 'cause he went round the doors knockin' folks up. Others, though, used to say that in his young days he'd been a bit of a boxer, an' he got called Knocker 'cause he knocked folks out.

Anyways, even in his sixties he was a fine figure of a man, an' his job meant he got plenty o' exercise. Every hour through the night, he went round the whole colliery, carrying with him his lamp an' his little wooden mell. In them days, hangin' outside every back door there used to be an ordinary bit slate, like they put on the roofs, an' if anybody wanted a call, why, they just used to chalk the time on it afore they went to bed. Like a big 2 if they wanted callin' at two o'clock, or a big 3 or 4 or so on. Then, as he did his rounds through the night, the Caller would shine his lamp on the slates to see whe wanted callin' when.

He needed the lamp, o' course, 'cause there was no street lights then, an' he needed his little wooden mell for brayin' on the doors wi'. The sounder the sleeper, the harder Old Knocker had to hammer, an' he'd keep on hammerin' away there until somebody came downstairs to open the door. In fact, openin' the door was the only way o' gettin' rid o' him, an' if ye kept on sleepin', why, the noise might easily wake your neighbours so there'd be some angry words in the mornin'. Once he'd called ye, though, Knocker had done his job, so if ye went back to bed an' to sleep again, it was your own fault an' "ye'd slept the Caller!"

Mind, talkin' about Knocker Jordan reminds us of a tale I once heard about him. It seems like there was two young chaps once thought they'd play a bit o' a trick on him, an' give him a bit o' a gliff. They dressed themselves in long, white sheets, an' in the middle o' the night laid in wait for him at the end o' Institute Row. Then, as Knocker turned the corner, they jumped out on him, wavin' their arms, an' moanin' an' wailin' someick awful! The idea was that he'd take them for a couple o' ghosts, an' turn an' run... but, no, they'd picked on the wrong man!

Knocker Jordan sees these two frightenin' lookin' figures, but he doesn't turn a hair. He just ups wi' his little mell, an' starts brayin' away at where the ghosts' heads would be if ghosts had heads. With all the practice he'd had hammerin' on back doors, he was a dab hand at it, and the two young chaps soon found out their heads weren't so hard as the doors Knocker had practised on. The wailin' an' moanin' that come from them then was far worse than afore, an' it wasn't long afore they took to their heels an' ran. Aye, they disappeared even quicker than real ghosts would have done...

Why, wi' the sheets ower their heads, Knocker didn't know whp they were... but next morning', it was easy to spot them! There was two chaps off work then, an' for a canny few more days, an' they went round the colliery wi' bandages wrapped round an' round their heads. Mind, Knocker realised they hadn't meant him any real harm, so, even when he knew who'd tried to put the wind up him, he didn't do anything about it.

Except for one thing... ever afterwards, them two young chaps were never sure at what time they were ganna get called! They might be havin' a nice sound sleep, not expectin' to wake until mornin', an' then about three o'clock, there would be this hammerin' on the back door.

When they went downstairs to find out what it was all about, Old Knocker would point to the slate hangin' up, an' show them he'd only called them at the time chalked on there. Then, when they said they hadn't put it on, Knocker would look puzzled.

"Why, if ye didn't put it on," he used to say, "I wonder whe did ...? Aye, I know... it must have been a ghost!"

(Lisle Willis, 1950s)

The actual start of work at the colliery had its own term: 'hanging on', from the attaching of a kibble of coal to the winding rope – a symbol that the colliery was in production:

hingin' on – "hanging on, the time the pit begins to draw: 'the... pit hung on', 'Frae hingen on till howdy ma'" (Wilson, G'head, 1820s); "hing-on or hang-on – a call from the banksman to the onsetter after any stop (the cause of which has been at bank), meaning recommence coal work" (Nicholson, 1888); "'Hang on'... was the signal to resume normal working" (Hitchin, 1962, p.79).

Training

In the nineteenth century, the contention was that children needed to start work in the mines as young as possible, or they would never become habituated to mine work. However, as work processes became more technically demanding, it was found equally convenient to dispense with child labour.

The solution was to offer training courses for youngsters of school-leaving age, and the NCB in particular offered attractive apprenticeships for electricians and mechanics. The following account, though from outside our area, illustrates the process well:

> ...I particularly remember the ad as the National Coal Board, as it was then in the 1960s offered a good wage scale compared to what I was then earning in other industries! I was then sixteen and a few months, a little older than was usual for a formal apprenticeship in the UK at that time. The usual age was to start at sixteen and finish at twenty-one. Needless to say I applied, I was granted an interview and had to take a written aptitude test and past both. I then had to take a medical and X-ray, again I passed both.
>
> A couple of weeks later I received an envelope with NCB stamped on it and I opened the same, finding they had accepted me and to report to Clifton Colliery at a set date.
>
> Clifton Colliery was just up the road from where I lived, in the old Meadows district of Nottingham. Clifton was also in the East Midlands Division, Number six Area of the National Coal Board, and the HQ was Bestwood Unit as all mines and workshops were now being called.
>
> Next stage was to let my Dad know! I had already asked how he felt about me working down a mine, and his reply was "over my dead body"! What would he say now I had been offered employment and I required his signature on the trade papers, commonly know as indentures!
>
> I waited until he had had his dinner and was relaxed and then promptly broke the news, "Dad, I've got a job as an apprentice electrician at Clifton Colliery"! His reply startled me! "You'll not like it" and that was all he said!
>
> He signed the papers and the long haul started in catching up with the rest of the class at tech college, I had almost six months of learning plus what was being taught each day. During the first year the syllabus was one week, (five days), at tech school and the following week at the Boards training centre.
>
> Tech school was where we learnt mining science, mining practice, mining legislation, mining history, workshop theory and practice and other classes.
>
> At the training centre, which was located at the old Hucknall Colliery site, on Watnall Road Hucknall in Nottinghamshire, we had to start our Statutory training as required by Law. Because we were all juveniles, we had to do twenty days surface training. That entailed wearing our pit helmets, overalls and safety boots, and learn how to operate safely around the surface operations of a mine without getting ourselves hurt. We also, a little later on, did the same in the underground galleries of the old mine. We took the same time, twenty days, which took into consideration,

pony haulage, setting supports, both face and main road. Rope haulage and other things to familiarise us with underground working.

The pony we had was more like a draught horse! Biggest pony I had seen and talk about cranky!! One morning the instructor had us all putting on the ponies gear, every time we tried to fasten the belly straps, the S.O.B. turned around and tried to bite us, so we all refused to go any further!! The instructor called us all wimps and said the hoss wouldn't hurt us, anyway he shoved us all out of the way and proceeded to fasten the harness himself. He was just reaching under the ponies belly when the pony turned around and grabbed the instructors elbow between his teeth, boy did he scream, of course we were all rolling about laughing!! It made our day!! but he wasn't a "happy camper" for the rest of the day, boy did his elbow swell up!

(John Waudby)

A special case was that of the Bevin Boys, recruited during World War 2 to help keep up the level of the workforce, when youngsters would normally be enlisted in the army. Usually they served as ancillary workers. Sometimes it worked out well, sometimes it led to disappointment...

We all arrived and a month to six weeks training down a dis-used mine. It was all the machinery and things but it wasn't very deep, the Morrison Busty, this training section. And it wasn't very dark. It was well lit, electric light and so it give me no inkling of what was to come. I suppose it was a gradual introduction of these people from London, from Inverness, all over the place and didn't know what a pit was. At least I knew what a pit was. They were going to be introduced to it in as nice a way as possible. Therefore they lit the place up and they made the shaft, the depth you dropped down, very shallow. In fact I've heard it said if you were late and you'd missed the cage, you could jump down. So they give the impression it was as pleasant as possible.

Then after the six weeks you lived in a hostel there which is still there incidentally, just at Annfield Plain where the Morrison Busty pit used to be, just on the corner going towards Stanley, those round nissan huts. That was the Bevin Boys hostel.

We all stayed together and you were given exercises. You had to run over these hills away above Annfield Plain. Boxing lessons for those who wanted to box. All supposed to toughen you up for the hard life to come.

... And then one magic morning, we were allocated, our slips, paper that said to which colliery we had been drafted. Now mine was Marley Hill. It's one of the last ones in this area to close...

And I got the shock of my young life. Because it was nothing like the training centre, it was hurry up and it was a long way down and it was a long way in. You walked forever before you even got to the place where you were going to work. There was none of this hewing with picks and filling into tubs and ponies. It was long wall face. It was just coming in then. Big coal cutters and conveyer belts that took the coal out to fill it into tubs and the tubs took it to the bottom of the shaft. It was mechanised as far as a pit could be mechanised in those days. I just knew nothing about this. I never ever wanted anything to do with machinery. I don't like noise. If I'm in a position where I could get a bit apprehensive, to be suddenly deafened by noise around you makes me more jumpy.

And I was eighteen months there and hated every minute of it. I've got to be honest about that. I used to, many a time I said 'I'd be better off in the army.' 'Why didn't I volunteer for the Black Watch?' Of course that was a guaranteed way, if you volunteered you could get into anything you wanted to. And I used to sit there and say 'my God what a ...'

(R. Barrass, Beamish 1924/25r)

End of work

The end of a shift was conveyed by three terms: 'howdy ma', 'kennor' and 'lowse'. The last probably refers to the return of ponies to their stables and the 'loosening' of their harness, etc. The other two remain obscure…

howdy-maw – "the conclusion of the day's labour, the last corf: 'Frae hingen on till howdy ma'" (Wilson, G'head, 1820s).

kenner — "an expression signifying time to give up work, shouted down the shaft by the banksman where practicable, and where not, signalled and conveyed into the workings from mouth to mouth or by further signalling" (Nicholson, 1888); "kenner – the end of the shift" (Wade, South Moor, 1966); "an expression meaning 'It's time to knock off working'" (Tootle, 1995, N.East). [Harry Tootle notes a variant 'kennell' in the South Midlands.]

"Wey hoo di ye knaa when it's lowse if ye divn't carry a watch?" – "Man, it's just instinct."

(*Ashington Col. Mag.*, January 1935)

louse – "meaning 'loose' or the end of the working period at the face or wherever the working place was. It is not the same as the end of the shift as it was still necessary to travel outbye and the shift didn't end until one was on bank" (Sharkey).

lowse – "loose" (Wilson, G'head, 1820s).

lowse – "to finish working; kenner" (Nicholson, 1888).

loose (laawz) – "to finish work. 'What time diz thoo louz?' or, to a stranger, 'What time do ye (yae) louz?' (When do you leave off working?)" (Palgrave, Hetton, 1896).

loose or **kennah** – "defines end of shift of work" (McBurnie, Washington, 1970s).

lowz – "untie, end of shift" (Dodd, Tanfield Lea)

lousen out – "example: all the fillers coming off the face together when it was time to start the journey outbye" (Sharkey); "'the pit's lowsed out' – stopped for the day" (J. Moreland, Dawdon, 1980).

An easy way to mark the change of shifts was to use the colliery hooter or 'buzzer':

buzzer (technical) – "The steam whistle or 'fog-horn' that warns miners of the times for returning to and from work" (Palgrave, Hetton, 1896).

buzza – "pit siren" (Dodd, Tanfield Lea).

buzzer – "a contribution from my wife is the saying, 'you're settin yerself ahead of the buzzer' (getting above your station, being forward). Again from Sherburn Hill area. The Buzzer being the pit alarm for changing shifts" (McGee).

> The buzzer at the pit was the time-keeper for the village: it started the first shift and blew the last shift. When the colliers didn't arrive at the coaling staithes on the River Tyne the pit was laid idle. The pit buzzer would be blown three times at 8.30 to say the pit would not be working the next day which meant poor wages and more worry for the miners' wives.
>
> (Mr Cawson, Kibblesworth, Beamish 1993/5)

> New Year was a big night. We used to go what we call first footing, this still carries on I believe. In fact people used to invite you, will you come and be my first foot. There was two, three houses, my older brothers have gone regular, and that was passed on from one to the other. I can remember two, or three houses I used to go to regularly and be their first foot. Go in and have a bit spice, and a drink of ginger wine. In those days you knew it was twelve o'clock because all the colliery buzzers blew. At 12 o'clock midnight, the ending of the old year all the colliery buzzers blew, and as soon as the buzzers stopped, everyone starting knocking at the doors. I think it's died out nowadays.
>
> (J .Agar, Beamish 1984/253)

Celebrations

With the aim of the pit being maximum continuous production, any holiday (other than the enforced holiday of a lock-out) was a matter of some celebration. While 'gawdy days' was the general terms for holidays noted by John Bell (*Bell MS*), sometimes it was used with the sense of unauthorised holidays ("Gaudy Day – it might be the day the first cuckoo was heard, or the turnips were ready in the fields", Douglass, 1973). [Gaudy from Latin *gaudium* 'joy'.]

More formal were special rituals associated with the pit shutting over Christmas:

tyup – "the last basket or corf sent up out of the pit at the end of the year. The name is got from a tup's horn accompanying it. 'Bussin' the tyup' is covering the coals with lighted candles, which the lads beg, boroow, or steal, for the occasion. It is an expression of their joy at the gaudy days or holidays which take place generally after this event" (Wilson, G'head, 1820s).

bussin'-the-tyup [decorating the ram] – "the tup was the last corf of coals drawn out of the pit on the last day of the year; and by way of showing their pleasure at the gaudy-days now commencing, the pitmen covered it with burning candles" (Heslop, N'd, 1880s).

The cawshun stowl maw heart away,	caution/special person
When he wiz helpin-up,	lending a hand
As roond the raws one heul doo day,	terrace rows...Yule dough
The youngsters hugg'd the teup.	
The teup, poor thing, wiz myed to bleeze,	blaze
The beer wiz myed te flee,	was made to flow
Till maw little Bob got as tight as ye pleese –	
Maw Bob's the lad for me! –	

(Alexander Barrass)

Another custom was the present of a Yule-dough or Yule-doo from the hewer to his putter. Originally a pastry rather like a gingerbread man, this could be commuted into a cash present.

Thor's a man o' mine, a hewer,	fellow worker
Weers a shirt o' flannen blue,	flannel
Which Aw fill'd away at Christmas	hid in a tub of coal
Kas he didn't bring me doo.	because...Xmas box

(Alexander Barrass)

Pranks (sconces) were a part of pit life.

In the blacksmith shop

He was quite a sensible person, mind. Only he loved playing tricks on folk. This time him and some other apprentices got up into the girders in the roof of the blacksmith's shop (the old loco shed with a high roof, but only low level lighting), directly above his victim, who was working away at an anvil or whatever. Then he pays out a long thread, invisible in the low lighting up above. And on the end of the thread is a live crab, its claws wriggling everywhich way, but held firm by the line tied round it, and all painted black.

Well, you can imagine the guy below, innocently hammering on a piece of hot bar, when round his ears comes this tickling, clicking sensation. He brushes it off, like a fly or a speck o' dust, but then it comes back. He looks up – and, well if it's not the biggest blackest spider in the world! and with a bite about it that would send anyone screaming from the building. Only standing back, he could just make out the little devils in the top of the roof, playing the trick. With an oath or more, he starting hoying anything he could lay his hands on – hammer first, then tongs – up at them, so they were soon scrambling to get down themselves, and out the way.

Yet the same guy that played this trick – and a lot others – why, he turned out to be the Assistant Engineer in time, would you believe it…"

(Trevor Charlton, Dawdon)

Organised sports were associated, in the modern era, with the local Welfare Hall, e.g. footy! Other customs might seem strange today:

Sports at Brough

I remember once we went to some sports at old Brough and there was a competition of a greasy pig. Whoever caught it, it was their pig. Three of us went in company. One of us would go down one side of the fencing, wire fencing where the crowd was standing, one would go down the other side and one would go down the middle after the pig. Now we had to be about 30 or 40 yards down and try to keep an opening and put our hands out and he would try to put the pig down that opening. It came off exactly. This lad and I was standing with our arm out and there was just a row through and he ran in front of the pig and he kicked it on the nose and it shot through this opening. I knew the only place it wasn't greased was the bottom of its legs, and I clicked [caught] it by the bottom of it's hind legs but it was that strong it pulled me onto my stomach and it was trailing me away over its back legs. And there was a bloke dropped clean on top of it and clung to it. I let him have the pig, but mind he had [to spoil] a new suit to get [it]. It was all grease. That's how we lost the pig. Now is there any more questions?

(Mr Garraway, Beamish 1983/248)

From its inception in 1873, the big event of the Durham pitman's year became the Durham Gala or 'Big Meeting'. Though later graced by the Bishops of Durham to honour the pit, a legend persists of a bishop who fell foul of the crowd:

Presently, Mother and I became aware of a disturbance near the speaker's platform and, to our surprise, a number of people began running towards the river. They passed over Dad [asleep], and this scared me so much that I hardly noticed a black-coated cleric heading the mob. The tumult shifted to the river itself and I saw boats performing some unusual manoeuvres. Later we heard that the Bishop of Durham had been thrown into the river for some remarks that had offended the men who heard them. This was afterwards amended. The new report said that he had run into the river as a way of escape. Perhaps he fell in...

(Hitchin, 1962, p.123)

A different version appears in the City of Durham Annual Lecture in 1983, entitled 'Miners & Bishops' by Michael Ramsay. While Ramsey recognised that Bishop Henson "had a deep hatred of socialism in any form" (p.5), he is acquitted of any offence against striking miners; rather, you may be surprised to learn, it seems that the miners were grossly unfair and unkind to the Bishop, who was probably unwell.

The whole of Durham City seemed to be a seething mass of bodies. Only the main thoroughfare was left clear for the parade. Lines of dancing boys and girls moved in unity to the music, which was provided by the brass bands that marched behind them. The tunes that the bands played expressed the feeling of gaiety and joy, which was felt by the crowd.

Next in the procession came the banner that related to the individual colliery union branch the men belonged to. The banner was 'Lifted High' by men whose names had been randomly drawn out of a hat. Carrying the union lodge banner was not only a labour of love; it was deemed a great honour to be chosen for this auspicious assignment.

Taking up the rear of the column were the families of the colliery workmen. In support of their men folk, they walked proudly behind the visual statement of their allegiance to the National Union of Mineworkers.

The black pennant, all too often forlornly attached to the top of the banner's side pole. This proclaimed to those that did not already know, 'Another miner and comrade has been killed, since we last met at Durham'.

(Tom Moreland)

A Northumbrian's Visit to Th' Big Meetin' a few months after the Easington & Eppleton disasters in 1951

Aa had a Satorday ti spend, ti waist it seemed a pity,
So off bi bus an' train aa went ti visit Durham City;
Aa knew it wus a Gayla Day uf which th' Miners' proowd, (1)
But nivvor for a minute thowt thut there'd be such a croowd.
Th' only way ti progress, wus followin' a Bannor!
(Thor seems a moral in thaat line), so aa joined in like mannor.
From th' Station ti th' narra bridge, wi haalted many times;
An' above th' noise of voices, rang oot th' Cathedral Chimes.
In Silver Street wi stuck agyen – aa thowt it wus for gud,
Yit ivvorybody laffed an' joked as if th' understud;
Aa hard nae angry voices, nae moanin' discontent,
An' when wi least expected it – th' band played – off we went.
Up past th' Three Hotels wi marched, an' whaat a lustry cheor
Sang oot when marchers knew for sure that Atlee had got heor;
Yis, theor he waas – 'Th' Gentleman'; who'd kept his pledge ti them,
Thaat's hoow th' cheor sae hartily; an' sum shoot "Gud Owld Clem."
It last wi reached th' meetin' place, an' wi broke oot from th' ranks,

Th' river lukked sae cool an' calm is aa sat on its banks –
An' ett th' tyesty sangwitches th' wife had myed for me,
An' washed thum doon reight hartily, wi a nice het cup a tea.

Sam Watson, from th' platform says – "This's th' best day ivvor,
Aa've nivvor in me life seen sae many folks heor – nivvor;"
Th' sun shon oot wi aal its might, an' not a cloowd ti dull
Th' bands an' folks still marchin' in, th' field wus nearly full.
On these two platforms there are men who've fitten for th' 'Caause';
An' whaat th' preached for 'eors hes noow becum th' Nation's Laaws; years
Aa felt sae proowd ti think these changes came withoot a shot,
A maricle it seemed ti me, aal bittorness disolved,
An 'both sides' sittin' side bi side, detarmined an' resolved –
That Nationalisation will succeed, wi willin' co'porashun,
An' thaat success'll benefit aal members uf th' Na-shun.
Aa hard th' Foreign Sec'ritry, an' Michael Foot M.P.,
Aa see'd the guests, sum Yugo-Slavs – who'd travilled heor ti see;
Aa wundor'd whaat they thowt uf this, a greit day in thor lives,
Aa think th'll tell it of'en ti thor sweethearts or thor wives.

An auld man waalked lang-side uf me, a stranger wi a stick,
Aa knew he'd been a pitman, an' once worked wi a pick;
Aa sade – "these bandsmen must feel proowd, thut they hev played inside," (2)
He torned ti me aal beamin', an' filled wi obvious pride.
"Aa've played in theor – aye lad aa hev, aye many 'eors ago,
Aa'll tell thu summit else lad perhaps thu'd like ti know:
Me son's conductor uf a band thut's played in theor th' day,
Aa've travelled in th' train aal neight, just for ti heor thum play."
Yor a lucky man aa mormored, an' then aa horried on,
An' aa left 'um theor tiv his glory, prowd uf his gud Son;

Aa marched ahint a bannor on its way ti th' Stashun,
An' aa waved ti Durham from th' train, lost in admorashun.

(Robert Straughan, 1951)

1. Always pronounced 'Gayla' in this case, though otherwise 'gahla'.
2. i.e. inside the Cathedral.

Disputes

With the interests of men and owners so radically opposed during the nineteenth century, it is not surprising that disputes over the terms of work were frequent, and local strikes not uncommon.

A major point of contention in the first half of the nineteenth century was the treatment of full tubs once they reached bank. Weighing gear was controlled by the owners; a tub containing too much stone or shale – in the owners' opinion – could be disallowed for payment, affecting hewers and putters alike.

The owner's view of loosely filled tubs is given in the following:

> They [hewers] will sometiems be so Roguish, as to set those big Coals at the top of the Corves, and make it look like a full Corfe, which Fraud when discover'd by the Banck's-Man, and the coals shaken in close appears to be little more than half a Corfe, is Noted by the said Bancks-Men, who do not empty that false Corfe, but setting it by as it is, when shaken in, lets it stand on the Coal-heap, till the Offender comes to Banck... the forfeiture is to give another full Corfe... or... the Offender forfeits six pence per Corfe, for every such bad filled Corfe to the Owner, which is Deducted out of his Wages.
>
> (*Compleat Collier*, 1707, p.38)

... which begs the question of whether it was really the hewer's job to break the coals down to a standard size. As regards the proportion of 'stone' in a tub, again – was it the hewer's job to break down lumps that combined coal and stone? And how on earth (or under it) was he expected to distinguish between coal and non-coal by the poor illumination of the odd candle or lamp? That stone would get included in the tub was almost inevitable – it was the way the offence was assessed and the hewer penalised that rankled.

laid-out – "when a tub was emptied and its contents spread out for it to be inspected for stone and foul coal, it was said to be laid-out. If there was too much stone or foul coal the collier would be fined or lose the price of the whole tub" (Tootle, 1995, N.East).

laid outs – "if a tub of coal contains more than a certain amount of stone it is confiscated, the stones and the hewer's token numbers are laid out for inspection" (Wade, South Moor, 1966).

The solution was for the men to have their own representative to check the assessment of the owners' weighman. A voluntary arrangement was suggested in 1860, but it was not until the Coal Mines Act of 1894 that this was made compulsory, with a checkweighman appointed and paid by the pitmen.

check-weighman – "the representative of the men, who checks the weight of coals at the surface" (Heslop, N'd, 1890s).

checkweighman (miners' technical term) – "name for both the owner's and the people's representative, each appointed to check the other's dishonesty, in weighing coal-laden tubs, as they come from the pit" (Palgrave, Hetton, 1896).

wyman – "weighman" (Dodd, Tanfield Lea).

Other causes of resentment included:

put-pay – "when the miners were paid by the fortnight the owners would often find a reason to hold back a portion of the men's wages until the next pay day. The amount owing could mount up over a period of time, and this was known as put-pay" (Tootle, 1995, N.East).

and

truck – "the name given to the system whereby wages, instead of being paid in cash, are paid either in goods purporting to be of the same value, or under conditions which force the employee to spend them in making purchases from his employer" – comparable to " 'butty' – in certain coalfields, notably in the Midlands, the men were not directly employed by the owners, but by a contractor, called a butty" (*HRCM*, ch.20) – the butty would own the local pub or shop, where he handed out pay and raked it back in. Prohibited finally by Act in 1842. Known also as 'tommy':

> In early 1831, meetings were held at Durham and Newcastle, each attended by upwards of 20,000 miners. At these great meetings, resolutions were passed to elect delegates to form a General Committee to petition Parliament for redress of their grievances; to send a deputation to London; to subscribe 6d (3p) per head towards expenses; to refuse to buy meat, drink or candles from the 'Tommy Shops'; to decline to sign the 'yearly bond' and to continue to work unbound thereafter.
>
> (Tootle, 1995)

By the middle of the nineteenth century, a provision for arbitration of disputes was not unknown. In the yearly bonds for 1869 quoted above (D/Lo/B/265) there is the clause:

> [In case of any dispute], such dispute or difference shall be submitted to the decision of two viewers of collieries, one to be appointed by the said owner and the other by the said workmen, and in case of their disagreement to the decision

of a third party, to be chosen by such two viewers before they enter on their reference.

It seems unlikely the viewers (colliery managers) would have much sympathy with the pitmen's cause. Nonetheless, in the latter part of the nineteenth century, it became usual to refer disputes to a Joint Committee, with six members appointed by the Union, six by the owners' association, and with an independent chairman. Issues that could not be settled between workmen and manager could be referred to this Joint Committee (*HRCM*, ch.23) – and this remained the procedure colliery by colliery, after Nationalisation.

joint committee – "a committee composed of an equal number of colliery managers and workmen, presided over by some disinterested person. The business of this committee is to settle all disputes arising between the owners and workmen at individual collieries" (Nicholson, 1888),

Until… with the appointment of Ian McGregor as Chairman of the NCB, there was increasing emphasis on closing collieries, and increasing concern about viability…

At Dawdon Pit

On this night at Dawdon Welfare
Kenny Henderson said:
Tak heart all me canny colliery lads
The pit is far from dead.
He showed us slides upon a screen
An' gav his point of view
Of how to reach the North Sea coal
And the things that we would do.

Thor was questions asked about the pit:
How lang could we survive?
Ten years he said we'd in reserve
But the sea-coal would keep us alive.
Then at ten to nine men got itchy feet,
They gave Ken Henderson a cheer – a big cheer
Then they queued up at the door
For two free pints of beer.

So Tyson's drove a tunnel out
Underneath the sea,
A waste of time and of good money
An' it's there for aal to see.
An' disappointed Dawdon men
Bitterly we realize
What the gaffors said that night
Was nowt but flaming lees.

Now with shearers machine-men are gannin' mad
Ripping out aal the coal
An' they're workin' themselves and us as well
Out of a job an' onto the dole.
An' with the thoughts of being on the dole
Staring us in the face,
The way the NCB's tret the Durham miner
Aa think it's a damn disgrace.

An' so now Aa think in five years' time
The pit it will close down
And there's no other work for us to do
In our little town.
Then the NCB will've done to us
What to others they've done before
An' the mining men in oor town
'll be mining men no more.

(Dave Mountford)

... and strikes

Ultimately, many disputes centred on the question of pay, fixed more or less arbitrarily by the mine owners. Attempts to reduce pay produced understandably bitter reaction as in 1831, 1875, etc. The Durham strike of 1844 led to evictions of workers and their replacement by new labour brought in by the Marquis of Londonderry from Northern Ireland.

What happened to the homeless, workless families? Hopefully,

> From the employment of men in new collieres, the men dismissed from old collieries are now at work, or there would be great distress in the trade.
>
> (from an official at Wallsend Colliery, *PP*, 1842, CR xvi, pp.624–5)

Frederick Grice in *Bonny Pit Laddie* (1950) describes a later nineteenth century strike, with families put in tents provided by the Union until the dispute was resolved; a miserable time, but official strikes at least meant a meagre strike pay from the Union.

> **Strike at Murton**
>
> ...the men staged their own protest march by carrying a banner of their union and another of three vests hanging on a line. This was because the main issue was over the new system of shifts at work. For weeks the strike went on and on, and debts grew, until with the coming of winter the wives took matters in hand. There was little coal left and the police guarded the stocks at the mine.
>
> One particular heap of coal was visible to all from outside the boundaries of the mine. This was always known as 'The Pea Heap', small coal sold for industrial purposes. As if by common consent the women gathered with buckets and shovels, and marched towards the Pea Heap. They were met by a line of police with truncheons drawn. Out before them stood Mr 'Johnnie' Bell, assistant manager, with a large sheet of paper from which he 'read the Riot Act', a warning which the women ignored. They shouted at the little man who turned and ran as they advanced. A number of us boys from school were able to watch from a discreet distance. It was not a pleasant sight. The women approached the police who made no retreat, and the women threw the buckets and shovels at the hated Irishmen. Urged on by those behind them some women reached the lines of stolid blue coats, but the truncheons stopped them in their tracks. Eye to eye they stood, then the women conceded defeat. Still hurling stones, they slowly retreated, and the police charged the crowd using their weapons indiscriminately.
>
> Not to be beaten entirely, the crowd ran towards the home of Johnnie Bell, only two or three hundred yards or so [away], near to the drill hall, where they stood shouting abuse at anyone within. Then someone shouted, "Look at all that glass in his greenhouse." It was a large greenhouse, which showed prominently over the wall, and the sight was irresistible. Stones rained down on to the greenhouse, until not a pane of glass was whole.
>
> (F.N. Platts, *The Canny Man*, pp.104–5)

In the twentieth century there have three strikes of major significance – the General Strike of 1926, begun by a lock-out of miners on 1 May 1926, following the Government's refusal to continue an agreement to sustain miners' minimum wage levels, and spreading rapidly with T.U.C. support into a General Strike of all union workers. This unity did not last, and from the 12 May the miners were left to fight their cause alone. By the end of 1926 they had submitted and returned to work. The episode is notable for the hysterical reaction of the anti-Union classes, who viewed the strike as akin to revolution.

> The mining communities are remote, hidden away, mysterious. If there had been several working collieries in London itself, modern English history would have been quite different. (For example, we should not have had the General Strike of 1926.)
>
> (J.B. Priestley, 1935)

...and the strikes of 1972, 1974, centering on Arthur Scargill and the Yorkshire NUM. There was concern over the level of wages under inflation and loss of jobs: North Gas was having an effect and 400,000 jobs had been lost in the coal industry between 1958–70 (Freese, p.235). The 1966 National Powerloading Agreement had changed negotiation from a county to a national level, and brought added status to the national union. In 1969 a small scale national coal strike for the reduction of working hours for surface workers had revealed a high level of unity in the industry – and the potential power of industrial action. In 1972, the NUM were able to mount effective picketing, blockades in effect, at points of distribution from coal stockpiles, as and when needed; and again, at a lower scale level in 1974, effective just the same because of wide support for the miners' cause. Twice, it seems, it caught the Tory government unawares. Their main response on both occasions was to declare a 3-day week which lost Heath the election of 1974.

...the strike of 1984–5 was an endeavour to stop a programme of pit closures and reduction of coal production, being introduced by Ian MacGregor, the new chairman (1982) of the National Coal Board. This time the tactics of 1972–4 did not work so well, and crowds of pickets were scattered by charges from mounted policemen; pickets were imprisoned; union funds seized by the Courts. Stockpiles of coal were high, and Nottingham miners continued to supply coal, severely reducing the impact of the strike. The lack of unity had been fostered by a previous National Incentive Scheme, bringing in bonuses for local productivity and setting coalfields, in effect, in competition. While some blamed Scargill for his management of the strike, the conflict and its end result were arguably unavoidable – economically and politically, coal was no longer wanted. By 1993 all the collieries in Co. Durham were shut down, and the coal industry of the UK was effectively over – its role replaced by imports of gas, oil and coal.

ca' canny – "a system of 'work to rule' adopted by the miners prior to the formation of their trade unions. This method of protecting their jobs had been practiced by the craft guilds for centuries" (Tootle, 1995). Also 'workie-ticket' – someone who did not pull their weight; "workie or workie-ticket – troublemaker, awkward customer" (Makepeace, South Shields).

candyman – "a bum-bailiff or process server; the man who serves notice of ejectment. During 'the great strike' [1844]... the pitmen recognised [among the recruited bailiffs] several faces that had been familiar to them on their pay-Saturday strolls through 'the toon' as the itinerant vendors who were called 'Dandy-candy, three sticks a penny'. Thus the term 'candyman' became generally applied in pit villages to those who served and carried out notices of ejectment" (Heslop, N'd, 1880s); "kandeemen – evict miners in strike" (Dodd, Tanfield Lea).

crake – "the miners union meetings were announced by the crake man going round the streets on a Sunday morning with a big wooden rattle, a crake" (Sanderson, Peterlee).

ester man – "another one for tha agyen: afore the waar alot on the pits were werkin short time some times day or two, other times langer; we had an ester man he used ta gan from street te street rattle a crake and tell the men te lye back till they were sent for. When the pit was ganna start werkin agyen and anounce that there would be a meetin in the miners hall. So there yer hev yer ester man. Arrl that went out when the waar started" (Darby, Seaham).

laid in – "in a colliery is when it is 'laid in' or given up working" (*Bell MS*); "laid-in – when a pit ceases working" (Wilson, G'head, 1820s); "laid-in – a pit that has ceased working for an indefinite period" (Nicholson 1888); "laid off – discontinued. The invariable description of a pit which is not working is 'laid off' or 'laid in'" (Palgrave, Hetton 1896); "laid in – pit closed e.g. coal exhausted, uneconomic" (Dodd, Tanfield Lea).

lying idle – "[pits] not working" (Nicholson, 1888); "ydel – pit laid idle" (Dodd, Tanfield Lea); "laid idle – a temporary suspension of work, and applies to a single individual or to a whole pit's crew" (Nicholson, 1888); "all the pits are idle the morn" [cry of the caller] (Hitchin, 1962); "Are ye working ? " – "Na, aam idle" (Dave Neville).

stick – "among colliers means when they confederate not to work without advanced wages" (*Bell MS*).

The Truculent Putters

"You know, it used to be laughable, the putters used to decide to strike, didn't they Sid?"

"What?"

"The putters would decide to strike"

"Oh yes that was what I was going to tell you"

"And they'd come round with a tin bath, you know, bashing the bath tin. 'The pit's off tonight, lads, the pit's off tonight!" They would LIE – the pit's off – didn't they Sid?"

"That was before the 1914 war, mind. I know the putters would go to work, they'd start on a Monday morning, they would all get in the yard and they would have a meeting before they'd start. One fella says, 'Look, I'll toss my cap up, if it stops up we'll go to work, if it comes back down – we'll go back home.' Right, mind."

(Mr & Mrs Taylor, Horden)

1921 Strike

The first strike that I could ever remember was in 1921. When it first started the people didn't think it would last long, it lasted for about 13 weeks. People were pretty hard up, the majority were hard up. There was no guardians... Fortunately our father, my father and mother were very strong minded, they had saved a little bit with the Coop. I remember I never went short during the '21 strike. I always had a shilling in my pocket all the way through. A shilling was a lot of money you know. I could go to the pictures or get an ice cream. But there were some very hard up mind. They just lived from day to day. Fortunately the weather was good, and everybody had gardens then, you know. They could supply their own material, vegetables that sort of thing. Well I think we lived on potatoes during that strike, and cabbage. I think we used to get a few bones, you couldn't buy meat so you had to get bones. I didn't know about it then but I do now. That was panacklety. We couldn't pronounce it. We used to have meat bones, potatoes and a slice of... Of course then a lot of the miners kept hens.

(J. Agar, Beamish, 1984/253)

I remember when the strike came. Oh it was horrible, the '21 strike. Your mothers had nothing. We had to go to the soup kitchens and you got pea soup. Well it was just green water more or less, just a few peas in. But the people used to cut the sandwiches up and make all these things, you know it was all voluntary and they did it all. You could have jam and bread and margarine and you could get sometimes a banana. It was cocoa, it wasn't tea, it was cocoa.

(Mr Carroll, Crook, Beamish, 1991/32)

Ballad of Orgreave

A notable episode in May–June 1984 was the picket of Orgreave coke ovens. Police combatted pickets with their devastating 'cavalry charge' – backed by police with riot gear, truncheons, shields, etc. It has become a strong visual symbol of the brutality of unleashed power.

It was at Orgreave
great were the masses of lorries
and the roads jammed with pickets
and the police on their horses with steel-toed hoofs
milled round and round
drunken centaurs them
to see if –

yes
this one
this man
the one with the bloody eye
makes a break
a run
out away
he thinks he can escape
he has had enough of being condense and beaten
and does a runner

the horse lifts its snout
scents the hominid in its mammal-trample splaying
and hinged limbs
at the order
gallops along the tarmac
get the bastard escaping
is running well for a half-blind,
turns
Tojohoto!
bangs into a supermarket door
and
like a new countryside
hides there-in

the cool, dark, damp and kindly interior of the supermarket
laced with soft product-music
a calm of yeast-musk and spiral notices called buyer-traps

bang! bang!
the head registers on the automatic open-door
and the helmet of the god
bounces once or twice on the top of the frame

the man is in the frozen pea aisle
the horse is at the checkout

there would be time to strew the path with hard-iced sprouts,
marble-head peas, carrots glued four-ways up
they would inhibit
but would they be truly sporting?

instead
the man holds a choc-ice to his bad eye
and pretends to notice the service lift
knowing body language to be irresistible to policemen

THE HORSE IS MOVED TO JINGLE AND STALK
down the tight aisles
regardless shoppers set baked beans rolling in terror
(tumbrils for the untested)
STILL THE HORSE GAINS THE CENTRAL CROSS
by the beef display and the family-size pizzas
most popular to trolleys, commanding the meeting of the aisles
and an excellent bargain if you have many children to feed
or a special visitor
then like a chessman
THE HORSE HAS TAKEN UP THE CENTRAL POSITION AND
whichever way the man moves he can

but he has not covered the emergency far exit
and its steps to the car-park
heavy single swing-door type with bars
the man has bluffed and
with a leap over the freezer
he is away
HEY! calls the horseman

WUH! calls the horse
There is a moment of almost-trot
as the horse
hits the broad aisle-way round the tinned peaches
where the mastery of man by the horse is at stake

but why look sillier than a silly runaway is looking?
the way is blocked with pallets of breakfast cereal about to be
loaded onto shelves;
what was meant to look good was a no-go
and the officer curls his lip in disdain under the perspex vizor
and the horse
and the horse, baulked of its prey,
lifted its tail.

Chapter 10: Hewing

Pitmen forming a ' bord'

Forming a 'judd'

Preparing to blast

Gathering the coal

It is in this art great changes have taken place over the years. Early on, coal was worked free by making cuts under and on each side of a large block of coal (the jud), then wedges were applied at the top of the seam to bring it down. In the nineteenth century, the same system, but with gunpowder used to dislodge the undercut coal was the norm; later the preparatory cuts would be made with a pneumatic pick. During the twentieth century, mechanical cutters took over the work, cutting the coal and loading it onto a conveyor belt in one process.

> The simplest form of coal mining, was coal hewing, where a man hewed the coal [ready for when] it was fired down. That was the simplest form of mining. Of course, I worked [after] compressed air was introduced in the mines, and they cut coal with a compressed air machine called a pom pom; it was a long arduous job; and then it was blasted down. Then came the electric cutting machines, a continuous chain which went round and round cutting the coal. Mining was totally different then.
>
> (Mr Sherwood, Beamish, 1984/250)

Overall strategy

Two systems have been used – 'bord and pillar' and 'longwall'.

Longwall implies the extraction of the whole of the coal seam in one operation. "The workings advance in a continuous line, and the space previously occupied by the coal is partially or wholly filled up with stone and refuse, upon which the superincumbent strata settle down. Either faces open out from the shaft and advance towards the boundaries (in which case roadways must be maintained strongly through the goaf) or roads are driven out first to the boundaries and coal winning proceeds by retreat, i.e. cutting towards the shaft" (*HRCM*, ch.4). There is a certain logic about longwall working. It simplifies ventilation as air can be brought to sweep along the coal face. Though used early on in Shropshire and Staffordshire, longwall in the North East was associated with automatic cutting.

Bord and pillar "consists in cutting up the seam into pillars – this work being known as 'working in the whole' and then extracting the pillars or 'working the broken'. Originally the whole mine was worked in its entirety before pillars were reclaimed, but this led to risks from pressure on the pillars, so it was more usual to work both "in tandem" (*HRCM*, ch.4).

> Nearly the whole of [Seaham] colliery is worked on the usual bord and pillar system of the country, which is preferred to long wall on the ground that the roof is hard and the bottom soft. The pillars are 40 yards square; the places are driven 44 yards centre to centre, leaving 4 yds for the stall roads. The broken is worked back, leaving the land weight to come down, which it usually does very rapidly, sometimes breaking square. The goafs are now very extensive.
>
> (*PP*, 1881, CR vol.x, p.v)

> Bord and pillar. This type of mining involves the extraction of a number of roadways (bords) in the coal seam parallel and at right angles to one another. In this way the coal seam is divided into a large number of rooms with rectangular pillars of coal left between them to provide a natural support for the overlying strata. The deeper the mine the larger are the pillars. In some cases the coal in the pillars can be eventually recovered by mining the pillars at the furthest point of advance and retreating to the mine entrance, letting the roof collapse in a controlled way as pillar after pillar is salvaged.
>
> www.competition-commission.org.uk

board or **bord** – "a wide heading usually 3 to 5 yds wide" (Tootle, 1995); "bord - the space allotted generally to one man to work in, in a colliery" (Wilson, G'head, 1820s).

board and pillar – "a system of working coal...in which between 30 and 60 per cent of the coal would be removed depending on the condition and the weight of the roof. The pillars would be worked out at a later date by using the 'retreat system'" (Tootle, 1995).

breast – "a coalface which is being worked" (Tootle, 1995, N.East).

face, feace – "the coal wall" (Brockett, Newc, 1820s); "face – the actual 'coal wall' where the coal is being extracted" (Tootle, 1995).

narrow work – "a 'stall' (working place) 3yds in width or under, was classed as 'narrow work', for which an extra price per yard above the hewing rate would be paid" (Tootle, 1995); "narrow-working – headway in a coal-pit" (Wilson, G'head, 1820s).

nook or **neuk** – "the corner of a pillar of coal" (Tootle, 1995, N.East); "nyuk – nook, corner, the corner of the working place or the working face" (Sharkey).

pillars – "the rectangular masses of coal between the boards" (Brockett, Newc, 1820s); "an area of stone or coal, left in place, unworked, to support the roof" (Tootle, 1995); "pilla – pillar area" (Dodd, Tanfield Lea).

win – "coal is won when it is proved and a position attained so that it can be worked and brought to bank" (Nicholson, 1888).

Hand hewing

> The Hewers are the same class of men which in the southern districts are called holers; as a general rule they are twenty-one years of age upwards, and it is only in cases of rare exceptions, that in the northern district any of them are under eighteen, but there are such exceptions. The hewer is called at an early hour, perhaps two in the morning. He rises, comes to the fire, takes breakfast, ties up some victuals in a handkerchief, and proceeds to the pit. He finds a whimsey man at the engine who lets him down the shaft, he walks onward through the horseway, and then over the barrow-way to his place of work. The deputy overman shows him what is to be done; he strips off the chief part of his clothes, he gets down on his hams and undermines the coals, and he also makes a perpendicular cutting at the side,

> from the roof to the bottom, he drills a hole and inserts gunpowder, and brings down a mass of coals at once. After about two hours the putters come to carry away his coals, and he assists in filling the tubs, and suspends an iron ticket with his number upon it to each of his tubs, that it may be put down in the count to his credit. He sees that the tub is properly filled, for otherwise there is a risk according to the articles of the bond that the tub will be forfeited and nothing allowed for it. He is also careful not to allow black stones to be put into it, for that incurs a fine, and might be detected in the day-time when the tub came to the bank, but if it be dark there is less danger and he runs the chance. About eleven o'clock he has done his day's work. He gives over, puts on his clothes, goes to the foot of the shaft, and ascends. He then goes home, washes his hands, and his face and neck, wipes his body with a towel, and sits down to his baked potatoes and broiled ham. He may if he think fit put on his good clothes, and walk about like a gentleman in the afternoon. He takes his tea a little after four, sits an hour or two by the fire, and then goes to bed and sleeps sound till the voice of the callman arouses him to his labour.
>
> (*PP*, 1842, CR vol. xvi, p.134)

> The coal is first holed or undercut with a special tool known as a pick or a mandril. That is, a groove one or two feet in depth is cut either in the lowest part of the coal or in the underlying fire-clay. The mass of coal is supported during this operation by sprags or props. When the holing process is completed several sprags are withdrawn and if the immense downward pressure of the overlying strata proves insufficient to break down this coal, wedges are drived in at the top of the seam or [after about 1830] explosives are used in non-gassy mines.
>
> (Jevons, qu. Benson, 1989, p.54)

coal-getter – "a coal hewer" (Nicholson, 1888); "coal-getter – a 'collier' or 'hewer' of coal. More often called a 'getter'. The term ceased to be used in many areas by the early 1940s" (Tootle, 1995).

cracket – "a low wooden stool or seat used by the hewer when under-cutting the coal" (Tootle, 1995, N.East); "pit cracket – a low seat used by a coal-hewer" (Nicholson, 1888); "cracket – was used or invented by coal hewers to rest or lean on their side whilst working" (Sanderson, Peterlee); "...sitting on a little stool or cracket, swinging his pick and levering the coal away from the face" (Grice, 1960, ch.7).

curvings – "the cut itself would become choked with dust which we called 'curvings'" (Hitchin, 1962, p.98); 'kirvens and nickens' – the preparatory operations for bringing down the jud or top, and which produce only small coal: "what he gat...frae out the kirvens and the nickens" (Wilson, G'head, 1820s).

double work – "where two hewers worked simultaneously in a single board; extra payments might be agreed for the inconvenience" (Colls, 1987).

hewer – "man who cut the coal with a pick and filled it into tubs" (J. Moreland, Dawdon, 1980); "the hewer of course was the aristocrat of the colliery labour force" (Benson, 1989, p.69), e.g. first claim on colliery housing; "kohl yoo-a" (Dodd, Tanfield Lea); "slush hewer – a hard working coal hewer" (Wade, South Moor, 1966); "mere physcial strength was not enough... he needed...a sure understanding of the dangers of underground work. This sixth, or pit, sense could be obtained only by long experience" (Benson, 1989, p.55).

When hewing in hoggers and drawers
A'm nyen o' your scarters and clawers — scratchers
Frae the trapdoor bit laddy
T' th' spletter, his daddy — pitworker
Nyen handles the pick like Bob Cranky

(ca.1812, Bell-Harker, p.124)

hewing – "the pitman's occupation of working the coal, with a tool called a pick" (Wilson, G'head, 1820s).

howk – "to dig or to hew" (Nicholson, 1888).

hag – "to hew" (Dinsdale, Tees 1849); 'ag – "to hack or cut with a stroke" (Brockett, Newc, 1820s).

holing – "the 'holing' made at the bottom of the coal by the hewer. Kirving was the same as holing" (Tootle, 1995, N.East).

jud – "a piece of coal ready for taking down, either by wedges or powder" (Wilson, G'head, 1820s); "jud – the portion of the coal about to be removed by blasting" (Brockett, Newc, 1820s); "jud – a portion of the seam, kirved, nicked, and ready for blasting; also, a portion of a pillar… in course of being worked away in the broken mine" (Nicholson, 1888); "jud or judd – a block of coal about 4 yards sq. kirved and nicked, ready for breaking down or blasting. Also called a 'lift'" (Tootle, 1995).

kiding – "holing or under-cutting the coal" (Tootle, 1995, N.East).

kirve – "to undermine the coal" (Wilson, G'head, 1820s); "kirving – a wedge-shaped excavation, made by the hewer with his pick at the lower part of the seam previous to blasting" (Nicholson, 1888); "kerve – the first operation in preparing a jud in a coal mine, for blasting, is the removal of a large portion of the foundation of the block" (Brockett, Newc, 1820s); "kirving – hollowing out the bottom of the coal in the workings of a colliery so as to let what is above to easily fall down without making much small coal" (*Bell MS*).

laa – "low e.g. mine working place" (Dodd, Tanfield Lea); "there was a face at Haswell Pit that was so tight, if you crawled on to the face and found your shull [shovel] upside down…you had to gan back to the high to torn it ower" (Johnson, Dawdon).

mell and wedge – [hewing without gunpowder].

Here agyen had awd langsyners	old timers
Mony a weary, warken' byen,	aching bone
Now unknawn to coaly Tyners,	
A' bein' mell-and-wedge wark then.	all... hammer

(Thomas Wilson, *Pitman's Pay*, Pt.2, re 1790s)

nick – "to cut the coal at each end, preparatory to taking the jud down" (Wilson, G'head, 1820s); "nicking – a vertical cutting in the side or nook of a working-place" (Nicholson, 1888); "nicking – a working at the face of the coal... the cutting of an upright cut into the face of the coal when it is kirved out below" (*Bell MS*); "nick – the perpendicular groove made in the sides of a jud" (Brockett, Newc, 1820s).

puttin' hewer – "a young man bound either to put or hew" (Wilson, G'head, 1820s); 'hewing putters' – "an intermediate class of worker was created [in 1884], the 'hewing putter'. They hewed but were ranked as putters, doing any putting which was required" (Tootle, 1995) – a step on the way to becoming a full hewer.

scapipen – "getting coal without blasting" (Wade, South Moor, 1966).

sprag – any sort of timber used to support the undercut or kerf. In the old hewing days the miner used the sprags to protect himself – after all he was taking the coal out at the bottom of the seam and it was necessary, in order to do that, to get his head and shoulders under the upper (non-excavated) part of the seam. Sprags could take various forms. Sometimes they would be a short vertical prop, possibly with a cap or a headtree on the top, set against the floor and the underside of the solid coal. It could also be an arrangement of props set between roof and floor and the face of the coal above the kerf" (Sharkey); "just ti thra a sprag in" – a spanner in the works (Darby, Seaham).

stub and feathers – "the stub is a wedge driven in between two tapered wedges in a bore hole to break down stone" (Wade, South Moor, 1966); "feathers – long narrow wedge-shaped pieces of iron or steel inserted into the back of a drill hole, between which a long wedge was driven to force the 'feathers' apart to break down the coal" (Tootle, 1995).

top – "a pit term for coal, when quite prepared for removal by wedges or powder" (Wilson, G'head, 1820s).

The Hewer

Aw needn't tell ye what Aw de,	I do
Aw'm here for a' te view;	all
The black marks that disfigor me	(1)
Prove clearly that Aw hew.	

Aw'm up i' the mornin 'fore the lark,	
Doon 'fore the brick o' day,	break
An' seun as Aw lay lowse me wark,	soon…leave off
The laddie hears me say:	
Chorus: (Tune "The Keel Row")	
O, hinney, put the led un in!	spare tub for filling
The led un in! the led un in!	
O, hinney, put the led un in!	
An' let's hed full!	have it
Aw elwiz sump, when i' the wall,	?undercut
As far as Aw can fend,	manage/reach
Then, smack! the roondie an' the small	round-coal
Aw skelps off the back-end.	cuts…standing face
For since the prices are se law	low
For yards, an' coal, an' clay,	(2)
Aw find it's maw best plan, ye knaw,	
Te keep the sump away…	?underway
Aw myeks a point, when i' the bord,	work-place
Te keep hor nice an' square;	her
Te curve hor in aboot a yard,	kirve/undercut
A yard an' six or mair.	
Aw nick hor up at byeth the neuks,	side-cut…both…corners
An' wedge or blast hor doon,	
Then fills hor up for priests and keuks,	cooks
An' fowks aboot the toon…	

When it's maw luck on kyevellin' day,	alloting of work-places
A broken place te win,	(3)
Then aal Aw de is bawl away –	all I do
"Come in! me lad, come in!"	
Aw slush an' fill like fire and fun;	I work hard
Aw've neether care or doots,	
Until maw token-bunch is deun –	done i.e. used up
An' then gans up me cloots...	on with my clothes
But let me place be where it may,	
I' brocken flats or hyel,	(4)
Aw'm there to box hor ivory day	?tackle her
Wi' picks Aw shaft mesel.	put handle on
For, de ye see, maw wife an' bairns	
Need meat an' Sunday claes,	clothes
An' if these come oot what one man airns –	earns
He mun gan all the days...	must go i.e. turn up
But, quiet noo, for lowse is call'd –	end of work
That welcome sound Aw hear! –	
Then Aw've not only sung an' bawl'd,	
But blunted aal me gear.	
Forby, Aw've got the hitch, an' mate,	besides...come to a break
The hitch is not te hew;	itch / hitch in the strata
Thor's nowt for me but just te wait	
Till the stonemen puts hor throo!...	(5)

(1) Coal dust, getting into cuts, would produce tattoo-like effects.

(2) Yards – special payment for unusual working conditions; clay – unlerlying strata at some seams, removal of which was paid at a special rate.

(3) Reworking the exposed pillars of coal after first hewing.

(4) Whole – the first hewing; broken – recovering the exposed coal pillars.

(5) The stonemen (sic) cut away intervening rock to restore access to the coal seam.

Tools related to working coal

A good source of power was essential for the winding engine, for pumping engines, and in time to operate tools and move coal to the shaft. A powerful steam engine on bank was the traditional solution from about 1860, but small stationary steam engines underground were not so satisfactory (*HRCM*, ch.7). About the same time, collieries began to use compressed air to power tools for face work underground, from a compressor run by a steam engine on bank. This arrangement persisted in many pits till well after Nationalisation. In 1901 the formation of the North East Coast Power Supply System – in effect a public grid – paralleled the beginning of a switch to electric power in the pits also. Usually this would be DC (direct current) from a generator powered by exhaust steam, coke oven gas or 'inferior slack' (coal) (*HRCM*, ch.11, 13).

> I know that Mainsforth had its own power generating capability with a bank of chaingrate stokers feeding Babcock and Wilcox boilers generating steam which drove turbines that produced enough electricity to run all the mine's machinery and supply all other power needs. To my knowledge oil never replaced steam at the mine. They also had a huge Bellis and Morcombe vertical compressor that made a hell of a racket and rattled the windows in the Surveying office continuously from Monday to Friday. For some reason they shut it off on Saturday mornings and the resultant peace and quiet was amazing.
>
> (Tony Sharkey)

aix – axe: "aix and saw" (Wilson, G'head, 1820s) – symbolic of the deputy's tools:

> A better birth turn'd up at last –
> The wages still but verra sma' –
> For sixpence did not seem a vast
> For carryen' Lukey's aix and saw.
>
> (Thomas Wilson, *The Pitman's Pay*, Pt.2)

bull pick – "a pick with one point and a hammer" (Sharkey).

clack – "an automatic valve used in pumping compressed air, etc." or "The lower valve of a pump" (Tootle, 1995).

coal shovel/ stone shovel – "different sizes of shovels used for different tasks. Shovel often pronounced 'shull'" (Sharkey).

eloy pick – "a pneumatic pick powered by compressed air" (Sharkey).

gavelick (pronounced geavlick) – "a strong iron crow, or bar, used as a lever, chiefly by masons and quarrymen" (Brockett, Newc, 1820s); "gaivlick – an iron instrument about 4 feet long used by quarry men and builders to paize [lever up] large stones, etc." (*Bell MS*); "gavelock – an iron bar used for putting up hurdles" (Luckley, Alnwick, 1870s); "g'yavlic – gavelock, crowbar" Dinsdale; "gablock – the collier's name for the Sylvester prop withdrawer. Gablock was synonymous with gavelock from the Old Norse *gaflak*, a javlin. A very old term for an iron bar which was used as a lever" (Tootle, 1995).

geer – "in a colliery is the working tools of the pitmen" (*Bell MS*); "gear – a collier's tools, picks, drills, wedges, hammer, shovel, etc." (Tootle, 1995, N East); "gear – work-tools, consisting of picks, drills, maul and wedge, shovel, cracket, &c." (Nicholson, 1888); "geer, set o' geer – pitmen's working tools: 'te get his geer sharp'd at the smiddy'" (Wilson, G'head, 1820s).

grape – "a kind of shovel (sometimes called 'gripe'), or huge fork-like implement used in filling coke, and by farmers for removing manure" (Palgrave, Hetton, 1896).

hack – a mattock; "a pickaxe with one arm" (Atkinson, Cleve., 1868); "with hack and shool" (ca.1806, Bell-Harker, p.84); "hack – a pick or tool, with which colliers cut or hewed the coal... With an eighteen inch blade it weighed about 7 lbs [3·175kilos]" (Tootle, 1995, North); "hack — a heavy pick, 18 inches long, and weighing about 7 lbs., used in sinking or stonework" (Nicholson, 1888); "coal cutter's hack – 2′6″ shaft with a head composed of one side hammer, one side pick... rolleywayman's hack had a 3′6″ shaft with a much heavier head, one side hammer, one side a flat curved blade; conveyor advancer's hack...was one side pick, one side axe" (Oxley, 1990).

hogger – "the compressed air hose" (Sharkey); "the hogger – a wire-covered rubber hose-pipe through which the compressed air poassed to the engine..." (Hitchin, 1962, p.101); 'holing picks' (Tootle, 1995).

holing shovel – "a short handled, round bladed, shovel for use in the confined space under the holing" (Tootle, 1995).

jack hack (round head and sharp point), 'pick hack' (sharp head and chisel point) (Palgrave, Hetton, 1896).

kevel – "a large hammer for quarrying stones" (Brockett, Newc, 1820s).

mandrel or **mandrill** – "a pick or 'hack' with one pointed blade, the other chisel shaped. Used for hacking down or hewing the coal. Also known in some areas as a 'mattock'" (Tootle, 1995).

mell – "a large wood or iron hammer" (Wade, South Moor, 1966); "large hammer" (Dodd, Tanfield Lea); "mell-and-wedge wark" (Wilson, G'head, 1820s); "mell / maul – a hammer used in driving a wedge to force down coal or stone; also used in drilling in stone to drive in the drill" (Nicholson, 1888).

peggy – "this is the term that Durham colliers applied to the handpick" (Douglass, 1973).

pick – "a tool used by a hewer. it consists of an iron about 18 inches long, steeled and sharpened at each end, and weighing from 3 to 6 lbs. In the centre of the head is a hole or eye into which is fixed a shaft of ash about 2 $^{1}/_{2}$ feet long" (Nicholson, 1888); "the tool used by the miner in many aspects of mining. The iron head was

18 inches long, sharp at each end, weighed 3 to 6 lbs and fitted into the end of a 2 $^1/_2$ft ash handle. The hewer provided his own picks and had them sharpened by a colliery smith called the "pick sharpener" (Tootle, 1995); " 'pikk shahpna' – smith skilled in tempering steel" (Dodd, Tanfield Lea).

shank – "describes pick shaft or hammer shaft" (McBurnie, Washington, 1970s).

sylvester – "device for hauling any object which requires extra heavy pulling. Consists of comb bar, handle with box attached. Chain attached to comb bar, also one long loose chain with crook attached to one end" (McBurnie, Washington, 1970s); "large rachet-like tool" (Roxborough, swDm); "Yes with a toothed bar and a handle used for pulling things with a chain" (Sharkey); "afterwards replaced by the 'terfor' a less robust but more adaptable wire-rope pulley winch" (Johnson, Dawdon).

> "Carrots! Man, it's ower early t'set carrots yit." – "Nar, it's not. Aa set mine this time last yeor and had t' borrow a sylvestre t' pull them up."
>
> (*Ashington Col Mag*, May 1935)

tommy hack – a combined hammer and chisel ended pick used by rolleywaymen. (Wade, South Moor, 1966); " 'tomahawk' – a type of hammer used by man laying railway in the pit. Head 1 ft long with chisel and hammer ends; shaft 2 feet long" (McBurnie, Washington).

topit – "an iron instrument used in boring, like a single brace-head, but much smaller; it is screwed" (Nicholson, 1888).

windy pick – pneumatic pick: "I'll use the windy to break this stone" (Dawdon Pit); "pneumatic drill" (Trelogan, New Herrington); "a windy pick...for breaking stones and hewing coals" (J. Moreland, Dawdon) plus "pompom" (Seaham), "jigger" (Winlaton).

Blasting

Gunpowder to blast mineral deposits loose was first pioneered in Hungary in the early seventeenth century, thence to Germany and England, e.g. Cornish mines in 1689 (*HRCM*, ch.6). The process necessitated drilling a borehole into the coal face, putting a charge of gunpowder into the far end of the hole, then putting a long 'needle' (or 'pricker') in and tamping it round with clay. The needle was then removed and a fuse substituted. Safer fuses were developed by the 1840s, electric detonators in the 1880s. From 1870s onwards dynamite was mostly used rather than gunpowder, but other types of explosive have been developed, tested and permitted since.

ajax – "high strength, high density, gelatinous, 'permitted explosive', which has a good water resistance" (Tootle 1995).

back-end – "In working a four or five yard 'bord', the hewer under-cut the coal as far as he could reach with the pick across half the width of the 'bord'. After making a vertical cut at the side he would then fire the coal. He would then work the other half of the board in the same way. This second working was known as the 'back-end'" (Tootle, 1995, N.East).

blasting out of the solid – "the blasting down of coal, without first under-cutting it. In 1877 the miners of Northumberland came out on strike to retain their right to 'blast out of the solid'. This enabled them to break down the coal quicker but left large amounts of small unsaleable coal which had to be 'gobbed'" (Tootle, 1995).

blow down – "to bring down coal or stone with gunpowder" (Heslop, N'd, 1880s).

bull – "a round bar of iron used in blasting in wet holes" (Heslop, N'd, 1880s); "an iron rod used for preparing a 'shot-hole', which had been lined with clay to protect the 'shot' in wet ground" (Tootle, 1995, N.East).

caddy – "powder box for explosive" (Geggie, Ashington).

cartridges or **plugs** – "a paper tube filled with gunpowder, which was rammed into the shot hole ready for blasting. If the hole was level or sloping down away from the hole, then loose powder could be used. In the early days a 'collier' would purchase the powder from the company store and make his own cartridges at home" (Tootle, 1995).

det – "detonator" (Sharkey).

dirl – to drill: "dirls me lug like wor smith's hammer" (Barrass, 1896).

dolls – "[Meanwhile] I had been rolling clay into cylindrical shapes about the diameter of the hole. These clay dolls were rammed tightly into the hole so as to throw the force of the explosion inwards" (Hitchin, 1962, p.101).

dollyshutting – "blasting down coal without undercutting" (Wade, South Moor, 1966).

drilla – "drills holes for shotfiring" (Dodd, Tanfield Lea); "then they would drill some holes in with a hand ratchet, just like turning a corkscrew affair, and put powder in it and that would blow the whole of that mass down, that was if it was hard" (Harry Letch, Beamish, 1977/161b).

fire! – "shouted by the fireman when is about to fire a shot" (Tootle, 1995).

flusher – "a 'squib' that fails to do its work" (Wade, South Moor, 1966).

kitty – "a length of straw about 4 inches long filled with gunpowder used as a fuse in blasting. It was placed in the 'pricker hole' which was open to the cartridge or shot. The end of the kitty nearest to the cartridge was closed, with the outer end open. When a light was applied to the kitty, it would move along the pricker hole like a miniature rocket and ignite the powder" (Tootle, 1995, N.East).

match – "there were several types used [e.g.] paper soaked in a saltpetre solution to form a touch-paper [or] greased twine or tape… They were often ignited with a piece of wire which had been poked through the gauze of a lamp and held in the flame until it glowed red or a small stub of a candle" (Tootle, 1995, N.East).

misfire – "the complete or partial failure of a blasting charge" (Riley, Blyth).

monkey – "drilling monkey – used by old-time miners as a drilling stand when fixed on a wood prop. For use with a worm and drill" (McBurnie, Washington, 1970s); "I first heard the term used at Newfield drift where the main product was fireclay (seggar) to feed the brickworks. But they had to mine the thin coal seam (which I think was the Beaumont, and they used to undercut the seam with hand picks (kerfing a jud!) and then blast down the coal. Drilling of the coal was by hand, using a scewed vertical post which was set between roof and floor to which was attached a hand cranked drill which somehow or other was engineered to extend into the coal as drilling proceeded. I believe the part of all this mechanism that was attached to the vertical post was the 'monkey'" (Sharkey).

powder – "a general term for explosives used in the mine" (Tootle, 1995); "pooda – mine explosive" (Dodd, Tanfield Lea).

powder box – "steel cannister in which was carried (by the workmen) 5 pounds of explosive. A variation of the law later allowed explosives to be carried in bulk in specially constructed cars or tubs from the surface to the face" (Sharkey).

powder-reek – "smoke caused by firing a shot in the pit" (Wade, South Moor, 1966; Palgrave, Hetton, 1896).

pricker – see main testimony, below.

shot up – "after kurving, you shot up, i.e. fired the shots" (John Kell, Leasingthorne).

shot-firing – "Tha's going shot-firing wi' me" (Hitchin, 1962, p.102).

shotstick – "a round stick on which a paper cartridge is rolled (mining term)" (Palgrave, Hetton, 1896).

smush – "to smoulder away, as touch-paper used by miners. The 'touch' is made by soaking in saltpetre" (Palgrave, Hetton, 1896).

squib – "a firelighter – a thin taper used down the pit to light explosives" (Geggie, Ashington); "squib – made at home by my father for pit use – used by my mother to clear flues of kitchen range especially where difficult to reach" (Merihein, Ashington).

stemming – "sealing explosive in a drill-hole either with clay or a silicone gel" (Temple, 1994, pp.19–20).

tadger – "a large electric drill used for drilling shotholes and holes for roof bolts etc." (Riley, Blyth).

worm – "used in early drilling methods. A long threaded steel bar about 10 threads to the inch, which when fixed in a suitable stand, screwed the drill forward to make a shot-hole. Short handle fixed on outer end, to turn the worm" (McBurnie, Washington, 1970s).

Making up Shots

You put the powder in, the deputy had the detonator, and he used to detonate the powder, then he used to stem the hole, shove like a powder, what we called Thames powder, you could get it in various lengths, two ounces, four, six. About an inch across. The deputy put that in, laid the shot cable, and fired it with a battery.

In the old pit, the old miners used to fire their own shots you know, they used to make their own shots as well, with brown paper, they had what they call a shot stick, it would be probably a bit rounder than that [indicates two inches], they used to put brown paper round the shot stick, fasten the end up, and fill it up with loose powder [shows how it slid if off the stick] – Yes, and fill it with loose powder. Mind I'm going back when I was a kid. And then fasten that end in, carry it in the pit in a bag, these shots. They used to know how much was required, they used to make them all at home, I've seen my dad making his shots here, there's a big fire on there, in the wintertime he was sitting there making his shots out of the loose powder, he used to keep the powder up there in a – I have a box what the powder used to come in, a square box. And sometimes it used to come in what they called a powder kit, [tin with] a round bottom, and there used to be a man come round with a cart, come round about once a fortnight and gather these powder kits in, until the time come when they got to what they call bomb powder, and that was compressed powder.

How would they fire homemade shots?

That was the day when they fired them with squibs. I showed you that puncher, they used to make holes with that till they started to get the drills. They used to put this pricker through this powder, and then they used to stem the hole up, withdraw the pricker and put a squib in, and the squib went off, backfired into the hole.

Stemmed with clay?

Yes or anything in them days, it didn't make any difference in them days as long as they made it air tight.

If coal wet?

I did a lot of wet work, we used to have what they called bagging – I never used the bomb powder, it was all new powder that I used, we used to use bagging, stuff made like, waterproof, then put the powder in and fastened it up again so that the water couldn't get in, you laid your cable already out and you hung onto the detonator, went back as quick as possible… It wasn't very oft it didn't succeed, aye.

(John Kell, Beamish, 1974/41)

Detonators

There's your powder flask there: It was a metal flask like this that you slung around your shoulder that carried the sticks of powder.

They used to get the detonators and I've seen them making them up in the house at night and the way they used to do it mind. They were making it was like a copper detonator and they used to put the long fuse in.

They used to get the fuse in a roll and they used to measure it, cut a piece off and light it and time it so that they knew if they put a two foot or three foot length of fuse how long it would take to burn to set the detonator off so that it would give them time to get out of the road. But they knew exactly how much fuse to put into a detonator but they used to be sitting in the house in front of the fire and cutting a length of and putting the detonators on. I mean how some of them wasn't blown up I don't know but it was that familiar with them it was just casual work to them. And that's what they used to do with detonators, biting the copper tight onto the fuse:

Once they'd put the detonator and everything into the hole how far back would they have to go?

What they used to do like I say was they drilled the hole first. They had a rammer generally copper it was so it wouldn't spark, shoved the black powder in, there was a hole in the centre just about the thickness of a candle, there was a hole in the centre where the detonator went into the powder and the fuse came up then they put clay in they shoved the clay in so that it was hanging out of the hole and then they lit it and they knew if they had fifteen seconds or half a minute to get out of the road. They would get out of the way, they would go well back where they were sheltered and whoosh! up it would go. They used to sometimes set two or three off at a time and they would have to count in case they walked on top of a one that wasn't off which has happened before with miners that have walked on them, two's gone off where they thought there was three and they've blasted them when they went in. Once again there's a little [?photo], that's them stemming in the shot there you see and these are your powder and your powder flasks.

(James Mackenzie, Beamish, 1993/10)

Shot Firing

You mightn't believe it, you had to buy all your own gear. You got your stand, you had your iron stand you'll have seen that if you've been in the drift. And you had your drill, and you had a thing called your worm, like a screw, with like a thing on there. And you had your handle, and your drill. Now you put your drill on your worm, and you set your grey stand, you set your stand tight again the top so it wouldn't shove out and you drilled your hole. Now after you drilled your hole, we'll say a four-foot hole, or four foot six or a yard what ever length you wanted. You had a copper pricker then, now your black powder was all in like bobbins, just like bobbins of thread tha knaas but black, it had a hole through the middle just like a bobbin of thread. Now you shoved your, you shoved your bobbins, we'll say four bobbins on your pricker on your copper pricker and you shoved them in like that. Now, you had a beater what you called a copper beater it had like a groove in the ends and you got your clay, your stemming, what you call your stemming and you stemmed right around that tight, tight and then you just screwed your picker and you pulled it out you see. It left a hole now you had a little blue squib just like a cracker. And you bit the end off, and you lit it with your candle, you were working with candles then up the drift, you just had a candle. You lit the candle and then you run away off. You run away off and fsst! the little blue flame would burn down the squib till it got to the powder and then it would shoot down the hole and then it would explode the coal.

So how long did you have to run away in then?

Well some men used to bite the end off so it would go off sharp. They would just get back to the tub afore it went off. It all depends which way your coal was gonna blow. If your coal was gonna blow that way, you were all right. But if it was gonna blow, you had to put a long squib on and get right around the turn, right down around the turn out of the road. Oh, that was dangerous work there was any amount of men burnt with that game.

Was there anyone hurt in the explosions?

There was a man called Smith, Ponty Smith, worked up the drift, he got a, his went off, and er, blew all his face oh he was marked for life. There was another man called Billy Middleton, he was burnt. There was a man along there, Billy

Littleton he got burnt as well using fire and shot. Then after that, they did away with the squibs, and they gave a fuse and it was like... you've seen the fuse what's on the pictures, and they've lit it and sssssss! And they used fuses after that, then they did away with the black powder. You mightn't believe it, er, in olden days you used to go to the store and buy your powder at the store, take it to work with you.

How much did the powder cost?

Well we used to pay I think it was fourpence a pound, off our note, for the powder, we had to pay the bosses fourpence a pound. Of course you were blowing the coal out to get more coal for them and they were charging you the fourpence, see the fourpence.

(Peter Talbot, Beamish, 1991/82)

Filling the tubs

Whether or not it was the hewer's job to shovel ('cast') the coal into tubs seems to have varied with local practice: "A hewer was a man between the ages of 17 and 70 whose job it was to break down the coal ready for the 'filler' to load the tubs" (Tootle, 1995); "hewer – man who cut the coal with a pick and filled it into tubs" (J. Moreland, 1980, Dawdon). An older hewer might well have an assistant, enabling him thus to work to an older age himself...

cast – "to throw coal by hand or shovel" (Tootle, 1995).

chum – "defines anything empty, e.g. a tub, chummins, chummings – Often wrote as plural for chum, when referring to a load of empty tubs" (McBurnie, Washington, 1970s); "tuemmen: empty tub, usually pronounced chummum" (Wade, South Moor, 1966); "tyum meant empty" (Hitchin, 1962, p.70).

fill – "to load tubs in the mine" (Tootle, 1995); "fill away – to clear coal after firing" (John Kell, Leasingthorne).

filler – "one who fills the tubs after the coal has been broken down" (Tootle 1995).

fullen – "full tub" (Wade, South Moor, 1966).

led-tub – "a led tub means a spare one for the putter to leave empty with the hewer whilst the full one is being put to the flat; the empty one being filled by the hewer against the return of the putter with another empty one" (Nicholson, 1888); "the empty or 'tume' tub is often called the 'led 'un' (= led one, i.e. the tub led in)" (Palgrave, Hetton, 1896).

odd un – "an extra tub, filled by or for the putter as a bonus: 'Aw'm running for the odd un...Frae gannen doon te lowse'" (Barrass, Consett, 1897).

scrattin' – "casual shovelling. Hens can be described as 'scrattin about' when they are digging up soil with their feet" (Douglass, 1973).

tyum, toom – see chum.

The Broken mine

In bord and pillar working, though pillars were left in place to make initial coal extraction easier and safer, reclaiming this coal was clearly desirable at a later stage – unless the pillars were to be left in place to avoid the effects of subsidence at surface level.

Rather than remove them at one go, Buddle introduced a system of slimming the pillars in stages. In 1810 he initiated a practice of leaving bigger pillars initially (unless substantial, squeeze (creep) could make pillars hard to extract). Following on the first hewing, the pillars were reduced, at least 3 rows behind the hewing operation. Later, wooden props were inserted and the last coal (the stooks) removed. Finally, the props were recovered and the mine roof left to collapse (see goaf).

broken – "the reworking of a colliery in the pillars etc left in first working the 'whole' coal" (*Bell MS*).

broken – "pillar working, the removal of the pillars left in the first working for the support of the roof" (Nicholson, 1888); also the broken mine, broken workings, etc.

broken jud –"a 'jud' in the process of being worked" (Tootle, 1995, N.East).

coming back broken – reclaiming more coal in return direction, until "only a forest of props supported the roof over a wide area" (Hitchin, 1962, p.105); "'Coming back brockens' – retreat mining in pillared areas where the pillars formed in bord and pillar operations were extracted starting from the inbye end and systematically working outbye" (Sharkey).

jenkin' – driving a 'board' within a pillar of coal (Wilson, G'head, 1820s); "'fast jenkin' – a bordway driven in the middle of a pillar" (Wade, South Moor, 1966); "jenkin… an opening cut into, or a slice taken off, a 'pillar' from 6 to 8 feet in width" (Tootle, 1995).

jud – "a pillar of coal about a third of all, left till last: 'working the jud... is considered the most dangerous part of the miners duty'" (*Bell MS*); "jud – a portion of a pillar in the course of being worked in a broken mine" (Tootle, 1995). [Properly a broken jud?]

judding – "system of mining where the second working followed closely after the first" (Colls, 1987).

last lift – "the last 'rib' or 'jud' to come off a pillar" (Tootle, 1995, N.East).

lift – "the slices or portions of a pillar of coal taken off when the pillar was being removed" (Tootle, 1995); "a slice of coal taken out of a coal pillar when 'cummen back brockens'" (Sharkey).

pillar – "mass of coal left to support the roof after excavation" (Colls, 1987). "Pillars were formed as part of the mining process, the roof was supported in the roadways by timber or steel supports" (Sharkey).

robbing – "partial excavation of pillars on a second-working" (Colls, 1987); "In bord and pillar working the putters not only got paid for the tubs they 'put' but also for any tubs of coal that they hewed and filled themselves and I knew of cases where they would hew the coal off the side of the coal pillars to do this. That certainly was robbing. It was also dangerous" (Sharkey).

stook – "the remains of the pillar of coal after it has been jenkined" (Wilson, G'head, 1820s); "this last bit is the stook" (Hitchin, 1962, p.106).

The goaf

Drawing the old timber [i.e. props] was necessary, in order to collapse the roof behind the supports and relieve the pressure of the face" (Temple, 1994 p.14). Recovering the timber could be managed at a more or less safe distance by using a chain round the prop and the pulling power of a sylvester, or more dangerously at close quarters with hammers and bull picks. The cleared goaf was left to collapse under its own weight – which it would do unpredictably, with the noise of clap of thunder – a shock and a relief to workers on shift at the time (*HRCM*, ch.4). [Sometimes, though, the goaf would be packed with sand to prevent subsidence]

> It is now found expedient from the high price of coals to attack the pillars of coal, and this work is more dangerous than the whole working. On that account two sets of hewers are employed, and they work very vigorou[s]ly, six hours each set. The pillars are undermined and thrown down part by part, until the whole be got away. The roof during this work is supported by props, and then the props are removed, but sometimes the roof will stand of itself without any support. It is more dangerous work than the first working.
>
> (*PP*, 1842, CR xvi, p.122)

bout – "used for safety in withdrawing timber from old workings. To enable drawer to keep a safe distance back: 6 ft or more long" (McBurnie, Washington, 1970s). [See pout.]

bowkin' – "word used to describe the sound of the unsupported roof falling after the timber had been removed" (Wilson, North Walbottle).

drawing timber – "withdrawing roof supports, e.g. from the goaf" (Sharkey).

goaf – "the space remaining in a coal mine after the removal of the coal" (Brockett, Newc, 1820s); "goaf – the space from which the coal has been extracted. it is usually of dome-like form, resting upon the wreck which has fallen from the roof of the exhausted space" (Nicholson, 1888); "gohf – goaf, space where coal worked out" (Dodd, Tanfield Lea); "at Dawdon roof allowed to collapse with little control as all work under sea with no subsidence damage at surface" (Johnson, Dawdon); "when the face had been advanced and the goaf lay on the ground / they stood there in amazement when they heard that awful sound" (J. Moreland, Dawdon, 1980); "an unsupported area which generally collapses with a spectacular 'thump' – terrifying when you first see it only yards from your safe supported area!" (Johnny Handle).

gob – mouth, goaf (Dodd, Tanfield Lea); "gob – a slang name for the goaf... Used throughout the British coalfields" (Tootle, 1995).

gob fire – spontaneous combustion in an abandoned sector of a mine.

> Spontaneous combustion in mines nearly always occurs in the goaf where the movement of air would be imperceptible. The generation of the spon. com. or initial heating is because of a chemical reaction between coal and oxygen. There can be sufficient of a reaction over time to gradually build up heat to the point where the material catches fire. Because of the extremely limited oxygen at the point of heating only "incomplete combustion" can take place and a major product is therefore carbon monoxide.
>
> In mines prone to heatings, very careful and frequent sampling and analysis of the mine air in return airways in working panels is carried on. A minute percentage of CO might be present anyway (it can be a by-product of shotfiring operations for example) but when the percentage starts to increase, this (with other signs, e.g., smell, sweating on steel) becomes an indication that a heating has started and steps have then to be taken to either dig it out or abandon the affected workings. Fortunately the Northumberland and Durham coal seams were not prone to spon. com.
>
> (Tony Sharkey)
>
> Also did you know that almost a whole lovely coal seam... Low Main (from 45 years ago memory) was 'sterilised' at Vane Tempest due to two seams being so close together (like 2 slices of bread without the hundred feet or so gap of stone in between) so as to create spontaneous combustion of the remainder after roof collapse in the goaf (waste) following extraction of one seam. The area/district had to be cordoned by brick barriers and constantly monitored.
>
> (Ken Johnson, Dawdon)

off – "worked out" (Tootle, 1995, N.East).

pout or **puncher** – "a tool used by the deputies when withdrawing timber out of a dangerous place. It had a shank about 8 feet long with a spade type handle and a head which was pointed and slightly curved towards the handle at one side and shaped like a hammer at the other side. It was used either as a ram to knock the props down, or to draw them out of the waste after they had been knocked loose. When in use it was supported by a hook and chain fastened to a roof support" (Tootle, 1995, N.East). [Compare 'bout'.]

prop drawer – a) "a tool designed for withdrawing roof supports from a safe distance," b) "the man employed to draw out timber for re-use" (Tootle, 1995).

pullers, pulling and to pull – "these were the guys who went on to the longwall face after the 'fillers' had 'cleaned it off' and moved the face conveyor forward into a new track. They then moved the 'chocks' systematically forward, withdrawing the other timbers as they progressed through the face. This allowed the goaf to collapse. The end result of all this activity was that the face had advaced the equivalent of a cut which was 4.5 to 5.0 feet usually" (Sharkey).

scour – "a roadway driven or being driven through goaf" (Sharkey).

stowbord – “an old working place into which refuse is put” (Wade, South Moor, 1966); “the hewers shall stow away or cast aside such quantities of small or refuse coal as the said owner or his agents shall require” (D/Lo/B/265).

waste – “old workings and air-ways” (Nicholson, 1888); “alternative to gob or goaf” (Sharkey).

> It was fascinating… I mean we had a permit – anyone, a fitter or an electrician – to travel underground, and in places where the normal miners were not allowed to walk. And sometimes you’d go into places that was devoid of anybody that was working and it was so quiet there was many a time in the early of the morning you used to sit down just for a couple of minutes, especially if you’d walked two to three miles underground… and you could hear your own heart beat, it was so quiet. And if you cast your eyes around and looked at the strata it was fascinating to see the form of leaves or mebbies a fish in the structure of the stonework. And sometimes if it got to a fault when they were following the different seams, you’d think that perhaps you were in a gold mine rather than a coal mine because the iron quartz, the pyrites… especially with an electrician or a fitter – they used to use high density light – not a diffused light like the ordinary miners used and it used to pick up all the facets of – well, for all the world, you’d think it was gold, sparkling back at you. And if the fault was very big, mebbies 10 to 12 yards, all of this structure [was] glistening till you got through it and then you got back into the normal strata of the mine.”
>
> (David James, Brancepeth)

> On the subject of old workings a somewhat ghoulish story still circulates: that in the modern period a gang of pitmen were sent to examine such a stopping and check the condition of the mine beyond it. The foreman oversaw the breaking of the wall and himself looked through the hole into the abandoned workings. After a pause, he turned back to face the workmen, looking very white and shaken, and gave orders for the wall to be rebuilt, without letting anyone else get a glimpse of what he had seen. Not unnaturally, a fair few versions exist as to what he saw that so shocked him, and one, which may be possible, is that he shone his torch on a carcass of a pony, still standing as in life, but reduced to skin and bones, waiting as though for someone to break down the wall and release him; but within seconds of the introduction of new air, this facsimile of life crumbled to dust and disappeared.
>
> (per Steve Barnett, Seaham)

Chapter 11: Putting

Hand putting

> Besides these Miners, called Hewers, there is another sort of Labourers which are called Barrow-Men, or Coal-Putters, these Persons take the hewed Coals from the Hewers, as they work them, or as fast as they can, and filling the Corves with these Wrought Coals, put or pull away the full Corves of Coals, which are set, upon a Sledge of Wood, and hauled all along the Barrow-way to the Pit-shaft, by two or three Persons, one before and the others behind the Corfe, where they hook it by the Corf-Bow to the Cable, which, with the Horses is drawn up to the top, or to Day, as it is their phrase, where the Banck's-Man, or he that guides the Sledge-Horse, has an empty Sledge to set the Loaden Corfe on, as he takes it out of the Hook on the Pit-Rope, and then immediately hooking on an empty Corfe, he leads his Stead-Horse away with the Loaden Corfe, to what Place of the Coal heap he pleases.
>
> (*Compleat Collier*, 1707, pp.36–7)

In the moving of coal from work-face to shaft there were also major developments. Earliest was the simple system of carrying the coal out in baskets (corves) on the backs of women and children. In the fifteenth century, on Tyneside, there is mention of 'barrowmen' – possibly using wheelbarrows on single plank barrow-ways. More efficient were 'corves' or square whicker baskets, loaded on sleds and pulled part or all the way to the shaft. This had the advantage that sleds can run on relatively uneven ground. 'Sledge horses' are noted in a Newcastle colliery in 1763 (*HRCM*, ch.7).

Thomas Wilson's *Pitman's Pay* is set in the Tyneside collieries of the 1790s, when putting was a communal task that everyone joined in, though not necessarily with good will:

The wark now plac'd, and pit hung on –	work
The heedsmen, whether duin or nut,	done
Mun ev'ry man and mother's son	must
Lay down the pick and start to put.	

Now then the bitter strife begins;
Pullen, hawlen, pushen, driven,
'Mang blood and durt and broken shins,
The waikens wi' the strangens striven.

Aw mind a tram byeth waike and slaw,	both
Just streen'd to rags to keep her gannen,	
Frae hingen on till howdy ma	from start to finish of shift
Ye hardly knew if gawn or stannen.	going
Just pinch'd to deeth, they're tarn and snarly,	ill-tempered
Yammering on frae morn till neet —	
Jack off the way blackguarden Charley,	swearing at
For at the corf nut lyen reet.	
While Charley damns Jack's hoolet e'en,	owlish eyes
His hick'ry fyece and endless growl;	seamed brown face
And sweers, if he agyen compleen,	
He'll splet his nell-kneed, wall-ey'd soul.	
A shower of coals, wi' vengence hurl'd,	
Suin rattl'd roun' the lugs o' Jack;	ears
Wi' threets he'd to the other warld	
Dispatch him sprawlen in a crack.	
Jack didn't like the journey then,	
And try'd to shun the deedly blast	deadly
By jouken down — nor shew'd agyen	ducking
His fyece till a' was ower and past.	

(Thomas Wilson, *Pitman's Pay*, Pt.2)

More efficiently, and increasingly useful as the journey got nearer the shaft and the vehicles accumulated, the corf could be loaded on a tram or bogie, and a series of these led by pony-power as a 'set'. While the railway for such sets could be inclined, the floor it ran on needed to be relatively even, so this system was suitable for the heavier traffic of the main passages, where it was worthwhile preparing the way.

The logic of putting is that at the coal-face only a single tub could be filled at one time by a hewer; there probably was not room for more than one! A putter was necessary to move a full tub quickly out of the hewer's way and replace it with an empty one. Ideally this work would be done by ponies, but this was impractical/uneconomic when a single tub was to be moved. The work of putting was undeniably tough, but served the purposes of the mine, since it prepared youths for the even tougher job of hewing.

> When the corves or tubs are filled with coals, the putters put the trams from the working place to the going headway, and down the Mothergate boards to the crane. [An average of 160 yds.] The minimum weight of the loaded corf or tub pushed by putters was 5 cwt [Hebburn Pit]; and the maximum 10 cwt [Cramlington Pit]. At the cranes, the 'craneman' hoists the corves on to the rolleys or waggons (10 foot long for 3 tubs, and 7 foot long for 2 tubs, at Hetton Colliery), and they are then drawn by horses, attended by the drivers...to the bottom of the shaft, where they are hooked on to the rope by the 'onsetter' and drawn up.
>
> (*PP*, 1842, CR vol.xvi, p.544)

arse flapper – "a large piece of leather often worn by putters which covered thaeir backsides and which was hung off their belts. The purpose was to give their backsides and lower back some protection when lifting tubs 'back on the way'. The inferior track into the working places made 'off the way' a frequent occurrence!" (Sharkey); "ahss flapper – putter's back protector" (Dodd, Tanfield Lea).

backskins – "At Shilbottle Colliery he has seen boys put coals under a height of 30 inches only. The little lads there, of 10, 12, 13 or 14, put the tubs by keeping their hands on the end of the tram, and putting their heads against the tub. The lads wear backskins there to keep their backs from hitting against the roof" (*PP*, 1842, CR vol.xvi, p.57).

barrowman – "a putter, one who puts or pushes the tubs of coals from the working places to the flats or stations. Formerly, before the application of tramways underground, coals used to be conveyed in barrows, whence the name" (Nicholson, 1888). [Another early name for a putter was a drawer.]

byard – "A leather belt worn across the chest. Used by the 'drawers' for pulling 'tubs' of coal" (Tootle, 1995, N.East).

cawdpies – "any accident happening to the tram or carriage" (Wilson, G'head, 1820s).

> Sic, then, was the poor putter's fate,
> Wi' now and then a stannen fray,
> Frae yokens, caw'd pies, stowen bait, ?collisions
> Or cowpt corves i' the barrow way.
>
> (Thomas Wilson, *Pitman's Pay*, Pt.2)

coin – see **koin.**

coup – "to upset or overturn" (Nicholson, 1888); "cowpt corves i' the barrow way" (Wilson, G'head, 1820s); "coup – to turn over a tub or machine part" (McBurnie, Washington, 1970s).

drags-man – "A man employed as a 'putter' or pusher in the 'working places'" (Tootle, 1995, N.East).

fast – "stuck or jammed" (Wilson, North Walbottle).

foal – "the youngest in the rank of putters in a coal pit" (Brockett, Newc, 1820s); "a little boy who was formerly employed to assist a stronger boy (called a 'headsman') to put; he pulled in front of the tub by a pair of ropes or traces called 'soams' whilst the headsman pushed behind" (Nicholson, 1888).

half-marrow – "among pitmen is when a man and boy put or push on the corves with a boy as partner; the boy is called a half marrow" (*Bell MS*); "a middle-sized lad, two such being required in a coal-pit, to put a corf of coals equal to a man" (Brockett, Newc, 1820s); "one of two boys who manage a team, of about equal age" (Wilson, G'head, 1820s); "a lad 16 to 17 years old who was not strong enough to 'put' alone. He would have a small boy to assist him known as a 'foal'" (Tootle, 1995, N.East).

hand-putter or **barrowman** – "one who puts without the assistance of a pony" (Nicholson, 1888); "a hand 'putter' would 'put' his tubs up to about 100 yds and he was usually paid by the 'score'. In the North East putters' 'places' were 'cavilled' for" (Tootle, 1995).

headsman – "a lad employed to draw the coal from the workings to the haulage road" (Tootle, 1995, N.East).

helper-up – "a lad employed to assist the barrow-man or putter out of a dip working" (Tootle, 1995, N.East); "helper up – young boy employed to help the barrow men, or in later years putters, out of a 'swally' or bad places" (Douglass, 1973).

koin – "to swing tub around, turn" (Dodd, Tanfield Lea).

koppel owa – "tip over" (Dodd, Tanfield Lea).

marrow – "a partner" (Nicholson, 1888); "a partner, a companion: 'gat a marrow gruff and sour'" (putting a tram) (Wilson, G'head, 1820s).

put – "to bring the coals from the workings to the crane or shaft upon a tram: 'Aw've hew'd and putten twee-and-twenty'" (Wilson, G'head, 1820s).

putter – "a boy in the workings of a coal pit who pushes or propels the corf or corves on a tram or rolley along the rolley way from where the hewer is working to the foot of the shaft" (*Bell MS*); "a person who conveys coals from the hewer. Putters are commonly young men from sixteen to twenty years old" (Brockett, Newc, 1820s); "a person who brings the full tubs from the hewer to the flat and takes the empty ones in to him" (Nicholson, 1888).

putting-hewer – "a young hewer who is liable to be called upon to put if necessary" (Nicholson, 1888).

rank – "the distance a 'putter' puts the coal from face to flat. The first 'renk' might be 80 yards from the hewer, and as the distance increased, the putter received an additional penny for every 20 yards. This was the case formerly, but putters are paid differently now" (Palgrave, Hetton, 1896).

twyne – "name given to the operation of the putter in switching the weight of his body to different positions to assist the tub round the turns" (Douglass, 1973); "and a flair for twinin' better than the rest" (W.B. Coombs, *The Putter Lad*).

The Putter

(Tune: "Wait for the Waggon")

Aw'm just a smaaly laddy,	little
Hardly aud eneugh te hew;	old enough to cut coal
But Aw've held me awn at puttin,	
Wi' the best Aw ivor knew.	ever
Give us plenty bate an' bottle,	food
Plenty beaf an' baccy chews,	beef
An' Aw'll bet maw bunch o' tokens	(1)
That frae gannen doon te lowse –	going down to work-end
Chorus:	
Aw'm running for the odd un,	(2)
Aw'm running for the odd un,	
Aw'm running for the odd un,	
Frae gannen doon te lowse.	
Thor's a hawf-a-dozen gannins	ways/branches
At the flat that Aw'm at noo,	
An' if Aw'd me awn i' choosin,	own (way)
Aw'd hev number one or two.	I'd have
But dash me, somehoo or other,	
Hoo it comes Aw divn't knaw;	don't know

But as sure's Aw rub me kyevel,	(3)
It's the warst one o' the saw...	worst
Thor's a hitch an' then a swally	dislocation...dip (in strata)
Filled wi' wetter like a ford,	water
An' a lot o' way aal twisted	i.e.rails
I' the clarty gannin bord;	mucky
Thor's law planks an' raggy kanches	low roof...stony juts
Where Aw've sometimes got a smack,	
An' it myeks ye twist yor gizzort	gizzard/insides
If ye chance te catch yor back...	
Thor's a short plate an' a lang un	L-sectioned rail
Near the double turn inbye;	away from the shaft
They've been fettled wiv a closer,	repaired...bridge piece
An' that closer winnet lye.	will not lie i.e.fit
O, that short plate an' that closer!	
Cud they speak, what wad they say?	
For Aw've tell'd them lots o' secrets	
When Aw've tummel'd off the way...	tumbled
Thor's a lang, law heavy pillor	pillar (of coal)
Inbyeside the canvas door,	
Where Aw horse the scrubbin full uns	(4)
Up for eighteen pence a score:	
Hoo Aw bliss that lang, law pillor!	bless (sarcastically)
Hoo that awful hitch Aw dreed!	dread
For its fearful wark this stickin	work...jamming
An' this shuvin wi' yor heed...	

Thor's a man o' mine, a hewer,	fellow worker
Weers a shirt o' flannen blue,	flannel
Which Aw fill'd away at Christmas	hid in a tub
Kas he didn't bring me doo.	because…Xmas box
Lork! ye shud hev heard him sweerin',	swearing
Hoo he'd bruise at ivory bat,	with every blow
While he chased me wi' the shot-stick	
But Aw lick'd him te the flat!…	beat.. assembly point
But the warst ov a' the evils	all
Thit a lad like me endures,	
Isn't wark, and isn't danger,	
But the lang ten dreary oors.	hours
For, ye see, a one thit's anxious	
Te command a canny pay,	
Is in shorter time exhausted,	
For throo a' the dowly day…	tedious, miserable

(1) Tokens would identify which tubs were to be attributed to which hewer, putter, etc.

(2) An extra tub, filled by or for the putter as a bonus (see Douglas, pp.61–2).

(3) kyevel or cavil — a lot deciding fair distribution of varying work-places; here numbers written out on the Deputy's saw.

(4) manhandle the full tubs, which rub against side or roof of tunnel.

I began putting a tram by myself without a partner last week, and get 4s a day. I like the work very badly; it is very hard work to run all day, and the sweat drops off you; the men constantly find fault with you; you cannot please them. I often have a battle with some of them; I sometimes lose; I lost one the day before yesterday. The men steal one another's dinners, and candles...

(William Hardy, age 17, *PP*, 1842, CR xvi, pp.160–1)

After driving you went to putting. A putter got a bunch of tokens from the weigh-cabin at the pit head with your number on and you put them on the tubs to say that you had put them. You took the empty tub into the coalface and the hewer filled that and you waited and took the full one out. You graded from there to what they called putting and hewing: that was like somedays you would go into the coalface and you would work like the men all day.

(Mr Cawson, Kibblesworth, Beamish, 1993/5)

If at first you dinnut succeed...

Aa cannet lift it, Aa cannet shift it,
Why, it's enough to mak ye cry.
Aa've chewed on till me arse is sore, struggled
Now Aa can't lift any more.
Aa cannet lift it, Aa carnet shift it,
An' Aa dinnet intend to try.
Aa's ganna put me gear away,
An' bugger off outbye.

(Lloyd, *Come All Ye Bold Miners*, p.65)

Tubs

Though dates will have varied, pit to pit, the transition from basket-type corves to wooden tubs on wheels will have taken place 1800–1820 (*HRCM*, chs 7, 11). The tub had the great advantage of providing continuous transport throughout the mine – making corves and cranes redundant – and forbye could be wheeled straight into the cage and out at bank.

Considerable variation remains in types of vehicles and the use of names; 'tram' for example, starts out as a sledge-like carrier for corves, but remains in use for a wheeled flatbed on which timber, etc. is moved round the workings.

bogie – "the tram or truck, used by the Newcastle Quayside cartmen" (Brockett, Newc, 1820s); "bogie – a low carriage with four wheels" (Wilson, G'head, 1820s); "down the pit, a bogey with an iron pin about two feet long, at each of the four corners, to prevent the timber and rails from falling off, would be called a horney tram" (Palgrave, Hetton, 1896); "bogey (or tram) – used for transporting lengths of long materials into mine working places" (McBurnie, Washington, 1970s). See also tram.

bottom-board – "the trap in the bottom of a coal-waggon" (Brockett, Newc, 1820s).

cat-band – [a band on a corf to take a hook] (Heslop, N'd, 1890s); "an iron loop placed on the underside of the centre of a flat 'corf bow', in which to insert the hook of the guss harness" (Tootle, 1995, N.East).

corf – "a basket for bringing coals out of the pit: 'lensda hand on wi' ma corf'" (Wilson, G'head, 1820s); "a basket made of hazel, with an iron bow by which it was attached to the winding rope" (Nicholson, 1888); "corves or baskets made of hazel twigs which carried about 4 $^1/_2$ cwt each" (*HRCM*, ch.11); "a basket of pined hazel rods" (Heslop, N'd, 1880s); "corve, curve – a small waggon, wheel-less but having iron runners, in use in the coal-pits" (Atkinson, Cleve, 1868); "kawf – coal basket (Dodd, Tanfield Lea). [corf, corfe or corve. M.Du. corf.]

> ...we must have two more Horses of a less Value, bought to Sledge out with, or draw the Corves as they come our of the Pit, on a Sledge on both sides the Pit.
>
> (*Compleat Collier*, 1707, p.34)

corf-batter or **corf-bitter** – "A lad who dried the wet 'corfs' over a brazier and cleaned off the dirt and mud before sending them back down the pit to be refilled" (Tootle, 1995, N.East).

corf bow – "a metal bow which was fitted to the 'corf' to hang it on the winding rope" (Tootle, 1995).

kibble – "a wooden tub, usually square, and of the capacity of about 20 gallons, used in conveying rubbish from one place to another: it is placed upon a tram. It is frequently made with a bow, similar to a corf" (Nicholson, 1888); "a large iron bucket used in sinking operations, also a small low tub with open end" (Wade, South Moor, 1966); "kibbil – carries stone in mine" (Dodd, Tanfield Lea).

laggans – "the pieces of wood which go to form a tub" (Palgrave, Hetton, 1896).

rolley – "a small waggon (with four little wheels) for conveying the corf" (*Bell MS*); "similar in construction to a tram but larger; a long carriage for conveying the corfs or tubs of coals from the crame or flat to the bottom of the shaft, drawn by horses on a rolley-way – the under-ground waggon-way along which the rolleys travel" (Brockett, Newc, 1820s); "rolley – a carriage used to carry corves along the horse-roads underground. The rolley was contrived as an improvement upon the tram, upon which a single corf was placed; a horse drawing one, two, or three corves at a time" (Nicholson, 1888); "rolley – what is called a 'trolly' in some parts, i. e. an open waggon for carrying heavy goods, such as beer-barrels or packing-cases" (Palgrave, Hetton, 1896); "rully, rolly – cart for horse" (Sterling, H'pool).

sled or **sledge** – "a wooden frame upon which the corves were drawn previous to the introduction of wheels and rails, and still used occasionally in leading to a stow-board" (Nicholson, 1888).

spider – "used to transport lengthy materials along roadways where no railway exists. Such as pipes etc which are slotted through between wheels and hung on to crook at end of rod" (McBurnie, Washington, 1970s).

rolley barrow – "a wooden wheelbarrow used to convey whicker corf of coals to shaft" – made entirely of wood, as per ex. found in waterlogged abandoned working at Whorlton. (*Newcastle Weekly Chron*, 18 March 1893).

timma tram – long tub to carry pit timber (Dodd, Tanfield Lea).

tram – "trams are a kind of sledges on which the coals are brought from the places where they are hewn to the shaft. A tram has four wheels, but a sledge properly so called is drawn by a horse without wheels" (Brand, *History of Newcastle*, 1789, vol.2 p. 681 – thus *OED*); "a small sledge, used in collieries, for conveying the corf" (*Bell MS*); "tram – a small carriage upon which a corf or basket is placed; or it sometimes means two boys who have charge of this carriage, the one drawing and the other pushing it" (Wilson, G'head, 1820s); "a small carriage on four wheels...used in coal mines to bring the coals from the hewers to the crane" (Brockett, Newc, 1820s); "a wooden carriage upon which the corves used to be conveyed along a tramway. The term still applies to the part of a tub to which the box is bolted" (Nicholson, 1888); "...very much the same as Bogey, q.v. Strictly speaking, a bogey has the flange on the wheel, while in the case of the tram, the flange is on the rail. Also, the tram had fast and loose wheels, having more play on the axle, to allow them the better to take a curve" (Palgrave, Hetton, 1896); "A tram... had a bogey like a coal-tub, but in place of a superstructure of wood it had four metal bars, one at each corner. Usually these were used for transporting props" (Hitchin, 1962, p.79); "flat bed vehicle, with uprights at corners, used to move timber around" (Roxborough, swD'm)... "Yes – among other things – cables, rings, gate end boxes" (Sharkey).

tub (too:b, toob, tuob) – "a coal-waggon used down the pit, holding from 6 to 8 cwt" (Palgrave, Hetton, 1896); "an open-topped box of wood or iron, bolted to a tram; used in conveying coals from the working places to the surface" (Nicholson, 1888); "wheeled box to transport coal in mine" (Dodd, Tanfield Lea).

wagons – "the wagons were hopper shaped, and had hinged bottoms to facilitate discarge at the staithes. This latter was open to the objection that it occasionally got shaken loose and the coal was prematurely deposited on the wagonway – a troublesome incident known to the miners as 'a cauld pie'" (*HRCM*, ch.7). A mine wagon. "The name is now used for large mine tubs" (Tootle, 1995).

Rails

When first upgraded from a mere sled, the tram had 'biscuit' wheels, that is wheels without a flange, and ran on L-shaped rails or plates which acted as guides. This system may have been suggested by cart ruts in mud or stone roads, thus 'rutways' on the foreshore at Ravenscar (N.Yorks) alum quarry.

Wooden wheels are first mentioned in use underground at Coalbrookdale in 1620. According to Freese (2005, p.91) it was Stephenson who built for mines "the first railways with the sort of flanged wheels and irontracks that future railways would use." And so the corf became a tub.

But heavy putten's now forgetten
Sic as we had i' former days   such
Ower holey thill and dyels a' spletten' –   floor... planks
Trams now a' run on metal ways.

God bless the man wi' peace and plenty
That <u>forst</u> invented metal plates; first
Draw out his span to five times twenty,
Then slide him through the heavenly gates.

(Thomas Wilson, *Pitman's Pay*, Pt.2)

bally (baa:li) – "a lever for turning points on a railway; so called from a big iron ball on the stem" (Palgrave, Hetton, 1896).

biscuit wheels – "tub wheels without flanges" (Tootle, 1995).

biscuit wheel rail – "an early type of L-section cast iron tub rail, used when using biscuit wheels" (Tootle, 1995).

check tyable – "It's the syam wi'sum folk wot reets to the papers, they're aal reet see far, then thee get off the way and thi've got to set back to th' check tyable ter get put on the way again. After some thought I realised he was referring to a tub getting off the rails underground" (Etherington, Hartlepool).

dogs – "large nails for underground rails" (Dodd, Tanfield Lea); "dogs – nails for fastening down tram rails" (Wade, South Moor, 1966); "dog nails – nails that fix plates/rails to sleepers" (Roxborough, swDm); "metal dog – spike to nail rails onto sleepers down pit" (Geggie, Ashington).

fishplate – "for joining rails" (Dodd, Tanfield Lea).

flat – "sheets put on the floor of the seam when the floor is soft" (J. Moreland, Dawdon, 1980).

flatsheet – "a landing plate. A rectangular or square iron or steel plate for use in twisting or turning mine tubs" (Tootle, 1995); "flat sheets – these were simply flat sheets of steel which were placed in the haulage track, both on the surface and underground and were used to turn the tubs in a different direction usually in situations where there was insufficient space for a 'turn'" (Sharkey); "flat sheets – in the old days these were square sheets of iron about 1" thick and nailed on to planks to assist in the moving of tubs and corfs. Nowadays flat sheets are used by rippers to help them in shovelling" (Douglass, 1973).

nails – "e.g. dogs, plates and joiners" (Dodd, Tanfield Lea).

off the way – "derailment" (Sharkey).

plates – "the last bit of track between the end of the rails into a working place and the face itself. 'Plate ends' meant that you had literally gone as far as you could" (Sharkey); "plait – plate, tub rail" (Dodd, Tanfield Lea).

platelayers – "the men who laid and maintained the tub rails underground" (Tootle, 1995); "plate-laying gang maintained tracks (underground only?)" (Barnett, Seaham).

plate nail – "a special type of nail used for nailing down iron plates used in the pit. 22 to the lb. 2 to 2 $^1/_2$ inches long with flat countersunk heads, round shafts and flat points" (Tootle, 1995); "plait nail – securing tub rail" (Dodd, Tanfield Lea).

plate rails – "cast iron L shaped rails, used underground for the 'tubs' to run along" (Tootle, 1995, Scots).

swapes – "tub rails bent to go round a turn" (Wade, South Moor, 1966).

thill – "the surface upon which a tram runs" (Wilson, G'head, 1820s).

> *So it was the hewers that laid the tracks was it?*
>
> Oh, yes, the man himself laid the track in the coal face, the coal hewer or the filler, never the wagon wayman, he laid the travelling base. Where they had an accident at Monkwearmouth lately, where they jumped the metals with the travelling cabs with about 10 men in you see. That's not the rolleywayman or the travelwayman – he mended the ropes as well. Ropes pulleywaymen, most times, it wasn't these arrangements then. In the coal face you kept advancing your own way to keep the tub after you where you were hewing or filling."
>
> (Mr Barton, Beamish, 1992 /98)

The route to the shaft

Mining operations spread out from the focal point of the shaft. It follows that (in board and pillar) the roadways nearest the coal-face are the newest and bear the least traffic. Once the putter reached a more established part of the route, the number of tubs multiplied, and were conjoined into sets and taken under power to the shaft. This could be pony power, or, especially when there was an incline, a form of haulage worked by a local engine.

bah tawn – "tub rail junction" (Dodd, Tanfield Lea).

barrow-way – "tram-way" (Wilson, G'head, 1820s); "tram road between the face and the flat along which the putters take the tubs" (Nicholson, 1888) "the underground road along which the 'barrowmen' worked" (Tootle, 1995, Newc).

bunker – "a high capacity hopper either above or below ground to store 'run of the mine coal' during a breakdown in the shaft or between the shaft and the washing plant. This allows the coal 'face' to continue production during the stoppage" (Tootle, 1995).

crane – "a hoist for lifting full 'corves' onto the 'rolley' for transportation along the main haulage road underground" (Tootle, 1995, C19 N.East); "crane – the junction between the branch railways and the horse roads in a pit, the coals being 'put' to this spot by the barrow-men from the working places. From the crane they were drawn by horses to the shaft. It is now called a 'flat' or 'station' " (Heslop, N'd, 1880s); "crane – formerly used to hoist the corves of coals from the tram to the rolley; the coals being put by the barrowmen from the working-places to the crane, and drawn thence by horses to the shaft. Upon the introduction of tubs the crane was abolished" (Nicholson, 1888).

crane-man – "A lad, 16 to 18 years of age, employed to work the crane loading 'corves' on to the 'rolley'. The point of loading was known as the flat" (Tootle, 1995, C19. N.East).

dilly – "self-acting incline. These are worked by full tubs descending hauling up the empty tubs" (McBurnie, Washington, 1970s); "dilly – a counter-balance mounted on a 'tram' used for hauling 'empties' up an incline." Or "A balance haulage incline" (Tootle, 1995, N.East). Compare jigger.

dish – "an area at bottom of shaft where the empty tubs are collected after being sent down the pit, and got ready to send inbye" (McBurnie, Washington, 1970s); "The section on an underground 'haulage road' where the 'sets' of empties stood before being hauled 'inbye'" (Tootle, 1995, N.East).

flat – "in a coal mine, the situation where the horses take the coal tubs from the putters" (Brockett, Newc, 1820s); "the point at the end of the haulage road to which the 'putters' or 'drawers' deliver the coal to be transported out of the pit" (Tootle, 1995, N.East); "marshalling point, underground tub standage" (Dodd, Tanfield Lea); "the station to which the putters take the full tubs, to be taken by the drivers to the engine plane or to the shaft" (Nicholson, 1888); "flat or pass-by – where pony transporters of tubs meet and change their loads over to each other" (McBurnie, Washington, 1970s) "'flat' usually referred to a close grouping of working places (coal hewers) in a bord and pillar district that was served by one putter and one timber leader. But that definition might be a bit pedantic" (Sharkey); "flat – junction for distributing tubs" (W.B. Coombs).

flat-lad or **flat-man** – "the man or older lad who worked on the 'flat' or 'landing' making up 'sets' of tubs to be sent out of the mine" (Tootle, 1995, N.East).

gannen or **going-board** – "when the flat or station is not at the end of the headways course at the face, the coals are brought down a board for one, two, or more pillars, as the case may be, to the flat. This board is called the 'gannen' (or going) board" (Nicholson, 1888); "gannen – a 'bord' down which coals were transported in 'tubs' on rails, as opposed to in corves or on runners" (Tootle, 1995, N.East).

greaser – "the greaser was a tiny reactangular hole set between the rails, and as the trains of tubs, the 'sets' passed over it, the axles were automatically greased" (Hitchin, 1962, p.66); "a saying I recall one used a lot was "Canny ower the greaser", meaning mind how you go. The greaser in question being a mechanism on the rails that lubricated the tub wheels and if care wasn't taken the tub could derail at this point. You would say this to someone who was departing instead of take care" (McGee, Sherburn Hill).

jigger – "a jigger is a self acting incline on which the weight of descending fulluns was used as the sole means (no external power) for hauling the chummens to the top of the incline. At Mainsforth we had a vertical staple (pronounced "stapple") shaft between the Harvey seam from where the coal was wound and the Hutton Seam above it. The fulluns from the Hutton were placed in a cage and the chummens from the Harvey were placed in the other cage. The weight of the fullens was the only power in the system and the whole thing was controlled by a man with a brake on the wheel at the top around which the ropes passed… I am very confident about a jigger being a self-acting incline. In the very steep seams at Dean and Chapter as we approached the Butterknowle fault we had many of them… In these cases no external power is used and control is exercised only by the application of a brake" (Sharkey).

kip – "usually an artificial incline constructed of bricks or blocks which carried the haulage track up to height where the tubs could run freely to a loading or marshalling point" (Sharkey); "kip – the landing place at the shaft bottom for the full tubs, when they are transported outbye to the shaft area" (McBurnie, Washington, 1970s); "kip – the highest point on the rollyway where the tubs are detatched" (Wade, South Moor, 1966).

koin – "to swing tub around, turn" (Dodd, Tanfield Lea).

landin – "a stopping place on the engine plane" (Nicholson, 1888); "pit tub standage" (Dodd, Tanfield Lea); "where the main set of tubs arrive from the shaft" (McBurnie, Washington, 1970s).

landing-lad – "a lad who prepares the sets of tubs at a landing and attends to the signals" (Nicholson, 1888).

lead – "to carry or cart: in the North they lead coals" (Brockett, Newc, 1820s).

plane – "a roadway along which men, coal and materials are transported by mechanical means or by gravity" (Tootle, 1995).

meetin's – "midway down the pit; or where the full and empty corves or baskets pass each other" (Wilson, G'head, 1820s); "wagons passing on gravity haulage" (Dodd, Tanfield Lea).

offtaks – "this was an underground location where the haulage ropes were disconnected from the train or 'set' and the tubs were redistributed" (Sharkey)... "Yes. Often at a junction where two rope haulage sytems met and the set was disconnected from one set of ropes and attached to another to continue its journey" (Roxborough, swDm).

rolley-way – "the way laid with iron on which the rolley travels" (*Bell MS*); "rolleyway – the horse road underground" (Nicholson, 1888).

Sets

> I became a driver, and have been at it half a-year. I like it very well; it is not too hard. I have to put the tub off the tram into the rolley; it is very hard, and if the putters were not to help me, I could not do it. We are 15 hours out of the house every day; I am very tired by night. I have a good appetite. I had a coal fall on my forehead, and the mark still remains, and will always remain.
>
> (*PP*, 1842, CR xvi, pp.162–3)

amain – "when tubs went over an incline without the securing rope being attached, so running loose" (Davidson, Ashington); "gan amain – uncontrolled tub or set of tubs running down an incline" (Sharkey); "amain – vehicle running out of control" (Dodd, Tanfield Lea).

binder – "an extra large roller used on haulage roadways to guide rope around curves" (McBurnie, Washington, 1970s).

bull – "the bull was a safety device for inclined rope haulages. In this case it was a static device. It comprised a length of I section girder located near the bottom of an incline. The length of the girder was about 1.2 – 1.3 times the height of the roadway. One end was attached by a hinge or pivot to a roof beam, so that in the lowered position it provided buffer against runaway tubs reaching the bottom of the incline where men might be working" (Roxborough, swDm); "bull – roof structure for stopping runaway tubs. Reverse to monkey but has to be dropped by lever or hand" (McBurnie, Washington, 1970s).

bump the set – "anyone taking unnecessary risks was described as 'he'll bump the set some of these times'. A set is a number of tubs or trucks pulled along by a rope from a fixed engine" (Wade, South Moor, 1966); "bump the set – get into trouble" (Dodd, Tanfield Lea).

cow – "a wooden or iron fork, hung loosely upon the last tub or wagon of a set, ascending an inclined plane. Its use is to stick into the ground, and stop the set, in case of the rope breaking" (Nicholson, 1888); "my recollection is that the cow was a solid steel 2–3 inch dia round bar that was attached to the back tub of an ascending set as a trailing safety device. If the rope broke, the set was prevented from careering down the incline by the 'cow' simply digging in to the floor and derailing the set" (Roxborough swDm); "coo – in mining, a pole having a fork of iron at the end [to prevent running backward]" (Heslop, N'd, 1880s); "axle cow – shorter type, hooks on to tub axle" (McBurnie, Washington, 1970s).

devil – "a device for detaching the rope from a set of tubs whilst in motion" (Wade, South Moor, 1966).

dog – "used to attach haulage rope to load of tubs. Easy to unloose from tub chain when required" (McBurnie, Washington, 1970s).

diamond – "a fixture on outside of tub-lines, to put tubs back onto rails when they have become derailed. An outside rail curved at each end sits on bed of concrete to guide tubs back onto rails" (McBurnie, Washington, 1970s).

dregs – "'drags' which were used to slow down or stop individual tubs or sets of tubs. Occasionally made of steel about 15/18 inches long, 1 inch diameter, with a point on one end and a "handhold" at the other but more often made of hardwood, round and with a point at each end – 15–18 inches long and about 2 inches in diameter. Dregs worked by sticking them in the spokes of the moving tub(s) where they jammed against the tub frame" (Sharkey); "drag — a piece of iron or wood put between the spokes of the wheel of a tub or rolley to check its progress where a dip of the way is considerable" (Nicholson, 1888); "I could stop a moving tub by spoking its wheels with a 'dreg'" (Hitchin, 1962, p.70); "dreg – a wood or iron stave put between the spokes of a tub wheel to prevent it from turning thereby retarding its progress" (Wade, South Moor, 1966); "dreg – A piece of wood shoved in between the spokes of coal tub wheels to act as a brake" (Griffiths, Horden). [If just one wheel were jammed, the friction between that wheel and the rails ought to bring about a braking process – see lockers.]

drivers – "boys who led horse-drawn full tubs along the main underground roads out-bye" (Colls, 1987).

dunched – "to run into with force as 'tubs dunching'" (Wade, South Moor, 1966).

lockers – "a short wood or steel device which was inserted into the tub wheel, this locked the wheel and friction between the wheel and the tub track caused the tub and any others coupled to it, to come to a standstill" (Riley, Blyth).

monkey – "device fixed between railway to hold tubs on heavy gradient. Weight on rear to keep the front end up, so it holds on to axle of tub" (McBurnie, Washington, 1970s); "a device set between the rails at the head of an incline. It allowed the ascending wagons to pass over, then lifted to form a barrier to stop the wagons if they break loose from the haulage rope" (Tootle, 1995).

pony putter – "a lad who brings the tubs from the working places to the flat with a pony" (Nicholson, 1888); "[someone who] used a pony to haul the tubs" (Tootle, 1995).

pusher or **creeper** – "mechanical device for moving tubs along slowly. Fixed in floor between the rails and runs under tubs, horns catching on axles of tubs" (McBurnie, Washington, 1970s).

run – "a set of tubs" (Nicholson, 1888).

set – "a train of tubs or wagons" (Nicholson, 1888); "a number of tubs the manager decides shall be hauled by any electric or compressed driven hauler" (McBurnie, Washington, 1970s).

set-rider – "a lad who goes with a set of tubs on an engine-plane" (Nicholson, 1888).

sprag – "a bar of wood inserted between the spokes of a coal-waggon, to act as a drag" (Palgrave, Hetton, 1896); "a wood or iron stave put between the spokes of a pit tub wheel to retard its progress" (Wade, South Moor, 1966).

yokens – "when two trams or carriages meet, going in different directions" (Wilson, G'head, 1820s); "yoken or **yoking** – the meeting or colliding of two sets of tubs; a collision" (Nicholson, 1888).

The Set Rider

(Tune: "Old Towler")

O Bob, maw luv, be sharp an' thrive!	
Tho' just a youngster yit,	
Thaw like's not seen in lad alive,	your like is
At bank or doon the pit.	above ground
Thor's nyen ov a' the scores Aw knaw	none
Aw'd gan se far te see:	go so
Maw little bit Bob is the best o' them a',	
An' Bob's the lad for me.	

Chorus:

O maw Bobby! maw laddie, maw lover, maw hobby!	(1)
O maw Bobby! maw laddie, maw lover, maw hobby!	
Be as sharp as thoo can, an' grow intiv a man!	into
Be as sharp as thoo can, an' grow intiv a man!	
For maw canny bit, bonnie bit Bobbie,	
Maw laddie, maw lover, maw hobby,	
A cortin we'll gan 'till the weddin' days dawn!	courting
Maw Bob's the lad for me!	
The cawshun stowl maw heart away,	caution/special person
When he wiz helpin-up,	lending a hand
As roond the raws one heul doo day,	terrace rows…Yule dough
The youngsters hugg'd the teup.	(2)
The teup, poor thing, wiz myed to bleeze,	blaze
The beer wiz myed te flee,	was made to flow
Till maw little Bob got as tight as ye pleese –	
Maw Bob's the lad for me! –	
He kept a door, then kept a flat,	
Then drivin days begun;	
What jobs the poor bit lad's been at!	
An' noo he rides the run.	(3)
He's near the deevil a' the day,	(4)
Hugs him whiles tail up te!	sometimes
Or tosses the dorty aud deevil away! –	dirty old devil
Maw Bob's the lad for me! –	
He's tell'd wor lads when Aw've been nigh,	told
Thit a' the hyel day throo,	whole

He's boond te keep a constant eye,	
On either bull or cow.	(5)
An' what wi' deevils, bulls, an' cows,	
He's sick as lad can be,	
Till he gets away hyem tiv his lass an' the news –	home to
Maw Bob's the lad for me! –	
But seun the time 'ill come te pass,	soon
When he'll get on te hew,	i.e. be taken on
An' hand the priest the needful brass	money
Thit keeps us pairted noo.	parted now
Then heart te heart we'll ventor life,	venture
An' a' thit fate can de;	
An' if he's a good man he'll find me a gud wife –	
Maw Bob's the lad for me!	

(Alexander Barrass)

(1) Hobby is a name for a colt, and a nick-name for a putter (implying strength?); but also a Scottish first-name.

(2) The teup was the last corf before the Christmas break, decorated with candles; 'tup' means literally a ram, an animal image associated with the corf. See ch. 9 'Celebrations'.

(3) To ride the run meant to travel with and supervise sets of rollies/tubs on a machine-drawn portion of the route. i.e. when they had to be pulled up an incline to the shaft by engine and continuous rope. It was a stage preparatory to becoming a hewer and involved occasional days of hewing work.

(4) "A device for detaching the rope from a set of tubs while in motion" (Wade, p.188); here a pun on Devil.

(5) Bull – leading tub of a descending train with built-in safety brake ready to engage roof; cow – last tub in an ascending train with similar device.

Running amain

Well there once was a serious accident; the sett broke away coming down my bank you see – Tommy the pony he was a good friend to me, and he would listen to the noise as the sett went up you know, he'd hear the rat-a-tat-tat, rat-a-tat-tat, rat-a-tat-tat, and that bank was somewhere between a quarter and a third of a mile long, and I used to listen; and this time oh it was a long time, it seemed to be a long time coming back – Tommy knew it was a long time in

> coming back because after a pause of so many seconds we'll say, you could hear the sett coming down – the full sett coming down – and you could hear it on the line – the noise traveling along with the plates you see – you could hear the tubs gain speed – Tommy whinnied to me – Tommy, wide awake – that pony – he knew there was something wrong and he yelled and yelled at me – whinnied at me – to get out the way – and I got out of the way – I went in one of the other old workings like the side of that fireplace there, not knowing what was going to happen – I think there was about fifteen tubs or more came away. So after everything settled down and the coal dust settled and there was no fall – roof fall – I waited – you've got to wait so long you see in case there's a roof fall you see – and I didn't know whether there was props knocked out or not, all I could hear was a bang and the coal dust and I kept my eyes down and my ears covered up... so I thought to myself, I'll go up and see what's happened – and I had a pile of tubs, about fifteen tubs piling all over my way you see, about the width of this room...
>
> (Mr Jackson, Beamish, 1984/259)

Ponies

Ponies are a favourite icon of the pit world, justly beloved, but now likeliest to be met with as miniature resin casts. Some pits in west Durham continued to work with pony power till they shut; in the east of the county, they more often disappeared in the 1950s, during modernisation, as trunk conveyors brought the coal to bunkers at the shaft bottom in place of the old sets and their ponies. And some of the best mine stories centre on ponies!

case book – "a book kept at the colliery, in which the name of every horse or pony, which has been off work for twenty four hours or longer together with the driver's name is entered" (Tootle, 1995, N.East).

choppy – "mixture of hay, corn, etc., used for feeding ponies" (Sharkey); "choppy – the corn life food for the pony: 'scrubbing, cowering, straining for the choppy'" (J. Moreland, Dawdon, 1980).

collars or '**braffins**' [on the ponies] (Hitchin, 1962, p.68).

cotterill or **cotter-pin** – "inserted in slot to fasten on part of certain types of equipment used" (McBurnie, Washington, 1970s); "particularly used to secure limbers to tub… but boycotted by many putters who preferred to be able to quickly get clear of Tub-Cowping-Up with risk of leg fractures" (Johnson, Dawdon).

draa – "draw: 'draa me whip'" [i.e. from stores] (Hay, Ushaw Moor, C20/2).

driver – "a boy who has charge of a horse in the pit" (Wilson, G'head, 1820s); "a boy, 13 to 15 years old, employed in driving horses on the main roads underground" (Tootle, 1995, N.East).

galloway – "a horse under forteen hands high, of the sturdy breed formerly common but now almsot extinct. They were used on the fells to carry ore over form the mines to the smelt mills etc." (Heslop, N'd, 1880s); "galloway – a pony" (Nicholson, 1888); "gallawa – pony, horse" (Dodd, Tanfield Lea); "Galloway – pronounced 'gallowa'. In Durham, all pit ponies were referred to as 'gallowas'" (Tootle, 1995); "gallerwer – horse" (Sterling, H'pool).

gallawa's byuts – “horseshoes” (Dodd, Tanfield Lea).

gears – “horse trappings” (Bailey, 1810); “sets of gears – collars, bridles, straps and chains” [for the ponies] (Hitchin, 1962, p.66).

granary – “Lastly there was the Granary (‘choppy-house’) – that was where the ponies’ food was kept once, and the oats ground up ready for them, but now it’s used by bricklayers” (Charlton, Dawdon),

heck – “a rack in which hay was fed to horses” (Wilson, North Walbottle).

jagger-galloway – “a pony with a peculiar saddle for carrying lead, etc. [e.g.] in Teesdale, near Middleton. Jagger, in the Scottish language, means a pedlar – jagger-galloway, a pedlar’s pony. Some of these itinerant merchants, as they are called, are yet in the practice of conveying their wares on galloways, a small, but spirited, breed of horses, from Galloway, a district of country in Scotland, famed for rearing them” (Brockett, Newc, 1820s).

jallup – “opening medicine, a purgative: ‘Noo jallup wes the stuff the’ use ta give the gallowas ivvery weekend ter mak them shite’” (Hay, Ushaw Moor, C20/2).

limmers – “the shafts of a cart or carriage” (Brockett, Newc 1820s); “limbers (lim:uz) – shafts of a carriage. The only name for shafts of a ‘tub’ down the mine, which are made in one piece and detachable” (Palgrave, Hetton, 1896); “limmers – wood shafts with an iron bow and a catch to clip on to a coal tub carried on the harness of a pit pony” (Wade, South Moor, 1966); “limbers provided a rigid coupling so that the pony could hold back on undulating ground” (Oxley, 1990); “limmers – yoke-like piece of equipment which is fastened to the horse/ponies harness and then attached to a tub. The limmers are similar to cart shafts except that they are not permanently attached to the tubs” (Riley, Blyth).

whip – “…you all had to have a whip – if you hadn’t a whip to hit the pony they’d tell yer, ‘Aa’ll send you home’. You had to get some long leather and make a whip of it and a bit stick – to hit the pony. If you hadn’t a whip – -‘Where’s your whip?’” (Mr Dawkin, Beamish, 1983/216); “neebody was allowed ter tak a gallowa without a whip, in case yer badly used them, like. In case yer hit them wi summing else, see” (Hay, Ushaw Moor, C20/1).

yam sticks – “…the collars here the yam sticks on where you fastened the chains and things to on these ponies where on a normal horse you see them sticking up there the metal yam sticks they were down over for the simple reason for the below working they wouldn’t catch” (James Mackenzie, Beamish, 1993/10).

yoke – “to ‘put in’ a horse (to a vehicle). This is distinct from ‘harnessing’ or putting the harness on his back. etc.” (Palgrave, Hetton, 1896); “to attach a pony to his limbers, which the pony carried along with him” (McBurnie, Washington, 1970s).

Care of ponies

There was horse keepers down the pit, underground stables, and they looked after the ponies, fed them and cleaned them and that, washed them at times. We used to have them for the full shift, you got used to the ponies, like human beings some of them. Some very nice ponies.

How small were they, the spaces you were in weren't very big?

You needed a good yard high for the tubs, and of course most places was higher than that. So we had one or two small ponies, just about a yard, same height as the tub, if the tub was catching the top the pony was alright, it didn't catch. Other places you had bigger ponies. That was for putting. The drivers they had bigger ponies still, I wouldn't say what hands they are, but they were bigger, they used to pull more tubs, sometimes three or six or so tubs, it just depends on the gradient.

Did you have the same pony every day?

Every quarter you got [allotted] to a different pony. Sometimes you got a bad un, it was a bad un if you got a bad un. The majority of ponies were nice, and they were pretty well looked after. Some lads was rough with them, but most of the lads was good with the ponies, they liked them. The better the pony was, it would help them. Some would follow you about all over, when you took the tub in and let the pony off, he would walk in to where the full tub was and turn around just ready to hang them on.

They knew the routine?

They did. Nice ponies, you got used to them and they followed you all over. Give them a crust of bread and they were there for the rest! Aye. Sometimes we took a tasty snack for them apples or something like that, but they got the corn and hay in the stable. You had water troughs in-bye, water for the ponies to drink, and hay, a choppy box, we called it, with choppy in the box if there was any spare at the time.

How old were the ponies when they went underground?

Round about two year old I think, or three, before they put them underground.

And did they stay underground, they didn't bring them out…?

Later on when we had the holidays – we never used to have holidays so they didn't come out. We got a week's holiday, then we got a fortnight, they were brought out and let them run in the fields.

Did they object to going back into the darkness after?

They didn't want to! …at Waldridge Fell Colliery, we had a drift, and the ponies come out every night, there wasn't a cage there, we used to walk them out. But the deeper mines, means that you couldn't bring them up, too many to bring up.

Were they usually shod?

Aye, they always had shoes on. The blacksmith used to go down and shoe them, every day. You weren't allowed to work a pony if he lost a shoe, you had to stop and try to get another out. The horsekeeper gave it to the blacksmith to put a new shoe on, he went down about seven o clock on the morning.

(Mr Rutter, Beamish, 1987/10)

You went with a boy who was qualified to learn you all about the pony – how to harness him in what were called limmas which had to be hooked on to the tub which the pony had to pull. You would have your own pony for two or three days. The fore shift used to take the ponies in and sometimes the ponies used to work all day. You would take the empty tubs into a flat and bring the full ones out to the landing which was a big place where the endless rope used to be hanging. A waggonwayman used to hang about thirty on the rope which used to pull them to the shaft bottom.

(Mr Cawson, Kibblesworth, Beamish, 1993/5)

Incidently, talking about ponies reminds me of a story told to me by a friend, Arthur Richardson, who at one time was undermanager at Mainsforth Colliery (a big pit in those days) who because of a health problem transferred to a very small pit west of Bishop Auckland, where all the pits were small. Anyway Arthur was in his office one day when he was told that a pony had cast its shoe. He acknowledged this information and went about whatever he was doing before he was told about the pony. And then it hit him! He only had two ponies at the mine and the news meant that 50% of his haulage capacity was now inoperable so he had to drop everything and get that pony shod again. He said he very quickly lost the 'big pit' mentality after that episode.

(Tony Sharkey)

Pony sense

I'll tell you about the experience at the Lily. [Lily Drift, Rowlands Gill.] I was driving, you weren't supposed to, you were supposed to be behind the last tub and I was traveling with 3 tubs with a black stallion pony called Rob, maybe 12 hands, he was one of the smaller ones on the particular area of way which had a fair bit of height. So you could drive horses 13.2 hands high. But he wasn't very big, maybe 12.2. And he used to go with 3 tubs and you weren't supposed to ride in the tub, you were supposed to be on the back of the last tub. But everybody broke the rule. Everybody used to ride in the first tub. It was highly dangerous. Because it would jump off the way when you were in a low part, then you couldn't get out the tub.

So I'm going in-by with this Rob; I drove him the most of the time I was there. I'd occasionally take other ponies out but wasn't often. I'd drive this Rob most of the time and I knew him. I didn't make a fool of the horse, he was just, he did what he was asked to do with me. I'm going in-by and I'd just passed what they call a deputies' kist. Which is just like a big wooden chest where they kept their pickaxes, their tools, whatever. And this rolleyway man, the man who mended the way that they put the tubs on was sitting at the deputies' kist having his bait. And I passed him "Hello Harry", "Hello there", and went on into the depth of the mine you see. And I'd maybe gone a hundred yards. I'd done this time and time again: And I'd gone this, about a hundred yards and suddenly this Rob stopped. And it was a slight down grade where he stopped. Very slight. So he wasn't feeling any weight in his collar, he wasn't pulling... if he felt any weight it was in his britchin. And he stopped and you could sense, he sensed something and I didn't. And

I'm sitting in the front tub. And it was this part that was fairly low and it was difficult to get out of. And I was saying 'get up' and cursing him, giving him his pedigree, threatening with 'God if I get out this tub I'll warm your backside up the...' and he started to back, really ram back. Now it's hard if tubs, even empty tubs, are on a slight grade, a very very slight grade, or nothing, like that, it's a very hard thing to back 3 tubs up. He does it through the brickin tub he wears on his harness and he's ramming back and the tubs are being bombed back over.

I'm saying 'have you gone out of your mind,' I'm shouting this, and he backed to a part where, he's still ramming back, I could get out the tub. And I had an acetylene lamp and this acetylene lamp had to be lit with a match. It had a little flint on the side but the flint didn't work so I needed a match. As I'm getting out the tub, I banged this light up on the [?rim]. Now you can't imagine because you haven't been down there, that if you are suddenly [left] in the dark, you haven't a light, it's blacker than the proverbial duck's backside. There is no gleam of light, turn you round once, if you turn round once when you're completely in the dark down a pit, you don't know which way you're facing.

You've got no indication. Unless with a little sense you'll try and feel the rails. Then you can still be fooled. Or you can put your hand up or wet your finger for the in-draught of air, if you know that the in-draughts coming in, well that's the way out, I'll go that way. If you know it's coming the other way. There's so many ways but you're completely blacked out, there isn't anything. And he's still, in the darkness, ramming back and there isn't room on the sides to get out the road. So I panic and I start shouting, hoping this rolley weighman will hear me. But there's no reply from him.

So I manage to scrub along the side, I don't know how I did it yet, the timber supports along the side that hold the roof supports in, I scrubbed along a space like that (just a few inches) and got what I could feel the last tub, and I knew which way then I would have to go. So I pushed myself up, feeling along the rails, going out-by until, shouting all the time, until he got off the kist and he says "what's the matter?" I can see his light appear, "what's wrong?" And I says "I had an old -----".

He says we'll get these tubs and this pony out the road. So we loosened the tubs off, we shoved them along to this deputy's kist where there was a lay-by, you could lay the tubs along, turned the pony around, led him out and went back. And here, the whole roof had collapsed.

Well I forgot to say in this part of my story, when he stopped and wouldn't go forward, I couldn't hear a thing and I was asking him, you know clicking my tongue and 'get up, get up' and he's ramming back, doing exactly the opposite to what you wanted him to do, there was this thunderous roar. You know the end of world, I thought. And that's when he backed far enough, I was getting out of the tub and losing my light. But this real ear drum busting roar you know. And when we went back, the rolley weighman and I, there it was, filled to the..., well it was still coming down, [you could] see the bits rolling out.

'Aye' he says 'the night shift will have their work for to get the shift that's in-by out.'

Somehow then, I'm going a long way about it to illustrate it, that he had a sixth sense, he had hearing far far more than a human being. He must have heard an easing of the ground above him or whatever he heard, he knew there was something coming down there. Another yard or two and we'd have been right slap bang underneath it. And that proved it to me, I'd heard this story before, how the pony knew when there was something about to happen and that if men observed and watched them closely, they were safer working with horses. I was convinced from that minute on and I never ignored a move that they made.

(R. Barrass, Beamish, 1924/25r)

Pony racing

People thought a lot about ponies, and if you took a couple of apples in, they could smell them – I remember as a putter I used to take apples in my pocket, but eventually, the pony would eat your jacket pocket out. They were really pets to some extent, you used to ride them in, have races with them.

Inside the mine?

Oh yes. Boys being boys, and young fellows, full of exuberance, 'I'll race you out Joe,' on its back, and away we'd go. And the pony knew it was going home anyway, so we were flat out.

(Harry Burns, Beamish, 2005/135)

The Granary

The granary was where they ground up the oats for the ponies for to eat. In the war-time there were short of workers – the drivers were all old men, and there was a woman running the granary – Sally Tasker. She was six foot, broad shoulders, wore big black clothes like Victorian style, and she was well over retirement age. She had worked there before the war, and they'd called her back to keep it going.

The oats came up in bags on the North East Railways. Each bag was a stone in weight, but she used to pick them up off the barrow, fix it on this hook and tip the oats into the hopper – and that unaided! She would be, well, the great great grandmother of that urchin Taska you see hanging about now.

(Gordon Patrickson, Dawdon)

Starting up

You were thrown in at the deep end.

Just handed me the tackle and said, 'Put it on him,' and left me.

Me and this pony, in a little space, about this size.

So I struggled, and eventually I got the bridle on.

I had no idea how it should fit though.

But I learned not to let a pony stand on your foot.

One thing I heard, was you should take the pony a little treat, to make friends, keep it gentle and quiet.

So I extended it this apple, but I did not know to do it on a flat hand, my fingers were curled under the apple and went straight in the pony's mouth. The job I had getting my fingers out again! Why, the skin was scraped, there was blood everywhere.

But the ponies loved to feed, OK. They would take the bait out your pocket as you walked along. You know, you would check for your bait, and all that would be left was a piece of paper.

Sometimes as you were walking along they would just lean over and bite you on the bum.

(John Williams, Haswell)

Spider and Darkie

Aa had this aaful gallowa caalled Spider when Aa was workin down the pit. Mind he wes a real little bugger. Neebody liked him cause he use ta kick an bite an bump yer with he's heed when yer warn't lookin – an sometimes when yer ware!

Anyway, there was one day Aa waalked inter the hosskeeper's ter get Spider out an draa me whip. Neebody was allowed ter tak a gallowa without a whip, in case yer badly used them, like. In case yer hit them wi summing else, see.

Why Aa gets Spider out an puts he's bridle on, an Aa aalways give him a couple o sugar bullets [sweets] an' an apple ter try an sweeten he's temper. But this partickler day Aa'd fergetten the apple, an Spider was hevvin nyen on't. He shoves he's greet snout inter me jacket pocket an there was nee apple.

"Gan on," Aa says. "Aa've fergetten it. Aa'll bring yer two termorrer."

Why the bad little bugger bares he's teeth an deliberately taks a bite outa me showlda. By lad! It hort an aall! Why one o' the deppities had left a shot stick lyin so Aa gets ahaad on't an whacks it reet across the top of he's leg. He squealed blue morder, an Jack Tate the hosskeeper come fleein out ter see what wes gannin on.

"What yer deein ter that gallowa?" yells Jack.

"He's just bit me showlda," Aa says.

"Why yer shoulda cracked he's airse wi yer whip, then. Mr Hairvey'll hev a fit if he finds out yer've hit one of he's pownies wirra shot stick."

"Aye," Aa says, "an that bloody gallowa'll hev a fit if he bites me again, cause Aa'll land me byeut reet up he's breed basket!"

By, he wes a bad bugger, Spider. Mind, he could pull tubs when he put he's mind te'it. He wes the strongest gallowa in the pit. Aa've seen him pull he's aan load an another gallowa's an aall. If ivver a gallowa brok down, or owt like that, the' aalways sent fer me an Spider.

One day we were gannin alang the flat, an he just stopped.

"Howway, Spider!" Aa shouts. "What's the marrer wi ye?"

But he just stood, so Aa thowt: "Reet, me lad!" So Aa gets me whip an Aa lays it across he's airse. Nee effect. Jimmy Bell an he's gallowa's reet behint an here we were howldin the flat up.

"What's the marrer, Jim?" shouts Jimmy.

"Spider winna move."

So Jimmy comes up. "Why man," he says, "he's load's ower hivvy. Gan on, drop the tubs off an tak him ter one side fer a rest."

Aa puts a chock in the back tub an gets down ter slacken Spider off. Next thing Aa knew, up comes he's hint leg an catches us just above me right eye. Aa've still got the mairk now. Look. Aye, Jimmy had ter tak us back alang ter the shaft bottom an Aa had ter see the doctor. By, he wes a bad un, that Spider.

Next gallowa Aa got wes a little black un. By, he wes a beauty! Dairkie the' caalled him. Mind, he wes neewhere near as strang as Spider, but he wes the nicest little feller Aa've ivver come across. Aa nivver had a minute's trouble outa that gallowa an Aa treated him like me aan bairn. Aa use ta tak apples an sugar bullets an when Aa had some straaberries riddy Aa use ta tak them an aall. By, he wes a little smasher.

Why one day we were pullin alang through a low bit in the Brockwell. By, it wes a bloody haird seam, the Brockwell. Anyway, Dairkie stopped. He waddn't move. So Tommy Nixon wes reet behint wi he's gallowa.

"Howway, Jim! Skelp he's airse for him!" shouts Tommy. He wes a bad bugger wi pownies, Tommy. Aalways whippin them.

Aa says: "Tommy, Aa've nivver had ter use a whip on Dairkie since Aa gorrim, an Aa'm not ganna stairt now. If he winna move, there's summing wrang."

So Aa gans up ter Dairkie an pats he's heed an taaks tiv im an tried ter lead him on a bit, but he just stuck he's feet in an waddn't budge.

"Howway, Jim! Gerrim uncoupled!" shouts Tommy. He wes an impatient bugger, Tommy. Got killed in the Waar, ye knaa, poor lad. Blaan ter bits, the' reckon, at the Somme. Anyway, just then we hord it. A greet rumblin up aheed, an the roof stairted ter shake. Tommy shouts: "Get the gallowas uncoupled, an run, Jim!"

So we both gets the gallowas out an runs like hell back towards the shaft bottom. An it wes just as weel cause the tubs we were pullin got buried an if we'd a stayed there we'd a getten it an aall. Aye, he saved our lives, Dairkie. By, Aa wes proud on him. There wes a dozen men trapped in the Brockwell, but the' got them aall out. Neebody got hort.

Anyway, next day Tommy an me got sent for by Mr Hairvey. He wes the owner, ye knaa. The Hairvey seam wes named after he's family, Aa believe. He wes an aad man. White-haired, he wes, a Quaker, an he use ta taalk like the Bible. By, he wes a lovely aad feller, a real gentleman. He says: "Thee, James, and thee, Thomas, did a very brave thing yesterday. Thee got thy horses out and put thy own lives in danger. It was a very Christian thing to do and I am proud of thee both."

Why, ye knaa, we were ownly young lads, an we didn't knaa where ter put oursels, we were that embarrassed. Aye, Aa reckon Dairkie saved me life an Aa cried when Aa lost him an moved inter coal hewin. Mind Aa made sure he went tiv a good lad. A lad caalled Emsley Ross got him. Treated him just like Aa did. An whenever Aa saw him after that, Aa aalways give him a couple o sugar bullets. By, he wes a good little gallowa. The best in the pit.

(James Hay, Ushaw Moor, C20/1)

Power assisted hauling

Where the route to be travelled by the coal sloped upward, the assistance of an engine was needed to draw the sets up the incline. This powered section was called a haulage way or engine plane. Originally powered by a horse gin, a stationary steam engine was introduced in the early nineteenth century, and later a local compressed-air engine (*HRCM*, ch.7), or in some cases proper loco engines were used for haulage.

beetle – "a small haulage engine driven by compressed air. The invention of Lishman & Young, used at the Newbottle Collieries in the North East" (Tootle, 1995); "beetle (or tugger) – small horse-power hauler either electric or compressed air driven. Can easily be transported and fixed up in very short time. Usually about 5 to 8 horsepower" (McBurnie, Washington, 1970s).

clip – "used to hang tubs on to endless haulage ropes. Collar pulls tighter as rope hauls tubs along" (McBurnie, Washington, 1970s).

endless rope haulage – introduced by Buddle 1844 – 2 engines, 1 each end, drawing full and empty wagons on an endless rope – e.g. at Haswell. Endless rope system needed two tracks, but only one continuous rope. Sets were hitched onto this as needed. Slower progress, but can work on only one engine (unlike main and tail rope system), and dependable and steady delivery (after *HRCM*, ch.7); "a haulage system consisting of an engine at one end and a return wheel at the other. A steel rope is wound round the driving drum of the engine, along the roadway, round the return wheel and back to the drum, where it is spliced to its other end. The tubs or mine cars, are shackled to this continuous rope. When the tub has been hauled in-bye, the direction of the engine is reversed, to bring it out-bye" (Temple, 1994, pp.17–18); "a haulage system using and endless moving rope to which the tubs attached using clips or lashing chain" (Tootle, 1995).

Both pits had endless rope haulage systems, which pulled the empties in as it pulled the full tubs out. These ropes ran constantly and the tubs were fastened together in sets by chain couplings and the sets attached to the moving rope using special clips. In the Betty Pit a top-rope system was used with the rope running above the tubs and fastened on with ham-bone clips. In the Mary Pit a bottom rope system was used: this ran under the tubs and they were fastened on with box-clips.

(Wilson, Walbottle)

haulage engine – "an engine employed to move coal, men and material, along the haulage roadways in a mine. [hence] haulage rope, etc." (Tootle, 1995).

loco – "applied to the battery powered 'loco's' rather than the diesels" (Douglass, 1973).

main and tail rope system – useful where the incline was irregular, undulating, etc. There was a powered drum at either end and two ropes – one attached to front one to rear of set – as empties go inbye, the tail rope winds itself up on drum and main rope unwinds; to draw full tubs up, reverse action (after *HRCM*, ch.7); main and tail haulage – "two engines, one at each end of the track, one to pull the set outbye, by the main rope, tuther to haul it back inye by the tail rope" (Temple, 1994, p.18).

> A brief story about taking a ride in a chum tub on the 'main and tail' heading out to 26 South Low Main, Dawdon, about a mile and a half further than the last stop of the 'Paddy mail'. It was quite illegal to ride so, and you had to quickly get in the tub in a canny stretch of high... then sit in the dark till you got to a longish stretch of high in-bye. On one occassion somebody elsewhere 'rapped howld', the set of tubs came to a halt under a brig... we had to sit in our respective tubs quietly and in the dark, because if we tried to exit upwards and the set moved... we'd be decapitated!
>
> (Kenn Johnson, Dawdon)

pig tail – "Durham name for a haulage clip. It clips the tub chain to a haulage rope" (Douglass, 1973).

rolleyway – "engine plane" (Wade, South Moor, 1966); "rolleewai – underground railway" (Dodd, Tanfield Lea).

rolleewai-man – "attends underground railway" (Dodd, Tanfield Lea).

tail rope – "as the full set began its descent, the leading rope was allowed to go slack and the full weight of the 65 tubs was taken by the tail rope" (Hitchin, 1962, p.109).

Ropes and wires

While ropes (including wire cables) are used in many contexts in a pit, the main winding rope was of critical importance, bearing the responsibility for many men's lives every day. Curiously, the miners themselves objected to having hemp ropes replaced with steel cables: "Their introduction [i.e. of flat wire ropes] in the North of England at the same time [1841], however, was a failure at the first attempt, as the colliers struck, saying they were not prepared to trust themselves to ropes of this material" (*HRCM*, p.173). Ropes of bessemer steel nonetheless came to predominate. Their structure is described as follows:

> The strands are usually laid round a hemp core, made of long fibre Ruasian hemp, or where clips are used, as in haulage, of Manilla hemp, which has a harder fibre and is less liable to deteriorate. This hemp core should be carefully treated with linseed oil or other preservativc, to prevent wasting from internal friction.
>
> (Kerr, *Practical Coal Mining*, 1901, p.191)

bleck – "pitch or tar used on ropes" (Tootle, 1995, N.East).

glinters – "curved sails to guide a rope on to a sheeve" (Wade, South Moor, 1966).

hedgehog – "the strand of a wire rope having, broken is carried along the rope by coming in contact with the sheaves or rollers and forms a ravelled mass or ruffle on the rope which is then said to be hedgehogged" (Nicholson, 1888); "hedgehog – this described the haulage rope after a strand broke and spiralled back along the rope as the tension came out of it" (Sharkey); "hedgehog – if a strand of a wire rope works loose and gets fast, it coils in a mass of wire on the rope. This is a hedgehog on the rope" (Wade, South Moor, 1966); "Hedgehog – occurs on haulage rope when one or more strands of wire are broken and they get fast at some point on roadway. The strands keep coilinq or rolling along the running rope forming a mass of uncoiled strands around the rope. These have to be cut off and the ends of the loose strands of wire knitted back into the rope [spliced]" (McBurnie, Washington, 1970s).

kink – "a twist in a coil of rope that would damage it if pulled tight" (Wade, South Moor, 1966).

ropemen – "men who repair and maintain rope haulages" (Riley, Blyth).

rowla – "roller supporting and guiding haulage rope" (Dodd, Tanfield Lea).

tarry-tout – "hemp rope tarred for use in wet conditions" (McBurnie, Washington, 1970s) "the old way of making haulage ropes and probably early winding ropes was to use a central core of hemp. Frequent oiling while in use gave it the tarry quality. I remember on Guy Fawkes night an adult might use a piece of tarry towt with one end of it smouldering, to light the fireworks" (Sharkey); "tarry towt: fibre strand in centre of a wire cable, acting as core, and lubricating the five surrounding strands of wire, e.g. when cable is flexed" (Orr, 2005); "tarry towt – a tarry rope" (Wade, South Moor, 1966); "could mak a meal of a piece of tarry towt n a tin o pease" (Hill, New Silksworth).

tar-ree-wagger – "old rope that is soaked in creosote" (Sterling, H'pool).

Chapter 12: Automation

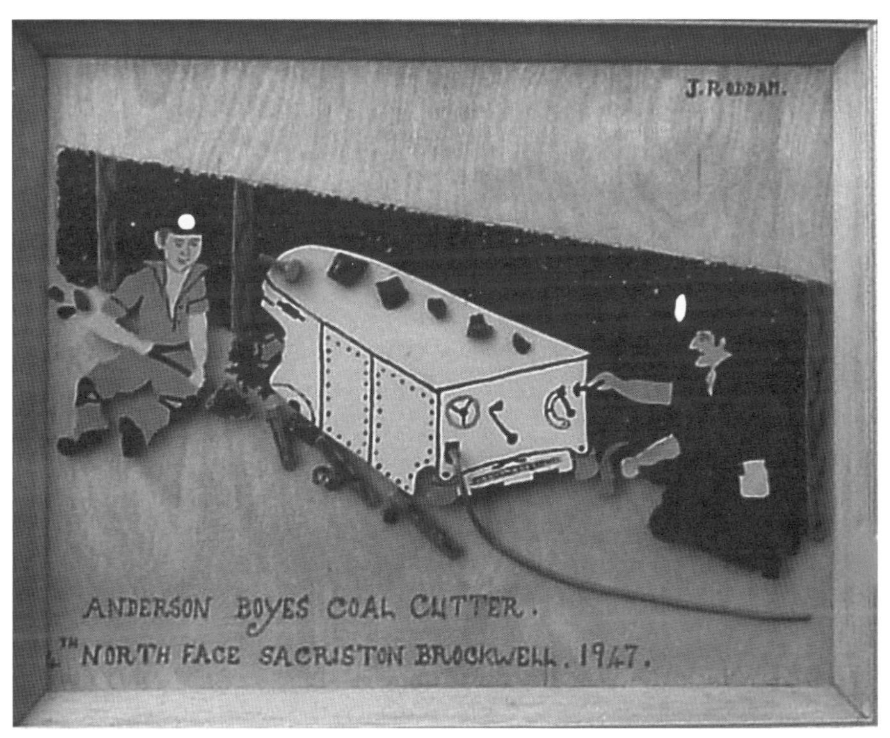

Automated cutting

This is associated with longwall mining, originally a manual operation but well suited to machine assistance because of the length of the coal-face. The process was not entirely automatic – first machines undercut the coal only (still called kerving). These disc-cutters were developed in the 1920s (*HRCM*, ch.5). If the coal did not fall under its own weight then explosives were used: "In some situations coal was undercut and shot-fired after drilling depending on hardness of coal for hewers to load onto conveyor after breaking up with compressed air 'windy picks'" (Jackson, Dawdon) Conveyor belts carried the cut coal to the mothergate for transfer to transport towards the shaft.

> The pit worked longwall faces which were up to 200 yards long and between 2 and 3 feet high. The cycle of work followed this pattern. The coal cutter and his marra would cut the face. This was done with an Anderson-Boyce cutter and removed a slice of coal from bottom of the face along its entire length to a depth of 4–5 feet. Next the driller would drill holes at intervals along the face: these would be charged with powder and the face 'fired' which would bring all the coal down in manageable size pieces. The fillers would then load the coal onto the face conveyor which ran the full length of the face This was done by hand using pan shovels ('shulls') – these were round and came in two sizes: coal shovels and stone shovels, the former much larger than the latter. Each filler was responsible for clearing his own stretch of the face which was known as a 'stint' and had to timber the roof as he went. The final shift of the day would see the bumpers come in and move the conveyor forward ready for the fitters. They would also draw out the timber from the goaf to allow the unsupported roof behind the face to fall.
>
> (Norman Wilson, North Walbottle Colliery)

Longwall face can be 'advancing' into relatively unproved seam/area…or retreating, where much of the cost of development has already been expended (Jackson, Dawdon). In advancing longwall, special attention was needed to advance and maintain the two side passages (mothergate and tailgate) which acted in effect like the 'nicking' in bord and pillar work.

> Bord and pillar mining is not particularly suitable for mining coal at very great depths, because of the size of pillars that have to be left. The main alternative is longwall mining, which has been practised for many years in the deep European mines, particularly in the United Kingdom and West Germany.
>
> (www.competition-commission.org.uk)

> In long-wall mining two galleries, called gates, are driven a distance apart in the same seam of coal and then joined by driving a gallery between them. This joining gallery exposes a wall of coal which becomes the coal face. On advancing long-wall face, the coal is extracted from the face and the two gates are advanced in line with the face. The face is

> ventilated by a current of air passing down the 'main gate', along the face and out of the tail gate. The main gate is sometimes referred to as the 'mother gate'.
>
> (Temple, 1994 p.14)

Fully automatic cutters, rotating drums (adjusted to the thickness of the seam) that brought down the coal in one sweep, were known as power loaders or shearers, working in combination with an Armoured Face Conveyor (AFC) to bring the coal to the mothergate.

> Longwall faces were faces moving forwards 3 or 4 feet per cut along a two hundred yard length... The whole face moved forward over 24 hours with coal cutting usually at night....some well organised faces could double manpower/shifts with 2 shifts of all activities including cutting.... and get 2 advances a day...but if anything went wrong it was costly to divert manpower elsewhere!
>
> (Kenn Johnson, Dawdon)

A.B. Meco-Moore – "The first genuine cutter-loader machine developed to perform two operations simultaneously on a longwall face and therefore do away for any need for blasting. First introduced into British mines in about 1934" (Tootle, 1995).

AFC (Armoured face conveyor) – "originally, armoured *flexible* conveyor, used in the North East in combination with coal-ploughs from Germany" (Sharkey); "it replaced the belt conveyor [at the face]... It consists of a series of steel 'pans', bolted together in sections, with loosely fitting 'pan bolts' that allowed the sections to be flexible. The parts act as guides for two parallel, continuous chains, that are threaded through the pans, over a driving sprocket at each end and back under the pans. The sprockets are driven by an electric motor in the maingate, sometimes assited by a tailgate motor. Steel bars known as flight bars are fitted between the two parallel chains. These flight bars scrape the coal along the pans and into the main gate, where the coal is discharged onto the main gate conveyor belt" (Temple, 1994, p.16); "the armoured face conveyor has three functions: it provides the track along which the power loader generally runs; it conveys the coal cut by the shearer to the main gate at the end of the face; and it serves as an anchor for the powered roof supports when they are advanced" www.competition-commission.org.uk; "The AFC was developed in Germany and by the sixties they were being installed on all the major longwall faces in Britain" (Tootle, 1995); "The AFC is used on a 'prop free front' and by using horizontal hydraulic 'rams' can be advanced (snaked over) as the machine progresses along the face thereby preparing the face for the machine's immediate return run" (Tootle, 1995); "It's AFC's and shearers that cut and load the coal" (J. Moreland, Dawdon, 1980); "[the AFC] runs the whole length of the face and consists of a steel trough built in sections. Steel flights within the trough, pulled by an endless chain or chains, drag the coal along the trough to the end of the coal face where it is taken away by conveyors" (www.competition-commission.org.uk).

Anderton shearer-loader – "an adaptation of the Anderton longwall cutter in which the jib of the cutter has been replaced by a shearer drum… Later models [1963] were capable of cutting coal in both directions and became 'bi-directional', and were called 'bi-di's' by the men" (Tootle, 1995); "designed to be mounted on the AFC and used the AFC as a track on which to traverse the face" (Sharkey).

arcwall cutter – an adaptation of the chain cutter to bord and pillar conditions. It operated on wheels on a rail along the coal face. At the banjo end (see next entry) it could be converted from a horizontal to a vertical cut (after Sharkey).

banjo end – the location on a cutting machine of the mechanism for transmitting power to a cutting chain (after Sharkey).

bottom cut – "the cut made by a coal-cutting machine at the base of the coal seam prior to the coal being drilled and fired" (Tootle, 1995).

brow edge support – "usually the inclined support legs and cross beam set against the face of the canch after it had been advanced in preparation for the next cycle of work" (Sharkey).

bumpers – "miners involved in the moving forward of the face conveyor belt on a daily basis" (Wilson, North Walbottle). See also pullers.

central gate – "long-wall extraction was sometimes arranged in such a way that two faces would share a single main gate and in this method the main gate was called the 'central gate'" (Temple, 1994, p.14).

chock fitter – "The man in charge of maintaining the coal face hydraulic support system. Sometimes called a 'Dowty fitter' (Dowty, manufacturers of hydraulic roof supports)" (Tootle, 1995).

codger – "rear box and roller at tail end of a longwall face around which the conveyor belt makes its return run" (McBurnie, Washington, 1970s); "return end of coveyor belt in pit" (Houghton). See also tension end.

curvings – "coal cutter would undercut coal on opposite side to face producing (painful to crawl through) curvings re coal chippings… the coal may then be spragged with wedges to prevent immediate collapse of undercut coal" (Johnson, Dawdon).

cutter – "name given to several different types of coal cutting machines, e.g. Disc, Bar, Chain, Percussive, Longwall, Shortwall and Universal." Also "The name for the operator of these machines" (Tootle, 1995); kutta – "coal cutter" (Dodd, Tanfield Lea).

cutter-loaders – "The first cutter-loaders came into use in the 1930s with introduction of the 'Meco-Moore' Cutter-Loader by the Mining Engineering Company, of Worcester… In 1943 the first Anderson Boyes version of the 'Meco-Moore' was in production, and by 1948, 165 machines were installed. The 'Meco-Moore' ceased to be used in 1966. The main draw back of all cutter-loaders was that they created a large amount of dust when cutting coal, this was over-come by water spray units fitted to the machines. They also produced a large percentage of small coal but with the improvement in coal preparation and the ability of the power stations to burn very fine coal this ceased to be a detriment" (Tootle, 1995).

Dosco – road header, etc. "Dosco's early successes were linked to the mechanisation of the coal industry.... Dosco has an extensive range of machines, ranging from the 17 tonne Dintheader and 18 tonne Dosco Webster Bucket Cutter Loader through to the 120 tonne TB2500 a 2 x 250kW twin boom machine for production applications" (www.dosco.co.uk).

Dowty prop – hyadraulic prop by Dowty Mining Equipment, in common use by mid 1950s. See ch.4 'maintenance'.

face-end work – "In 1968 90% of coal output was 'cutter-loaded'. At each end of the face a stable had to be cut in advance of the face to provide a profile for the machine to begin the next cutting run. Much of the work of cutting these stables was done by hand, which reduced the benefits of mechanisation" (Tootle, 1995); "a problem eliminated with further mechanisation" (Sharkey).

flit – "to move a coal cutting machine from one place to another under its own power" (Tootle, 1995). [Dialect: 'flit' – to move abode.]

forepoles – "usually a pair of cantilever girders mounted in brackets attached to the last two or three rings and which projected beyond the last ring to support the roof between the last ring and the face of the canch" (Sharkey).

hand-filled – "to fill coal using a shovel on to a face conveyor as opposed to machine-loading" (Tootle, 1995).

jib – extension of the cutter that supports and guides the cutting chain; "a projecting arm or jib carrying an endless chain, the links of which are armed with cutters" (*HRCM*, p.69).

kansh – "All the while the gates were being kannshed… heightened and in the case of the mothergate an armoured tunnel was constantly over the conveyor so that stoneworker activity did not degrade or prevent coal-getting" (Jackson, Dawdon).

kerf – "the cut under the coal in mechanical coal-cutting" (Tootle, 1995).

kongt – "machine failed" (Dodd, Tanfield Lea).

mothergate – "there are two headings/roadways... the mothergate has a conveyor system carrying the coal outbye to a loading point or other means of carrying coal via main roadways to shaft. The mothergate also has (usually) a rail track for material haulage and has cables hanging on the arches leading to the face electrical (FLP = flameproof) transformer. The mothergate is usually of larger steel arches and girth than the other roadway the tailgate. Mothergate also equals air intake" (Jackson, Dawdon).

neuk – "the extreme ends of the coal face; in the first phase of mechanisation" (Douglass, 1973).

open end – "when the 'gates' at either end of a longwall face are driven in advance, the coal exposed at either end of the face is the open end" (Tootle, 1995).

pans – "originally 'shakerpans', which were used on longwall faces to move the coal. The name was extended at a later date to include bluebird scrapers and panzer face conveyors. [Also] iron troughs bolted together and used in steep inclined seams. The coal was allowed to flow down under its own gravity" (Tootle, 1995).

panzer – "a chain conveyor, armoured flexible conveyor, AFC" (Riley, Blyth) [Gm for tank].

power loader – "the coal is cut by a machine called a power loader which travels along the coalface normally on top of an armoured face conveyor (AFC)... The cutting element of a power loader consists of a rotating drum fitted with hard metal tipped picks. As the machine moves along the coal face it cuts into the coal which is then loaded on to the AFC by the action of the rotating drum" (www.competition-commission.org.uk).

pullers, pulling and **to pull** – "these were the guys who went on to the longwall face after the fillers had 'cleaned it off' and moved the face conveyor forward into a new track. They then moved the chocks systematically forward, withdrawing the other timbers as they progressed through the face. This allowed the goaf to collapse. The end result of all this activity was that the face had advaced the equivalent of a 'cut' which was 4.5 to 5.0 feet usually. The face was then ready to be cut" (Sharkey, swD'm); pulla – "man moving supports to support face" (Dodd, Tanfield Lea).

riving and chewing – "tearing and pulling (coal)" (Briscoe, 2003).

scufflings, scuffler – "the stuff that was produced by the cutting machine as it cut (usually at the base of the seam) across the face. The 'scuffler' was the poor soul who worked close behind the machine clearing the scufflings from the jib and helping to prevent the material from being carried back into the cut. One of his jobs was to install supports (sprags) in the jud to prevent the coal from spalling over and to keep the undercut clear. The purpose of cutting was to provide a 'free face' for the explosives to do their work later" (Sharkey).

shearer – "the shearer extracts coal from the seam by means of a revolving drum, to which is attached a series of tungsten steel picks. The picks are so arranged on the drum as to follow the path of a helix, with the effect that coal is 'screwed' onto the AFC" (Temple, 1994, p. 17); "the physical extraction of the coal at the longwall face is carried out by a power loader. The type most frequently used today to cut and load the coal is the shearer, which essentially involves a rotating drum fitted with hard metal tipped picks that break the coal from the coal face and vanes that load it on to the AFC" (www.competition-commission.org.uk).

spalling – "In modern mechanised mining, cleat is unimportant when laying out a mine for coal production. But it still has importance when entries are driven approximately 'on end', i.e. headways, because the sides of the entries are parallel to the cleat and spalling [shedding] of the sides can occur; the opening becomes wider and roof support may become critical. In the old, hand-got days the headings were driven narrow because of the difficulty in mining and consequently any 'spalling' of the sides didn't matter that much because the place was narrow to start with. In mechanised mining it's the amount of equipment to be accommodated and the ventilation requirements that govern the width of the roadway, irrespective of its direction" (Sharkey).

sprags – "also known as 'holing props'. On an undercut longwall face, one of the scuffler's jobs was to set the sprags in the cut so as to prevent the undercut coal from collapsing before it could be brought down with explosives. The sprags in this case were almost any piece of wood that was available to him as he followed the cutting machine along the face. The kerf left by a cutting machine was usually about 6 inches high, so props, chockwood or planks all served as sprags" (Sharkey).

stage loader – the tranfer point between the face conveyor and the mothergate conveyor.

tailgate – "air return and main material (props/ straps/ timbers/ chocks, etc.) supply route via rail tracks and latterly by wheeled all-terrain vehicles" (Johnson, Dawdon).

tension end – "hewn/loaded coal would move along the face on the conveyor from 'tension end' [tailgate] to 'codger end' [mothergate] where it tumbled on to a series of conveyors going outbye along the mother gate" (Johnson, Dawdon).

The Stoneman's Song

Johnny Handle wrote this in 1958 at the insistence of a stoneman, one of the 'forgotten race' of mine-workers, who promised him a pint for a song or else...

Now the coal is off and the fillers have left the flat
And the deppity comes and he asks we what we're at
So we tell him and he stems the holes we've drilled
And the shots gan off and the packs we build
Doon the Brockwell seam in the North off Number Five West.

Now we build packs from the stones that's in the gate,
And we get them neat and tidy weel afore bait.
For there's girders to <u>hump</u> and girders to set, — move forward
And <u>side</u> to take off that aa dor bet; — extra stone
Doon the Brockwell seam in the North off Number Five West.

So the belt is rolled and set down in the new tracks,
And we draw oot the chocks while lyin' on wer backs,
And we set them again in their new place,
Te stop the weightin' on the face;
Doon the Brockwell seam in the North off Number Five West.

Now aa'm alreet the morn for a sup, aa knaa,
For me marra's reckonned up that he's won the snaabaal draw. accumulating lottery
With a hoosey card and a pint in me hand
Aa'l forget aboot that no-man's land,
Doon the Brockwell seam in the North off Number Five West.

(Johnny Handle)

The song describes the advancing of the mothergate/tailgate as part of the longwall cutting process: "the arched girders are brought in on a tram along the rolleyway and bolted into place... If the shot holes have not been put in the right place, there may be more stone ('side') to remove, with picks and mells to enable the girders to fit... the rubber conveyor belt is dismantled at the joints, rolled up, and rolled back along the new space left by the extracted coal; metal rollers to support the belt are moved forward" (Johnny Handle).

The electrical side

bat end – "panel end of an electric cable" (Ho'ton, C20).
gate end box – "an electric panel used to control and distribute power to face machinery" (Riley, Blyth).
jonker – "coupling box for electric cables" (Ho'ton, C20).
lektric – "electric" (Dodd, Tanfield Lea).
lektrician – "it's fitters and 'lectricians maintain the cold steel grey" (J. Moreland, Dawdon, 1980).
pommel – "the end of a trailing cable designed to fit into a machine or a switchbox" (Sharkey).
switches – "a bank of electrical panels".

The Pit 'lectrician

The Switch is tripped – and the Cutter's stuck,
the Cuttermen's mad and curse their luck;
the cry goes out for that magician,
the poor and slighted pit 'lectrician.

So 'Sparks' is hunted until he's found,
in his little workshop underground;
turns from the vice with a stifled sob,
he's working hard on a Government job.

He packs his bag and fixes his lamp,
and for half a mile he has to tramp:
a dirty track – he staggers along
and cheers himself with a little song.

He inspects the switch along the road,
and sees it had tripped on overload;
he pulls the plug from out the socket,
locks flap, and puts key in his pocket.

"How-way" the cuttermen shout unseen,
the deputy says – "where hae yi been?"
but 'Sparks' just gets right on with his tests,
ignores these stupid untimely jests.

He twists and groans to remove the plug,
his end's O.K. – oh he's no mug;
says in a voice that's very bitter,
"This is a job for Harry the fitter."

The overman comes with face all sweat,
says "have you not got this job right yet?"
hurts his toe as he kicks the cutter,
what he says then – I wouldn't utter.

Harry arrives with his bag of gear
he takes off the lid and says – "Oh! dear,
we'll have to send her up for repairs
she's all to bits – and we've got no spares."

He 'phones out for The Commando boys,
they handle these cutters just like toys;
are all strong men – with hairy chests,
brim full of pop through vigorous tests.

Within an hour – and at the double,
bringing new cutter with little trouble.
Out with the old one, in with the new,
that's the way these Commandos do.

'Sparks', he soon fixes the cable plugs
the pick-chain starts with easy chug-chugs;
then into the cut with awful rows,
there's just time to finish the place 'for lowse.

The Commandos run back to report,
for the boys just treat these jobs like sport;
'Sparks' and Harry, all grime and grease,
envy the Cuttermen on bi the 'piece'.

The overman now that things are right
is whistling a tune with heart so light;
his spirits have surely been reborn
for he knows the Flag will fly the morn.

(Robert Straughan, March 1947)

Comment

Typical of a pit electrician and fitter saying it's each others job and typical of an overman kicking a machine (I've done that loads of times...but it's ok when you wear 'steelies').

The 'plug' he speaks about is the 'electric cable end' which goes into the cutter (cutters are now called shearers, doscos, dinters & Norse miners). In the days of that poem (1947) a 'cutter' was used to take a slice of coal out of the bottom about 12" thick then you drilled holes in the coal above to insert explosives (my job in the late 70's on some 'headings').

When the shot was fired, the gap at the bottom which the cutter removed acted as a "free face" so the coal would just drop rather than explode outwards which would happen if there was no cut or free face.

(Norman Conn, Seaham)

Conveyor belts

Associated with automatic hewing, a system of conveyor belts carried coal from the working face to a sump near the shaft under continuous power. First introduced in 1902, when the coals would be cast on by hand, conveyor belts were particularly useful in thin seams with a limited vertical working space. They became the essential accompaniment to automatic coal cutters (i.e. to keep pace with them): an AFC (see section on automated hewing) running across the face would deposit coal onto a belt to begin its journey outbye. And farewell to the pit pony.

belt conveyor – "A moving endless belt, from 18 ins. to more than 6 ft. wide, on which coal was carried. A series of conveyors [in sequence] would be used to carry coal from the face to the shaft or in some cases up a 'drift' to the surface. It was driven by a drum to which it returns after passing around a tail pulley. Belt conveyors could vary in length from a few yards to over a mile" (Tootle, 1995); "When the coal cutter reached one end of the face the undercut coal was hewn/ filled onto either a bottom belt (lower layer of large rubber band) or top belt (very unusual but we had this at 10 North Maudlin) or an armoured all metal conveyor, nicknamed 'Beien' (after early German manufacturer, but usually 'Huwood of Team Valley'). This took the form of a large metal rung/ chain stile/ ladder constantly moving horizontally… but you could lose a leg trying an illicit ride on that beggar!!" (Johnson, Dawdon).

clip – "flexible metal 'zip' used to join sections of belt together" (Charlton, Dawdon).

cable belt conveyor – "a heavy-duty, high capacity, conveyor belt which uses two stranded steel ropes, one on either side of the belt to provide tensile pull. Moulded rubber shoes along the edge of the belt grip the steel ropes, which support the belt and provide the motive power. Cable belt conveyers can carry coal up steeply inclined roadways for long distances" (Tootle, 1995). Fire susceptible belting was replaced in the 1950s by PVC belting.

Lastly, if conveyor belts seem the last word inlabour-saving autmoation: "Any large timber or machine parts that couldn't be transported on the conveyors would be pulled in by ponies" (Wilson, Walbottle).

Paddies mail

In contradistinction to the above, we may note "Paddy's Mail – man-riding train" (Moreland, 1980); "a set of steel plate carriages, for man riding, pulled back and forth by main and tail engine… at Dawdon this went inbye about two miles from shaft to east end of Hutton seam" (Johnson, Dawdon); alias "man-set – mine cars for transporting men underground" (Temple, 1994, pp.19–20); "manriding set – an underground passenger train. One version of it has [rows] of seats facing outwards… the other is like a big dipper train having room for perhaps four or six men, and pulled by a loco" (Douglass, 1973).

Bad Geordie

It got me in a bit trouble, this one, and I never knew why. It was only an ordinary sort of joke, the sort of thing a hewer would play when he'd finished drawing on the notices or hoying bits coal at another's back and feigning innocence, or standin' round discussin' how we allus tak the wrang turn and end up on a work-face so dorty and dusty when visitors always arrive at the neat, clean dust-free example that seems almost reserved for them – little notions a face-worker'd get when he was bored, that is. Like I was. So I devised this plan of upsetting the gaffor. Which is what it's all about. There was all these rules about pitmen travelling on special man-riding trains and pitmen not travelling on the coal-bearing belts; which is OK but sometime you feel like a change, and a month or so back they'd fired someone for taking a short-cut on the belt when he'd missed a proper train. Well that wasn't fair, we thought. Rules is rules, and if they didn't get brokken, there would nae point makkin' them in the first place.

Anyway, we knew they was keeping their eyes out for anyone infringing their precious man-riding rules, so I got up this dummy, just a set spare orange overalls, stuffed with newspaper and wood, and a plastic bottle for a head, and some goggles and a helmet. Stupid-looking thing, but I put it on the coal-belt anyways, and then as it rattled off into the distance, I waited a bit, and then I whizzed the handle and phoned through a warning that this rule-breaking maniac was on his way, doing stunts on the coal-belt, and they'd likely catch him coming in any minute now, and oughta give him what-fettle for risking the safety of us all with such a bad example, just for showing off like. I made it sound right virtuous, like, a sort of genuine bit grievance, not a bit tattle that wasn't true or what, so they'd be sure to check up.

Mebbies I overdid it, for instead of waiting for the belt to hoy my man out into their hands, or tumble tragically into the staple where all the lost coal lies in its low-level bunker, they pulled the switches that stopped the belts altogether, and deputy and overman and under-manager strode forth in person to accost the wrong-doer where he stood, or lay. I hadn't thought they could trace the phone below, but mebbies they just waited till they spotted the gadgie on the conveyor and pulled the plug then. I saw the belt stop, in-bye where I was; so I thought a minute, and changed over with someone working the next stretch, to distance myself from the belt and the phone. In case there was trouble.

Was there trouble! They were so evil to the hewers next the belt I had to come forward mysell and rescue them; 'What's amiss here?' I asked (knowing full well). 'Some idiot playing pranks on the belt – you was it?' 'What prank, like?' 'A dummy, I guess, but it's caused that end trouble, you'd better own up if it's you, or there'll be a shift of you laid idle, I reckon, just to sort it out.' 'No need for that sort of talk (sez my marrers). No one round here knows aught about a dummy.' And this was where I stepped in: 'I did see summat; a man, riding up on the belt; and I reported it like I'm supposed to; only I didn't say naught to the others, in case they thought I was telling tales, ye knaw.' 'Don't you play innocent with me; it was a mock-up, a dummy, you could surely tell that; and it's caused a vast o' trouble, I can tell you.' Well, I didn't look guilty for I never said I had made the model, I just said it was me saw it moving up in the distance and phoned, and that I thought it really was a man and a dangerous act altogether. I was just as much a victim of the hoaxer as onyone else, I insisted. But I was summoned to the manager's office thereafter, just the same, which was unusual, and I didn't think it very sporting of them at aal, mind.

It went something like this. 'Your model, was it?' 'What model?' 'The dummy on the belt.' 'I never saw a dummy, I thought I saw a man.' 'So what was its head made of?' 'Heed?' 'Thing under its helmet, you fool.' 'No, I meant, head. That what its head was made of.' 'Am I stupid?' 'Nae, it's me that's aggrieved to be thought a fiul, for I never would a reported what I thought was a breach o' rules if it led to all this.' (I sez, trying to restore a little dignity to the occasion.) Fool, indeed. 'Alright, I'll not say you made it, but what did it look as though it was made of?' 'Made of? As I reckon'd, it was a man in an orange outfit, one of us, ridin' on the belt. It could have been sitting, or lying doon, now I recall. And it turns out it's a dummy, and ye've seen it, so ye'll knaw what it's made of yersells.' 'Do you want your job?' 'Do I get ma one free call to the union?' 'Don't play games; there's summat very wrong, and if you don't co-operate with us, well, I can't help you.' 'Do I remember asking you to help me?' 'You saw nothing odd about it?' 'I on'y ever saw it in the distance, ye knaw. I wish I hadn't now. I wish I hadn't said a thing about it.' I was quite aggrieved, you'll understand, for their benefit. And that was that. It wasn't my affair, I told them, and I couldn't supply any details at all.

I didn't find out why they were so worried till a day or two later. It seemed some under-manager had been on hand, and decided to investigate the call, come up to the figure on the belt, took hold of it, shook it, its helmet come off, 'heed' an aal, an rowled a good way ower the coals. Then he sort of gasped and collapsed – the undermanager that is – and had to be took to hospital. Heart trouble. 'That must ha' been some scary dummy ye made there, man,' my marra said to me, but I shushed him on the matter; naught to do with me. But I thought I had to show a bit concern. So I made a point of going up to the deputy, who was there as well, as I'd heard, and telled him I was sorry to have made a call that caused such trouble and asked him what had upset the boss so? He may have knawn I was taking the piss or not, but he must've been keen to knaw mare hissell, for he telled me a bit, to get summat out of me in return, I'd guess. According to him, they'd soon enough come up to this figure on the belt, stopped in its motion like the coal it was sitting on, for they was all agreed the body was deed still, just like a puppet, which it was by the way. Only they didn't see that at first, but the under-manager went straight up the body, pulled it round to face him – either to have a yell or check it was OK – could have been either – the deputy wasn't that close – but he could tell he was fashed about something – and then when the body swung round, it was almost as though the thing lowped up at him – an then the helmet fell reet away, and the under–manager gollered something terrible and collapsed. Thought he'd shook his head off or killed the poor bugger, seem'ly. 'Scary was it, then, this heed?' I asked. 'No', he replied, 'when I picked it up all I found was an empty orange-bottle wi' a big friendly orange on its label, and some clumsy goggles, wouldn't fool anyone.' ''xeptin a fiul.' 'Don't jape on about it; it was bad enough a notion to send one man to hospital, seemingly.' 'Now haud on, did you see auht scary?' 'I just telled you, no.' 'Then I think I'm owed an apology. I did the proper thing, and get telled I'll be sacked, and all along it's just some hyper yuppy gettin' hissell aal shocked at my expense! That's a union matter if ever anything was!' But of course I never did mak a fuss. The under-manager had only himelf to blame for what he saw, unless Bad Geordie was makkin one o' his rare appearances, as a warnin' like…

It was a notion I did not share wi' the others, tho mebbies I should of, for the whole belt bust up a day or two later and varnigh killed two men. Then there was that to worry about, and naebody said any mare about the dummy trav'lor.

Chapter 13: Safety & health

Precautions and rescue

While major explosions dominated press coverage and public attention, everyday accidents that merited little reporting took a greater toll of pitmen's lives. From 1850 to 1900 an average 1,000 pitmen per year were killed in such small-scale fatal accidents (Benson, 1989, p.37).

The issue of mine safety was of vital importance to pitmen and pit owners alike, if for slightly different reasons; yet good intentions did not always work out. Refuge holes, designed to shelter workers while sets of tubs passed, were found used for storing wood, or fouled as toilets (Benson, 1989, p.34). The increased use of Davy lamps led in some cases to an unfortunate relaxation of ventilation precautions (*HRCM*, ch.8). The use of gunpowder to bring coal down from the 1830s on, which made the hewer's job easier and boosted coal production, was in turn a major factor in an increased number of explosions (*HRCM*, ch.8). Hewers often adopted their own defence strategy – absenteeism, as perhaps the only way a worker could sustain mind and body in view of the hardships of the job (Benson, 1989, p.59).

Mine owners had the capacity to enforce safety precautions, but not the obligation – as shown here from the yearly bonds of 1869:

> It shall be competent for the owner or viewers of the said colliery to prevent the use of gunpowder, either wholly or in part, at his or their discretion; and to introduce and enforce the use of the Safety Lamp...
>
> (D/Lo/B/265)

In fact, naked candles continued in use long after this, in parts of the mine not considered at risk from gas.

Respirators in the nineteenth century comprised little more than a mask fitted with a wetted sponge – no use against carbon monoxide. Breathing apparatus was more effective: a smoke helmet was a device supplied with air pumped down a long tube. An early version of a self-contained breathing apparatus comprised a large bladder or goat skin filled with air. From the mid-nineteenth century on, oxygen under pressure was available in portable cylinders; after the Seaham disaster of 1880, higher pressure oxygen in copper cylinders was developed. In 1907 a great improvement was made when liquid air replaced compressed oxygen in these reservoirs (*HRCM*, ch.19).

> In an explosion most of the available oxygen in the area is quickly used up, producing CO^2 and the chemical reaction continues with the reduced oxygen combining with the carbon to produce CO. Many more men lost their lives due to the CO in the air than through the initial explosion. Self rescuers, developed in the late 50's/early 60's were designed to filter the CO from the air that a man was breathing while trying to escape.
>
> (Tony Sharkey)

One simple precaution – when tokens were no longer a measure of work done – was their issue as part of the safety check process:

> Time office – underground worker would collect 2 tokens (one brass, 1 silver) – both with his own unique number on – then to lamp cabin for self-respirator and lamp (deputy gets special safety lamp) – then to shaft where hand in silver token to banksman, who shot it by compressed air to the time office, where hung on a board. Brass tally stays with miner during shift. When shift over, the worker hands in brass tally to banksman who sends it to time office where it is placed on top of the silver token, so easy to see if anyone missing.
>
> (Steve Barnett , Seaham)

A general government duty to regulate for mine safety became an increasing feature of the last quarter of the nineteenth century, e.g. an effective mines inspectorate; yet progress was alarmingly slow. It was not until 1902 that the first rescue station was established, in Yorkshire. In 1914 it was required there should be a rescue station within 10 miles' reach of every colliery, linked to them by phone, and manned 24 hours a day. There would also be stationed a fire engine in case of surface fires. This meant at last that there could be prompt reaction to any disaster by trained crew (some full-time, some part-time) with appropriate apparatus – whereas previously the miners of each colliery had to cope as best they could by themselves (*HRCM*, ch.16). For good coverage of rescue issues go to: www.healeyhero.co.uk/rescue/menu.htm.

Rescue Training

Did you just decide you wanted to be in fire rescue or were you picked out?

No, chosen. The undermanager approached us; Mr. Fletcher. The only thing that we got out of it, we got a shift away from the pit for which we got paid, and our traveling expenses and meals; expenses for our meals. But we trained with a full dress on as we call it and that – apparatus. And there was the smoky conditions, then there was the low conditions. They had a wooden dummy there on a wooden framework for a stretcher, Frankenstein as I called it, bah what a blinkin' weight it was. It was soaked 'cos the gallery was underneath the tennis court i' the fire station.

We would either have this body to rescue from behind a fall or would be building 'stoppings' as we call them, but the stones that we had there, why they were round stones you seen the stones that's lying about on the land and that… And there was the pack, the dress itself, and when it was filled it was 42 lb in weight. Now the tubes, 'cos you had your pack on the back; the marrow [partner] of that was a box filled with caustic soda, and on the front you had your breathing bag. Now, the air come away from there round all these tubes before it come to your mouth. Now seemly the length of those brass tubes was the same length as what your breathing tubes are in the human body and the idea of that was that by the time it got to you it was of the temperature you'd normally be breathing outside because if you breathed straight from the pack it froze your lungs. See it was liquid.

It was hot cold water. If you put your fingers in it or caught any on our fingers, if you left your hand too long on the bottle [you got a burn]; yet you had to fill it with a glove on or your hand would freeze. And the bottle was shaped like that. And I've just forgotten now how many pounds of that we used to put in her. I don't know whether it was fourteen or not.

It must have been very cumbersome having all this equipment on after being used to be just working in next-to-nothing.

Why, there's the pack would be about that thick, and then there was your breathing bag would be about like that and it was in the leather case – why that was on the front of you, and you imagine, there's one of the seams was that high that we're in, the other one was a bit higher, so it will give you an idea what -- you hadn't much room for to sort of manoeuvre inside. See, if they were working through a fall, why they'd make as small a hole as they possibly could but big enough for them to get through, see, and that's where the danger used to be at times.

(Henry Richardson, Beamish, 1983/217)

Oh, you got lectures. Practical and lectures. They had galleries built there just like pit collieries. There was a coke stove lit in the gallery with the fumes in the gallery you know: You had to learn to wear your apparatus which was a oxygen tank and you had to learn how to rescue men and all that in those seams you see. You got lectures. You went there every day for fourteen weeks.

(Mr Younger, Beamish, 1984/246)

Well of course when you were going into the danger zone and that [i.e. after an explosion], you had a length of rope you each kept hold of, and of course the leader, he had one of these little toy motor horns on the apparatus; there was one for stop, two for to go forward or three for to go back, see. And then the man at the back, he had a one and... he'd repeat it, see.

(Henry Richardson, Beamish, 1983/217)

An alarm

So I starts to do my duties, a short cut to the face to get the shots fired, to get the pillars going... when there's a collection of putters and men come on to me, I was on the far face of the district. "Jimmy, there's clouds of smoke coming in." 'Clouds of smoke?' " "Aye, you cannot get to the flat". So I goes and [checks] it. Checks up, are you all here? Yes. Always [check] numbers, straight away. "You, John, you take the back place, I'll lead the way." We take the ponies as far as ever we can, find the place where if they cannot travel, if they are too big we can put them in. So away we started. When I got round this back pillars, they hadn't been travelled for months and months, some had boards on, we had to take them off to get men and boys through, to what was the landing. A few [pillars] down, I says to this lad away with me, ["Get this] stopping down."... "Right oh..." Calls the men, "fetch the ponies through here..." I says "Tommy don't come in here lad, landing's clear, nobody there." Goes away from the landing to the drivers' flat. There was a bit of a hill to go up and down, the ponies could only pull two tubs at a time, and they were the biggest ponies we had in the mine, them drivers. When we got over the breast of the hill, oh there was a fire a'blazing, and the two boys were sitting there keeping them fires blazing. Well the first thing I did, we'd just reached the choppy box, the water cistern, I emptied the water straight down on them, I said "Lads, you know what you've done wrong? What's the meaning of it?" "Oh, we're just having a bit clart on [much about], there's nae baccy so we're not going to work". And that was the most frightening experience of my life in the mine.

('Jimmy and others', Beamish, 1974/48)

Injury and illness

Underground workers – even the youngest – might expect a number of injuries during their working life, as reflected in the uneasy saying "he's getten his lames." A common injury might be a fractured limb, which could only be set and rested. While the miner was healing up, the mine owner neither wished to lose his long-term labour nor pay unduly for someone not to work. 'Smart money' was therefore paid, at a modest level, on the understanding it would be later deducted from wages.

More seriously, the loss of a limb might leave a miner only fit for light surface work, or unable to work at all. Some support might be gained via the Poor Laws in the nineteenth century, but the emphasis was on self-sufficiency. This too was part of the pitman's creed – "...the belief that if they only kept going most weaknesses [illnesses, etc.] would 'backen themselves', as they said" (Grice, 1960, ch.17).

When miners were killed in explosions, a public subscription was surely mounted to help care for widows and orphans. However, the resulting Trust was sparing in its payments, and widows were basically expected to work and maintain themselves. True, miners would have a collection among themselves to aid the dependents of a comrade killed in an accident, but the issue of insurance became increasingly important to miners.

Private insurance clubs – run by the mine owners – had predictable problems. Friendly Societies, and their offshoot Permanent Relief Funds were more trusted and more effective. Commercial insurance was also available, and by the mid-1890s more than half of English miners were insured with The Prudential (Benson, 1989, p.187). The need for savings against future need was widely appreciated, and despite the miner's reputation for being a rash spender, Trustee Savings Banks and 'Penny Banks' were popular formats.

Work-related illnesses were less obvious, were usually slower to develop, and more difficult (in terms of nineteenth century medical knowledge) to relate to specific causes. Rheumatism was a common occupational disease, while the term 'miner's asthma' covered a range of respiratory illnesses. "Above the age of 40 almost ALL miners are the subjects of chronic bronchitis and asthma" (qu. Benson, 1989, p.45, re 1863). As late as the 1920s the risk of breathing coal and stone dust was scarcely recognised: it was considered that "it is in time all again eliminated" (*HRCM*, ch.18). The sad condition of older mine workers presented by Alexander Barrass was a depressing reality too little appreciated in a time of no state pensions.

In recent years, a clearer insight into the causes of diseases associated with mining has been achieved, and with the winding up of British Coal, ex-miners and their families have been encouraged to submit claims for compensation. A sad, but appropriate ending to the saga of English mining.

From a symposium in Easington, 2006:

ralloused – stiff joints/seized up.

tewed me pluck out – worked hard.

giz a gos – give me a bit of your drink.

pullies – soot/coal dust round eyes.

From Ronald Orange re Bebside (Horton Grange Colliery):

stannin' hacky – in danger: "we're stannin' hacky heor, marra".

bonny on – in difficulty: "we're bonny on heor lads".

haakin' an' coughin' – of miners trying to bring up phlegm.

cowp yer boilie – be sick.

> Of course there was no ambulances in those days either you know. I remember one of my older brothers, he got his leg broken down the mine. He was brought home in what we call the colliery cart… That's what they used to leave the coal in you know.
>
> (J. Agar, Beamish, 1984/253)

anthracosis – "a disease of the lungs caused by the inhalation of coal dust over a long period of time" (Tootle, 1995).

bet – "used for the site of an injury, e.g. bet knee, bet foot" (Wilson, North Walbottle); "rheumatism [i.e.] 'beat hand, beat knee, beat elbow'" (Benson, 1989, p.44); "beat hand or knee – blistered from hard work" (Brian Davidson, Ashington); "beat hand – a hand which, from being blistered with hard work, has festered" (Nicholson, 1888); "sciagma" (Douglass, 1973).

caisson disease – "a disease caused when men remain too long in the pressurised atmosphere which was needed during 'caisson sinking' and returned to surface without going through a decompression process. Also known as the 'bends'" (Tootle, 1995).

dust – "miners' respiratory disease" (Dodd, Tanfield Lea).

fever van – "used for the colliery ambulance transporting injured miners" (swDurham).

kittle – "dangerous or risky" (Tootle 1995).

lamings – "the collier's name for accidents of any description to men or lads working in or about the mine" (Tootle, 1995, N.East).

miner's asthma – pneumoconiosis, from coal dust in lungs (Benson, 1989, p.45).

miner's phthisis or **black spit** – from stone dust in lungs (Benson, 1989, p.45); "black spit – Pneumoconiosis. A disease of the lungs, caused by the inhaling of coal dust. It was not confined to miners, but also afflicted men and women employed on the surface screening plant" (Tootle, 1995).

morphia – "a pain killing injection given after certain serious accidents" (Riley, Blyth).

nystagmus – "rotary oscillation of the eyeballs" (qu. Benson, 1989, p.45) – it involved headaches, giddiness, allergy to light, etc. triggered by returning to daylight after the poor lighting underground; "stag – short for nystagmus which was an eye disease brought on by working in extremely poor light" (Sharkey).

a pneumo – "miner with pneumoconiosis" (J. Moreland, Dawdon, 1980).

skaith – "danger" (Wilson, G'head, 1820s).

skumfish – "lack of air causing illness or death" (Dodd, Tanfield Lea).

spelk – "a splinter of wood that has stuck into the skin" (Wade, South Moor, 1966).

wark – "to work; to ache" (Wilson, G'head, 1820s).

Dust

(Tune: "Blaydon Races")

Ah went te Dawdon Colliery 'twas on the tenth o' June
Nineteen hundred an seventy fower on a summers eftennoon
Ah tuk a bus fra Deneside me heart heavy wi' forebodin'
Neet shift is a lousy shift e'en when yer on Power Loadin'.

Chorus:

Oh! me lads ye shud see 'em gannin
The shears fra the 'retreaters' leave the advancin faces stannin
The way 'em lads flee aboot the'll end up wi thrombosis
An if yen dinna wear yer dust mask ye'll get Pneumoconiosis.

Noo when yer in the night shift yer nivver naw where yer gannin
If yer on the 'miners' they arlways seem to leave 'em stannin
They shuv ye on somebody else's caunch – ye feel it is a snub
'Specially when the fella that shood be there is drinkin i' the Club.

Ah arlways gan fer an X-ray when it comes roond wor way
But ah naw if ah gan what the doctor's ganna say
Yis ye've got the 'dust' me lad – o' that there's definite traces
Yit wor 'Ruler' the Computer says that wi ha' dust approved faces.

Mind we can play won part by seein' te the working of arl sprays
An' that we divvent cut top n' bottom an' the shearer level stays
An' when the dust comes thick an' heavy, divvent stand there chokin
Weer yer dust mask an' ye'll delay that final last cage token.

(Ernie Taylor, Dawdon)

Problems of pressure

These problems have been partly dealt with under 'passages' earlier (see ch.4), but play a particular part in the roll of mine dangers. The pressures from strata above (and below) the open roadway could evidence itself in anything from small trickles of dirt to a roof fall; and explosions would almost inevitably bring with it the blockage of roadways through broken timbers and roof falls, leaving men and boys trapped. The expectation of such events – as in Barrass' 'The Pitman's Dream' was in itself daunting enough – "the dim light given by safety lamps, the machinery moving in the darkness, the feeling that an immense weight of rock threaten to crush in the roof, that poisonous gases or deleterious dust may be present in the air, or that an explosion or inrush of water or outbreak of fire may occur, all contribute to the alarm" (*HRCM*, ch.18).

breaker, brikker – "a fissure produced in the roof of the mine, from the pressure on removing the pillar" (Brockett, Newc, 1820s); "a vertical break in the roof, e.g. immediately adjacent to the side of the entry or roadway" (Sharkey).

creep – "a heaving or bursting upwards of the floor of a coal mine" (Brockett, Newc, 1820s); "the rising up of the thill in excavations in a seam of coal, occasioned by the pillars not being left sufficient, or not having a sufficiently large surface to prevent their being forced into the thill by the superincumbent pressure" (Nicholson, 1888); "floor heave in roadways" (Sharkey).

fall – "a falling down of the roof or stone" (Nicholson, 1888); "a 'fall' – collapse of the roof. Reasons can include, inadequate or no support, incompetent rock, dislodged supports" (Sharkey).

fissle, fistle – "to make a crepitant noise or faint crackling. This takes place in early stages of creep" (Nicholson, 1888).

floor heave – "sometimes called floor lift. Occurs when strata weight is transferred into a soft floor either through the support pillars or consolidated goaf. Sometimes in bord and pillar workings it can occur if places are driven too wide. Can be a serious problem in advancing longwall" (Sharkey).

nip – "the effect produced upon coal pillars by creep; a crush or squeeze" (Nicholson, 1888).

roll – "causes undulation in the floor when floor of seam rises towards the roof" (Sharkey).

shivery – "broken; as shivery post, broken post" (Nicholson, 1888).

spangued out – "a prop forced out by pressure" (Wade, South Moor, 1966).

working – "'working' was an expression used to describe the movement of the strata and the creaking and cracking of wooden supports when strata weight was being redistributed. If the support was inadequate a fall would probably result. Sometimes the 'working' would be accompanied by fine material falling from the roof and this served as a warning of a fall to the miner" (Sharkey); "fyess wawkin – danger of roof collapse" (Dodd, Tanfield Lea).

Roof fall

Yes, we had many hard times at the pit but with God's help we made it. I remember I was working with Tom Whitfield at the coal face – what was called double working – when the roof collapsed on top of the coal tub. We couldn't get out. The timber was cracking and breaking around us and we thought our time had come. We were barred in. All the officials at the pit came to try to get us out and after seven hours they got the tub pulled out far enough for us to get out. What a relief. Not many months after that the pit closed forever. I had teamed up with my brother Ernie and we worked right to the finish of the pit. When we brought our gear out – picks, drills and the worm for drilling – I said that is the last time I'll go down a coal mine again and sure enough I kept my promise. That was 1932.

(Mr Cawson, Kibblesworth, Beamish, 1993/5)

from 'The Pitman's Dream'

...Aw said <u>afore</u>	before
That <u>Aw'd</u> <u>gyen</u> off te bed,	I'd gone
Te de the pitmen's daily snore	
As <u>seun's</u> Aw'd wesh'd an' fed.	soon as
An' not 'till <u>maw</u> last breath Aw draw,	my

'Till kennor's call'd on me belaw,	end of work signal
Will Aw forget the seet Aw saw	sight
I' these few winks Aw hed.	had
Aw thowt Aw'd nearly holed the lift –	finished working on a pillar
Aw'd fill'd a score an' fower –	24 tubs i.e. a day's stint
That kennor'd closed may weary shift	the call to end work
An' Aw wiz given ower;	stopped
When lowk! the gove gans thud! for thud!	excavation… goes
Crack gans the timmor i' maw jud!	timber… work-place
An' though the weel-built chocks were gud,	layered props
The top began te lower!	roof
The bottom heaved, an' myed the way	buckled upward
Unfit for tub te gan on;	
An' then maw led un, truth te say,	spare tub
Wiz brickin where twiz stannin!	was breaking up
Te myek things warse Aw bowlted past	I bolted
The half-full tub, an' stuck hard fast!	
An' there Aw lay te wait the last	
O' the darkest oor that ran on.	hour… approached
Noo, Aw wiz in a sorry plite! –	plight
May such ne mair betide us! -	no more befall
The putter lad had teun his skite;	taken his exit
So'd Broon, thit work'd beside us!	
The deppity, i' leathor hat,	deputy
Wiz lying fyece up at the flat,	face…landing
An' Aw wiz yellin' -- God knaws what –	
I' the jud thit sowt te hide us!	coal section…sought

Bill Broon an’ me work’d back te back;	
An’ oft when at wor bate,	our meal-breaks
We’d had some confidential crack	talk
’Boot chapel things ov late.	
An’ Broon, although when i’ the lift,	?work in ‘broken mine’
He often tried te tyek maw shift,	take
Possess’d the gud man’s special gift –	
The pluck to welcome fate.	
Aw’ve heard him sweer – “Aw wadn’t fear,	swear
The darkest deeth cud meet us:	death (that) could
For when Aw put maw picks up here,	i.e. finish with
The lads at bank ’ill greet us.	up above i.e. Heaven
Why, man alive,” Aw’ve heard him say,	
“What is thor here to pleese or play?	
Or whe’s the man can put away	who’s
The end the mun defeat us?	that must
“Thor’s nowt for huz but ploddin on	there’s nothing for us
Throo all thit Heavin may send us;	
Te use the oors weel one by one,	hours well
Till that one comes shall end us.	
An’ if we de the best we can,	do
And act as brothers man te man,	
Till we’ve trod throo life’s little span,	
Then Heavin ’ill sure defend us!”	
Aal this, of course, wiz very nice:	
But here, amang the styens,	among the stones
Aw thowt far less o’ his advice	
Th[a]n maw poor achin byens.	bones

An' then maw canny wife at hyem!	lovely... home
An' then, the bairn thit bore maw nyem!	child... my name
An' then, what wad become o' them?	
Thinks Aw, God only kens!	knows
Still, bowk! the gove gans thud, for thud,	goaf
An' diz maw [hole in] clivor.	does... properly
But just as that aud brocken jud	coal-section
Was buryin' me for ivor;	
An' just as Aw'd said maw last prayers,	
Maw marra drops in unawares,	work-mate
An' gollers up wor garrot stairs –	yells
"O Geordie! Hoo's yor liver?..."	i.e. do you want a drink

The Pitman wakes, and finds he has been dreaming. However, the moral of the tale is sharply pointed out in the reaction from his audience:

"Back, back!" the delighted screamed,	
Transported for the while;	
"By hokey, marra, but ye've dreamed	mate
I' reely splendid style!	
Te risk such dangers for such pay	
Wad turn the maistors blue!	Masters, i.e. pit-owners
An' what a thing twad be, Aw say,	it would
Shud such a dream come true!"	
"Come true! Aw wonder at ye men!	
The thing maw dream describes	
Is happenin ivory noo an' then	every
Te pitmen ov all tribes.	
The tuther month Tom Dodds wiz lost,	other

Last Monday, Harry Lee:
Coals! man, O what coals sometimes cost! –
The next one may be me!..."

(Alexander Barrass)

Problems of gas

Methane is as much a feature of the vegetable origin of coal as the coal itself.

> The gas was adsorbed into the coal structure as the coal was formed. It also collected in bedding, cleat and fracture planes, and was released as mining progressed in varying amounts from negligible to large amounts and occasionally as sudden outbursts which could dislodge very large amounts of the previously solid coal.
>
> (Tony Sharkey)

> The chemical analysis of coal shows it to contain the same elements as wood. It consists mainly of carbon, and compounds of carbon and hydrogen. Plants and other vegetation consist of oxygen, hydrogen, carbon and nitrogen, in various amounts. After being buried by strata, the vegetable matter underwent chemical changes. Various gases, such as carburetted hydrogen, or firedamp [CH4], carbonic acid gas [CO^2] and water were given off, leaving a greater percentage of carbon and a smaller amount of the other elements.
>
> (James Tonge, *The Principles and Practice of Coal Mining*, 1906, ch.3)

It is as well to be clear about the main gases involved, as these can have popular names that confuse the identities. ['Damp' by the way, comes from the German 'Dampf' meaning fog, vapour, steam.]

In the eighteenth century two basic types of gas were distinguished – 'styth' or 'foul air' (better known as chokedamp since its effect was to suffocate) and 'surfeit' or 'fiery air' (better known as firedamp):

> But what is worse of all if he be altogther unacquainted with this sort of sinking Labour, he may loose his Life by Styth, which is a sort of bad foul Air, or Fume exhaling out of some Minerals, or parting of Stone... and here an Ignorant Man is Cheated of his Life insensibly, as also he by his Ignorance may be burnt to Death by the Surfet, which is another dangerous sort of bad Air, but of a fiery Nature like Lightning, which blasts and tears all before it, if it takes hold of the Candle...
>
> (*Compleat Collier*, 1707, p.23)

The term 'chokedamp' could in fact be used of more than one gas, e.g. Carbon dioxide (a product of complete combustion) and Carbon monoxide (a product of incomplete combustion). More certain of identity was the dangerous firedamp, an increasing problem as mines reached greater depths and faced greater pressures in the strata.

Firedamp (methane, CH4)

Recognised in 1670s, also that it was lighter than air (*HRCM*, ch.18).

"Firedamp is a mixture of Methane and air which is (theoretically) explosive when the methane forms between 5% and 15% of the mixture. It is most explosive at about 9.5%" (Sharkey); "fire-damp – the inflammable air, or carburetted hydrogen gas of coal mines" (Brockett, Newc, 1820s); "fire-damp – light carburetted hydrogen gas. It is found in most coal mines; being most abundant in the vicinity of slips and dykes" (Nicholson, 1888).

> During the decay of the vegetation which finally produced our coal seams the firedamp was adsorbed and during the process of mineralisation due to earth pressure and heat more firedamp was liberated, only to be occluded in the interstices of the forming coal and retained under a pressure which is often considerable. During the process of mining coal the occluded firedamp escapes, often with a characteristic hissing sound, and in a quantity sufficient to foul the air current to such an extent as to produce an explosive mixture.
>
> (*HRCM*, ch.18)

Products of an explosion include carbon dioxide and carbon monoxide (CO) where the carbon of the coal has combined with the oxygen of the air.

Afterdamp (carbon monoxide – CO)

The after product of the combustion of firedamp, the carbon of the methane having combined with the oxygen of the open mine. Carbon monoxide is poisonous in itself, producing dizziness, unconsciousness and death in a short space of time. Victims appear rather swollen and pink of skin.

"After-damp – the residual gases after an explosion in a coal pit" (Brockett, Newc, 1820s); "after-damp – carbonic acid; stythe. The products of the combustion of fire-damp" (Nicholson, 1888); "practical miners also knew that most of those who lost their lives in explosions were suffocated by afterdamp, and many a rescuer after an explosion has been killed by afterdamp" (*HRCM*, ch.18).

Though the impact of carbon monoxide is primarily as a poisonous gas, "CO is in fact a combustible gas but it will only burn (or explode) at percentages (over 12%) when support of life would be impossible" (Sharkey).

Whitedamp (carbon monoxide – CO)

Another less common name for afterdamp. Perhaps derived from the concept of it spreading in the way a cloud of dust would, after an explosion?

> But lo! yon light, erewhile so bright
> No longer lights the scene;
> A cloud of mist yon light has kiss'd
> And shorn it of its sheen.
>
> A cloud of mist yon light has kiss'd,
> See! how long it steals,
> Till one by one the lights are smote,
> And deep the doom prevails.
>
> (Joseph Skipsey, 'The Hartley Disaster', 1862)

"whitedamp – a tasteless, almost odourless gas, the product of incomplete combustion, usually associated with gob fires..." (Tootle, 1995); "white damp – carbon monoxide" (Freese, 2005, p.48).

Black damp (carbon dioxide)

So-called because it extinguished miners' lamps.

Blackdamp or chokedamp [sic] – a mixture of nitrogen and carbon dioxide present in mines. The gas will not support a flame, nor life. In the early days of coal mining, the mine was shallow, and the only gas the men had to contend with was blackdamp. It was so called because of presence in large amounts could choke or suffocate anyone coming into contact with it" (Tootle, 1995); "black damp or stythe which put out their lamps, causing panting, sometimes suffocation" (*HRCM*, ch.18).

Chokedamp

While Nicholson identifies this with carbon monoxide ("choke-damp – the product of the combustion of fire-damp or carburetted hydrogen; called also after-damp"), Freese (2005, p.47) more usefully identifies it with carbon dioxide.

> Chokedamp was air with a deficiency of oxygen. CH^4 and CO^2 are not poisonous gases but when present in the air they replace oxygen and when the volume of oxygen falls below about 17% a flame lamp would be extinguished; heavy breathing and some distress will start to be experienced when the oxygen content goes below 14%, and if the oxygen falls much further suffocation can result.
>
> (Tony Sharkey)

Stink damp (Hydrogen sulphide, H^2S)

Also 'sulfuretted hydrogen'. "Stink damp or sulphuretted hydrogen is formed by a chemical reaction between pyrites and water and is very poisonous. Fortunately its smell is very repulsive (rotten eggs) and it can be easily detected by smell long before it reaches dangerous levels" (Sharkey).

Detection

As these gases are invisible and largely odourless, the question of detection was an important practical consideration (never mind the name or the chemical composition).

An early and fairly effective system was to use canaries or mice – their rapid respiration and consumption of oxygen meant they were more quickly affected by impurities in the air (*HRCM*, ch.18). In fact, canaries were of most use after an explosion, as a quick guide for the rescuers.

> Why you didn't use canaries up at Crook, they used wild birds – we used to call them 'Frenchies'; Redpolls: and after they'd had so much of it they used to release them again because they found out the canary got immune to it if you kept using the same one over and over and over again. He showed us a one that'd – was overcome with it, and he opened the door and he opened the window and – it wasn't long in picking up, mind: and away it went. I say, with canaries, you had to breed them or buy them in like, and they had a chap was authorised to catch them, these Redpolls – and we found out that canaries became immune to them. They could stand it a bit longer, see. It was false security.
>
> (Henry Richardson, Beamish, 1983/217)

> The 'canary in a coal mine' stories originated because after an explosion canaries were taken into the mine and helped indicate the presence of CO by falling off their perches. They were much more susceptible to the effects of the gas than human beings. But canaries were not everyday features of underground life. I remember on the first day I went underground being shown the cages of canaries that were kept in a special place in Dean and Chapter lamp cabin.
>
> (Tony Sharkey)

Mice had the advantage that they might be expected to be present uninvited (originally descending with the ponies' feed?). It was not unknown for miners to query the safety of a working area where they noticed no mice running about.

A more reliable method, regarding methane, was to check the flame of a safety lamp:

> A blue triangle or gas cap formed on the top of the flame in the presence of Methane gas. The height of the triangle helped to determine the percentage of methane present at the inlet to the lamp. When the percentage exceeded 5.5% (approx) the flame would spire into the roof of the lamp and extinguish itself.
>
> (Tony Sharkey)

Carbon monoxide, however, did not provide any warning via a lamp flame at low levels, though it might have an odour "resembling the scent of sweet flowers" (qu. Freese, 2005, p.48).

As to firedamp, prevention was the priority, before dangerous levels could build up. Being lighter than air, an early (seventeenth century) precaution was to send a fireman round the mine, before the day's work began, to combust any small pockets of firedamp:

> The 'fireman' wrapped himself up in old clothing previously soaked in water, and entered the mine carying a long pole, to the end of which was fixed a lighted candle. Upon nearing an accumulation of gas he dropped down on all fours and crawling forward pushed the candle towards the roof. This ignited the gas, the fireman meanwhile lying flat on his face until the flame had passed over him. He then rose and retreated from the mine, leaving it in a fit state for the men to enter.
>
> (*HCRM*, ch.8)

The more accepted method of dealing with firedamp was to use ventilation – which would both dilute the gas to safe proportions and eventually draw it out of the mine altogether. Airflow was checked via an anemometer, the presence of methane via a methanometer:

> The methanometer was a relatively new device. I don't know when it was introduced into coal mines but of course one of the problems it had originally was that it was electrically powered. Making it work without blowing up the place in which it was being used was a necessary development. In many parts of the world they are part of a mine official's normal equipment and they are also built into coal getting machines.
>
> (Tony Sharkey)

> AFD – standing for Automatic Firedamp Detector (firedamp, a mining term for methane or CH^4). A methanometer was a portable CH^4 detector that was about the size of a large mobile phone, the deputy carried this on his person at all times so he could detect methane anywhere he was.
>
> (Norman Conn, Seaham)

> And we had to visit what they call the goaf – places where the coal had been extracted. Well they used to draw all the timber out and let the roof fall, well the outlets of them had to be tested for gas every now and again and it all depended on the pressure… if it was a very low pressure then of course you had to be very careful because then of course that's where the gases used to come off the faces you see. Then we had to make sure the airway was clear. He had an anemometer which measured the air that was passing. So he had had to have one of those. Used to make sure that there was sufficient air going into the faces.
>
> (Michael Curran, Beamish, 1991/38–39)

> Firedamp in the goaf expanded and contracted with the decrease and increase of atmospheric pressure. A sudden fall of atmospheric pressure could allow large quantities of firedamp to migrate into the mine air.
>
> (Sharkey)

agate – "on the way, agoing: 'The fire burns agate'" (Brockett, Newc, 1820s).

blaw – "a sudden escape of gas from the strata or the coal into the workings" (Tootle, 1995).

blower – "a fissure in the broken strata of coal, from which a feeder or current of inflammable air discharges" (Brockett, Newc, 1820s); "blower – a strong current of methane gas issuing from the strata" (Temple, 1989, pp.19–20); "a sudden outburst, or flow of 'firedamp'. The blower could continue for many days or weeks. The pressure of gas could at times reach as high as 300 to 400 lbs. per sq. in, and then gradually decrease. The quantity of gas given off was sometimes enormous, filling the workings in a matter of minutes…" (Tootle, 1995).

blue divel – "blue devil – the ignition of localised pockets of gas. From the resultant blue flame" (Oxley, Burradon).

cap – "the blue top, or lambent flame, which appears above the ordinary flame of a candle or lamp, when it is burning in an atmosphere of air mixed with fire-damp" (Nicholson, 1888).

clean – "free from 'firedamp' or any other gasses" (Tootle, 1995, N.East).

dadd – "to beat out a small fire of gas, or a small accumulation of gas" (Tootle, 1995, C19, N.East).

fiery – "producing inflammable gas" (Nicholson, 1888); "as in a fiery mine (or pit)" (Sharkey).

fizzle – "a faint crackling noise caused by gas escaping from the strata" (Wade, South Moor, 1966).

foul air – general term for bad, possibly dangerous air; "'the air's foul', means that the circulation is bad" (Douglass, 1973).

gas – "a term used by miners for carburetted hydrogen or 'firedamp'" (Tootle, 1995); "Methane was presupposed when the term 'gas' was used" (Sharkey).

marsh-gas – "an old term used by miners for Methane" (Tootle, 1995).

scumfish – "to smother, to suffocate with smoke" (Brockett, Newc, 1820s); "scumfinch'd – soaked in sweat" (Trelogan, New Herrington); "scumfish – to suffocate" (Wade, South Moor, 1966); "skumfish – lack of air causing illness or death" (Dodd, Tanfield Lea). [Fr. discomforter.]

self rescuer – "a stainless steel canister, about the size of a small tea caddy, carried on the belt at all times. When the red lever on top was pulled, you could pull out a small respirator with a mouth piece, noseclip and webbing straps to hold it in place. It contained an air cooler, smoke and dust filters, and most importantly, a substance called Hopcalite, which converts carbon MONOXIDE into carbon DIOXIDE…" (Riley, Blyth).

styth – "foul air; a black suffocating damp in a colliery" (Brockett, Newc, 1820s); "Through smoke and styth" (Wilson, G'head, 1820s); "stithe – carbonic acid gas, often found in old workings, and evolved in most shallow mines" (Nicholson, 1888); "stythe – bad air" (Wade, South Moor, 1966); "styth – mine gas, CO^2" (MD, C20).

stoppings – "a barrier of plank, brick or stone...in a coal mine" [to prevent spread of fire] (Brockett, Newc, 1820s).

swelted – "overcome by heat and perspiration" (Brockett, Newc, 1820s) [OE sweltan – to perish].

Big Geordie Gray

(Tune: "Cushie Butterfield")

I'll tell ye a sad story of big Geordie Gray
Its fair shocking the way that this lad went astray
One dismal Monday foreshift, in the merry month of May
He went down the 'Pit', but never saw another day.

Chorus: He was a big lad and a bonnie lad
An' he liked his beor
He forgot his self rescuer respirator
An' now he's not heor.

It was just after bait time – they had to run for their lives
And run hard they did for their bairns and their wives
Big Geordie ran like hell – just like the rest
But on reaching those 'fumes', poor Geordie went west.

Geordie's marra's got to bank – all safe and all sound
And along with the Manager the reason they found
As to why poor Geordie will never come back
His 'self rescuer' was lying unused in its rack.

The moral of this story is as clear as day
Always carry your rescuer – don't hide it away
A bloody nuisance it might be – but I hope and pray
Ye'll not all gan the same way as Big Geordie Gray.

(Ernie Taylor, Dawdon)

Explosions

A small explosion confined to one road was called a 'flush'; if several roads were affected it was called a 'fire'; but if the explosion affected the whole of the working district, it was known as a 'heavy fire', the term 'blast' being confined to those explosions which travelled to the mouth of the shaft.

(*HRCM*, ch.8)

Nineteenth century safety precautions – with good reason – centred on the risk from firedamp.

Much danger arises in the mines from the escape during the working of the imprisoned gas called 'fire-damp' (carburetted hydrogen), which is highly explosive when mixed with air, and when ignited produces the much dread 'choke damp', or 'black damp' (carbonic acid gas); so that a good system of ventilation and the use of the Davy lamp are very necessary.

(Woodward, *Geology of England & Wales*, ch.4)

...but as the toll mounted – New Hartley in 1862 – 204 dead, Seaham in 1880 – 164 dead, West Stanley in 1905 – 169 dead – the suspicion arose that something else was involved.

The Haswell explosion of 1844 that killed 94 supplied the first evidence: the effect of the explosion travelled through the mine in a way not expected with a localised 'blow' of gas. It was posited that "the coal dust swept by the rush of wind and flame from the floor, roof, and walls of the words would instantly take fire and burn..." (*HRCM*, ch.8) – a supposition supported at the time by Faraday.

A similar puzzle attended the Seaham explosion of 1880 – resulting from a shot fired in an area of stone, where there should have been no gas. The likelihood was that the running footsteps of the miners retiring with the usual zest after lighting the fuse had raised a cloud of coal dust from the floor – and this had been the base of the devastating explosion that followed. This theory was rejected by the Coroner, and it was not until an explosion at Altoft Colliery in 1886 that it was possible to demonstrate the crucial role played by coal dust.

Coal Dust – Although coal dust cannot be termed a gas, it is, nevertheless, one of the chief causes of the pollution of the air in mines, and is now recognised as a most frequent cause of explosions. It is contended by some that an

> explosion of coal dust and air is impossible without the presence of fire-damp. Like many others, the author believes that the presence of this latter gas is not always necessary, and that a mixture of finely divided dust with air may be ignited owing to an unsuccessful shot or a defective lamp, and cause an explosion of such an extent that it is only limited by the extent of the dust.
>
> (James Tonge, *The Principles and Practice of Coal Mining*, ch.15)

Remedies included using alternative 'safety' explosives, watering down the dust, or laying stone dust on the roadways (dust with 40% or more of limestone dust in it was found not to ignite) – the latter was the favoured solution, though with a doubtful benefit to miners' respiratory health.

> Coal dust explosions greatly expanded the destructive effect of an original explosion of methane and the resultant explosion of a cloud of coal dust raised into the air by the initial explosion could be devastating. As knowledge of the dangers of coal dust improved legal requirements to ensure that any deposits of coal dust lying in the mine were diluted by spreading inert dust (gypsum or limestone dust but generally referred to as 'stone dust') in such a manner and in quantities sufficient to render the resultant mixture non-flammable even when raised into the air. Later, the law required the placement of barriers (essentially flat wooden trays on which large quantities of stone dust was placed) high in the roadways, which when disturbed by an explosion would disperse the stone dust into the air (in the path of the explosion) and suppress it. Experience in the last quarter of the twentieth century indicated that the various methods of dust suppression were having a great effect on minimising the magnitude of explosions.
>
> (Tony Sharkey)

barred in – "trapped undeground by fall of roof, etc." (Johnson, Dawdon).

blast – "an explosion of foul air in a coal mine" (Brockett, Newc, 1820s); "an explosion of fire-damp" (Nicholson, 1888) "the sudden rush of fire, gas and dust through the underground workings following an explosion" (Tootle, 1995).

bowk – "belch, earth tremor" (Dodd, Tanfield Lea).

fire – "to explode, 'the pit has fired' meaning there's been an explosion underground" (Tootle, 1995); "fired – exploded" (Nicholson, 1888).

happed up – "caught by a fall, buried" (Tootle, 1995).

manhole – "refuge hole between legs or rings, dimensions should be 3ft. by 4ft. by 6ft. and they should be whitewashed and numbered. Distance apart depended on the type of roadway and gradients, usually 10 yards or 20 yards. They provided a safe place in case of runaway tubs, etc." (Riley, Blyth).

reek – "smoke" (Nicholson, 1888).

refyooj hohl – [in mine]. (Dodd, Tanfield Lea).

stonedust – "crushed limestone (calcium carbonate)" (Riley, Blyth) [used to counteract coal dust].

stour – "dust" (Nicholson, 1888); "dust floating in the air: 'midst dust and stour'" (Wilson, G'head, 1820s).

Reactions

Though explosions affected directly and terribly the victims' families, we are left to gauge the effects via public reactions. The major explosion grabbed public attention and raised public sympathy in a way that is both a credit to nineteenth century sensibility, and yet a sad indictment of public indifference to the miners' lot at other times. A positive response was the generosity that boosted public subscriptions for the families of the deceased miners. Less admirable, in general, was the outburst of poems in the press that followed such an explosion. Joseph Skipsey's, *The Hartley Calamity* of 1862 (which I do not reprint) seems to me of no great standard. The following extract from a poem after the 1880 Seaham disaster has more literary stylishness, but that perhaps only serves to distance it from the 'simple' heroes it celebrates.

'Nay, I'll stay with the lad!'
Down in a deep, black seam,
Huddled together, dying and dead,
Far from the day-world over head,
Face to face by a sudden fate,
With a horror of night precipitate;
Hidden away from the merciful Sun,
The death and the burial all in one,
By their fifties cut off in vain,
More than a battle counts its slain;
Huddled together man and horse,
In the grip of the fire-damp's watchful force, –
Unsung heroes of simple mould,
All unchanged from the race of old,
To the olden truths, with a martyr's cry,
Out of the depths they testify;
And never has rede been read, I deem, advice
Nobler than that in the deep, black seam,

Of love and courage the message sad, –
Only, 'Nay, I'll stay with the lad.'...

(From scrapbook in Newcastle Central Library)

The most effective of these commemorative poems is surely Tommy Armstrong's on the Trimdon Grange explosion of 1882. Though Victorian sentiment ranks high in much of its content, the opening and closing sections have an impact not often met with in any poetry and provide solemn anchors for the whole. Unusual for Tommy Armstrong, it is written in 'standard' English; his son thought so well of the song, he placed it first in the collection of his father's work he issued in booklet form in 1909.

Trimdon Grange Explosion
(Tune: "Go and leave me if you wish it")

Let us not think of to-morrow,
Lest we disappointed be;
All our joys may turn to sorrow,
As we all may daily see.
To-day we may be strong and healthy,
But how soon there comes a change,
As we may learn from the explosion,
That has been at Trimdon Grange.

Men and boys left home that morning,
For to earn their daily bread,
Little thought before that evening
That they'd be numbered with the dead;
Let us think of Mrs Burnett,
Once had sons but now has none,
By the Trimdon Grange explosion,
Joseph, George, and James are gone.

February left behind it
What will never be forgot;
Weeping widows, helpless children,
May be found in many a cot, — cottage
Homes that once were blest with comfrot,
Guided by a father's care,
Now are solemn, sad and gloomy,
Since the father is not there.

Little children, kind and loving,
From their homes each day would run
For to meet their father's coming
As each hard day's work was done.
Now they ask if father's left them.
Then the mother hangs her head:
With a weeping widow's feelings,
Tells the child that "father's dead."

God protect the lonely widow,
Help to raise each drooping head;
Be a Father to the orphans,
Never let them cry for bread.
Death will pay us all a visit,
They have only gone before;
We may meet the Trimdon victims
Where explosions are no more.

(Tommy Armstrong)

Of prose accounts, the following notes on the Brandling Main explosion of 1815 has the merit of careful observation, from the surface point of view:

The subterraneous fire broke forth with two heavy discharges from the John pit (the downcast), which were almost instantaneously followed by one from the William pit. A slight trembling as from an earthquake was felt for about half-a-mile around the workings; and the noise of the explosion, though dull, was heard to three or four miles distance, and much resembled an unsteady fire of infantry. Immense quantities of dust and small coal accompanied these blasts, and rose high into the air, in the form of an inverted cone. The heaviest part of the ejected matter such as corves, pieces of wood, and small coal, fell near the pits, but the dust borne away by a strong west wind, fell in a continued shower from the pit to the distance of a mile and a-half.

In the village of Heworth it caused a darkness like that of early twilight, and covered the roads so thickly that the footsteps of passengers were strongly imprinted in it. The heads of both of the shaft-frames were blown off, their sides set on fire, and their pulleys shattered to pieces; but the pulleys of the John pit gin, being on a crane not within the influence of the blast, were fortunately preserved. The coal dust ejected from the William pit into the drift or horizontal part of the tube (i.e. the passage between the pit and the chimney stack) was about 3in. thick, and soon burnt to a light cinder. Pieces of burning coal, driven off the solid stratum of the mine, were also blown up this shaft. By twelve o'clock, by means of the gin at the John pit, which was worked by men in the absence of horses, thirty-two persons, all that survived, were brought to daylight...

(Rev. J. Hodgson on the 1815 explosion at Brandling Main, qu. *HRCM*, ch.8)

Explosion at the Lambton Colliery in 1850

This more racy account of an underground explosion in November 1850 at Lambton Colliery survives from the hand of a pitman who was a youth at the time. The style of this piece suggests the work was intended for a general audience (thus the avoidance of dialect and technical terms); it is affected to the modern ear, but all the more typical, perhaps of the High Victorian literary expectations. Not impossibly, it was rewritten by a 'professional' writer, but if it has lost something of its authenticity, it has gained in the way of adventuresomeness.

So it was on the morning in question, when about a hundred and eighty men and boys, as usual, entered the pit, and threading their way through the long narrow passages to their respective places of toil, commenced the duties of the day without the slightest apprehension of immediate danger or sign of impending peril, and over the wide area of the mine work generally was soon in full swing.

At one point, however, the explosive gas had been slowly accumulating entirely unnoticed, whilst the current of air passing within a few yards of the spot not only left it undisturbed, but gradually increasing; and slowly it stole along the narrow passage to where a coal-hewer had for two hours been toiling *within a few feet of death*. Yet, all unconscious of his awful nearness to the eternal world, he kept diligently plying his pick, whilst the subtle invisible foe crept on, inch by inch, nearer and nearer, till it silently hovered over the naked light, and there came the fatal touch, the sudden flash, and the roar of hissing flame, instantly scorching the stalwart toiler into a blackened corpse. 'The angel of death spread his wings on the blast,' as it swept through the mine with increasing fury, creating consternation and terror, to some as short-lived as it was sudden, for with one wild shriek for mercy 'Their hearts but once heaved, and forever grew still.' [Quotes from Byron.]

In less than two minutes the work of destruction was over, leaving here and there, as was afterwards discovered, timber and tubs, horses and human bodies, scattered or wedged together by the force of the blast. The main road being blocked by a heavy fall from the roof, the air-currents were for some time suspended, leaving the deadly choke-damp [carbon monoxide] to make short work with those who came under its power. The stir and din of busy toil had suddenly given place to the fearful stillness and gloom of death, and for the time it seemed as if the grim king of terrors swayed his sceptre uncontrolled. [Ref. to Job 18:14.]

The explosion had occurred a considerable distance from where I was working. My place, being only seventy yards from the shaft, was reached by a single passage, entirely apart from the main line along which the explosion had swept, so that a solid mass of unworked coal separated me from the course the blast had taken. I had just returned from the shaft with an empty tub when the explosion occurred. The shock was terrific, and powerful enough to be felt on the surface; to use the words of the Psalmist, 'The earth shook and trembled; the foundations of the hills were moved and shaken.'

Knowing too well what it meant, I seized the lamp, which owing to my sheltered position had not been blown out, and ran for the shaft, about six yards from which I met a dense cloud of dust and deadly choke-damp, completely filling the seam, slowly and solidly moving into the drift where I stood. But not the slightest sound or movement was to be heard, all being still and silent as the grave. The busy workers I had left there five minutes before had disappeared, and the well-known voices all seemed hushed in death. The sudden silence was terrible, and the awful feeling that all hands were lost and there was no hope for me made it more terrible still. Thoughts of father and mother, home and friends, of Christ and God, flashed through my mind more quickly than I can write them. The cloud of dust and choke-damp was coming nearer; and whilst I knew that to retreat was almost certain death, and to go forward seemed almost equally fatal, yet therein lay my only chance – to struggle through and climb the shaft if possible.

Committing my soul to God, I rushed into the cloud. A stifling feeling seized my chest, and my breathing at once became slow and thick; yet, with one violent effort in the struggle for life, I climbed over the tubs and timber which had been blown together, reached the top of the cage which rested thereon, and so stood within the shaft. Gasping and hopeless, I leaned against the framework, when a tremendous draught of cool, fresh air crept slowly over me, and I *breathed* again, with strange sensations, the '*breath of life*', [Genesis, ch.2, 6, 7, – and in well-known hymn] for life it was – unexpected life – as the pure air of heaven silently drove back the poisonous fumes which in a few moments at most must have extinguished the already flickering lamp of life...

With the current of air which had so relieved me hope revived, and leaving my position I pressed my way round to the back of the shaft, where we usually ascended, passing as I went the dead body of the poor lad who a few minutes before had helped me away with the tub. Just at that moment I was startled by a voice feebly asking, 'What is the matter?' and turning round I found a man lying amongst the timber where he had been thrown, just again becoming conscious. He was very much shaken, and lifting him up, I helped him into the cage in which we were accustomed to 'ride' (i.e. go up). On trying to signal to the surface we were suddenly lifted and rapidly drawn up the shaft, excitedly praising God for our unexpected deliverance from the jaws of death.

On reaching the surface my mate was conveyed at once to his home, and he ultimately recovered. Prompt action being necessary, I was anxious again to descend, in the hope of rescuing any who might be near to the shaft. Being greatly relieved by a few minutes in the fresh air I entered the cage, when two men who had just arrived at the pit joined me, and we at once descended, leaving all above very anxious as to the result...

(George Parkinson, *True Stories of Durham Pit-Life*, London, 1912)

More realistic, perhaps, is the confusion and uncertainty in the following testimony:

Coroner: What are you?

Ralph Marley: A stoneman.

Q. Now, on Tuesday night, what seam were you working in?

A. The main coal.

Q. What portion of it?

A. What is called the skirting way – the staple?

Q. How far from the shaft?

A. About 1,200 yards.

Q. From which shaft?

A. The high pit, No.3.

Q. Will you go on and tell us as to anything that occurred during the shift from the time that you went in to the time of the explosion?

A. We went down about ten o'clock at night, and went in-bye, and saw the air-ways and everything, and got to work about a quarter to eleven o'clock; and at twenty minutes to three o'clock we were going to commence work again, after getting our baits, and I felt the shock. I was furthest in-bye.

Q. You felt a shock. Did you hear nothing?

A. We heard nothing, just felt a shock. I said, 'I did not like the wind.' I said to my mates that were sitting beside me that the pit had fired; and the mate that I was working with, he went off and went in-bye to some other place. He went to see if there were any falls.

> Q. And you found no fall?
>
> A. I said to Smith, 'It's no use working, there is something the matter. I don't like the look of matters.' A man named Wilkinson came up, and he went up-bye and saw the smoke; and I said directly, as soon as he saw the smoke, 'The pit had fired away out-bye'.
>
> Q. You went to the shaft and saw the smoke?
>
> A. No; he went so far out toward the shaft.
>
> Q. And he found smoke, and then you made out?
>
> A. We went through, the two of us, and came away until we got into the fresh air.
>
> (*PP*, 1881, CR x, p.8)

Lamps and lighting

The basic illumination for the first coal miners was the candle. A lump of plastic 'clay' sufficed to fix the candle to some useful projecting surface. The naked candle survived in use much later than generally supposed, partly because some parts of a mine would be gas-free, partly because of its cheapness and convenience:

> In the first working or whole working the men use candles exclusively, and are safe in so doing, as we can guide the air into every working part so as effectually to carry off dangerous gas. But when the men are at pillar-working, that is removing the pillars, no candles are at all allowed, and the Davy-lamp alone is used; and for this reason, that it would be impossible when so large openings are made, and a vacant space left beyond, for us to secure the men against sudden danger from a large portion of the roof falling in, and throwing a huge flood of gas, and dashing it against the light. [Shelley, Sth Hetton]
>
> (*PP*, 1842, CR xvi, p.57)

In the eighteenth century, safety consciousness led to the introduction of a flint and steel mill: "turning a steel wheel against a flint emitted 'an abundance of sparks' giving light. Colour of sparks also gave warning of degree of concentration of fire damp" (*HRCM*, ch.10). A strange, surreal illumination that must have seemed.

The big step forward was the invention of the safety lamp, independently by Sir Humphrey Davy and George Stephenson. The Stephenson model was understandably favoured in the North East, to the extent that some people trace the origin of the title 'Geordie' for an inhabitant of Tyneside back to this model of lamp.

In 1815 George Stephenson was working on a safety lamp on the principle, "that if a lamp could be made to contain the burnt air above the flame, and to permit the firedamp to come in below in a small quantity, to be burnt as it came in, the burnt air would prevent the passing of the explosion upward, and the velocity of the current from below would prevent its passing downward" (*HRCM*, ch.10). Firstly, an adjustable slide was used to regulate admission of air; then three small tubes from below. Eventually, he decided that small holes or perforations would do as well, with the air passing through two sets of these in the form of an outer and an inner sleeve (the inner sleeve partly glass).

Sir Humphrey Davy was also working in 1815 on a safety lamp, and by 1816 had settled on the wire-gauze cylinder, though which an explosion could not pass. Sir Humphrey won national acclaim; but the validity of Stephenson's work was appreciated in the North East, where he was awarded a substantial prize in 1817. (See further detail in Jeffrey Smith, 2001.) To Buddle, verifying their practical effectiveness in the presence of gas, it seemed "We have at last subdued this monster."

The use of the safety lamp took a while to become accepted, its cost and relatively low light telling against it with conservative mine owners and men. Various improvements and other models were introduced over the years, sometimes unofficially:

> We had Davy lamps. We used to cut out a Nestles Milk tin to put on the back. When you were walking in bye the light off the lamps in front used to dazzle you. When the air was bad the lamps went out and many's the time we walked for miles with our foot on the rail to guide us because we had no light. At certain safety points you could put your lamp into a machine, turn the handle and it was lit by electricity.
>
> (Mr Cawson, Kibblesworth, Beamish, 1993/5)

A cap lamp had clear advantages for the working miner, focussing on the work in front of him while leaving his hands free. An acetylene lamp was the first type experimented with, about 1910, and gave one of the best lights of all. A portable electric lamp, to be held in the hand or fixed on the cap, was being developed about the same time, and ultimately prevailed through its convenience and safety. One drawback was it gave no signal of firedamp; but the development of the methanometer eventually covered that lack.

On main roadways, fixed oil lamps would be the nineteenth century standard, gradually replaced, 1880 on, by electric lighting. And so it remained till the end.

acetylene lamps – "the base of the lamp was filled with small grain carbide, above this was a container for water with an external stopcock to control the flow of water. As the water dripped onto the carbide acetylene gas was produced. The lamp gave a better illumination than the oil lamp and could also be used for gas testing" (Tootle, 1995). Use ended in 1947, as deemed unsafe.

bonny leets – "at one time the officials had spotlights on their cap lamps which gave out a long beam. The workers could thus see them coming at a great distance and would shout out 'Here's a bonny leet coming'" (Douglass, 1973).

bull's eye – "a type of hand-held miner's lamp, no longer in use" (Tootle, 1995); "An' the lantrin', we used te caal it a 'bull's eye', and yet, Aa warned [warrant] that any self-respecting bull would be ashymed te hev an eye like it. D'ye mind, hinnies, the bit ov reed glass and the bit ov green glass on th' revolving shutter?" (Elliott, Tyne, 1910) [origin: bull's eye lens].

cap lamp – "an electric lamp developed in the 1920s, worn on the front of a miner's helmet with a cable running to a battery carried on the miner's belt, the battery being recharged at the end of each shift" (Tootle, 1995); "No lamp was numbered 13. Brass on lamp gives status: Max = Manager; Min = miner" (McBurnie, Washington, 1970s). Cap lamps were powered by an acid battery: "The acid battery is ideal in size and weight for use in hand-held and miner's cap lamps" (Tootle, 1995).

Clanney – "a term used by the miners for 'Clanny's Safety Lamp'" (Tootle, 1995, N.East, 1810s); **chenny** – pit lamp" (Thornley).

clay – "a substance used by pitmen as a substitute for candlesticks" (Wilson, G'head, 1820s); "a pitman's candlestick, made of a piece of clay" (Heslop, N's, 1880s); "Me fathor showed me the way / T' spit t' soften the clay, / And clag it onto the prop t' howld me low [light]" (W.B. Coombs).

Davy lamp – "a lamp invented by Sir H. Davy in 1815. It consists of an oil-vessel, gauze cylinder around the flame, and a gauze cap" (Nicholson, 1888); "Jack Davy lamp or Jack lamp – a Davy lamp with the addition of a glass cylinder outside the gauze" (Tootle, 1995); "Davy – a name given to a lamp prepared by Sir Humphrey Davy, to be used in the collieries after the year 18" [i.e. 1818] (*Bell MS*).

Davy man – "the man who 'trimmed' and repaired the 'davy lamps'" (Tootle, 1995, N.East).

fluorescent tubes – common lighting in main roadways underground.

Geordie – "the pitmen have given the name of Geordie to Mr George Stephenson's lamp in contra-distinction to the Davy, or Sir Humphrey Davy's Lamp" (Brockett, Newc, 1820s); "Geordy lamp – "a lamp invented by George Stephenson in 1815. It consisted of an oil vessel, a glass chimney with a perforated copper cap, surrounded by an iron shield perforated with large holes. The air was admitted through large holes at the base and through small holes at the top of the oil vessel. It is now made with a wire gauze in lieu of the perforated iron shield" (Nicholson, 1888).

lamp-cabin – "where the safety-lamps are cleaned and trimmed for the workmen" (Nicholson, 1888); "lamp rooms – the surface building at a mine where the electric and 'flame safety lamps' are stored, charged and maintained. Generally known as the 'lamp cabin'" (Tootle, 1995).

lamp man – "issued/maintained lamps" Trelogan (New Herrington, C20/mid); "The man employed at the mine to clean and maintain the collier's lamps. He is usually responsible for booking the time the men enter and leave the mine" (Tootle, 1995).

lamp station – "the lamp stations are the only places underground where a 'flame safety lamp' can be opened and relit. Before the invention of the electric lamp, should a collier accidentally 'loose his light' he would take the lamp off his 'drawer' [putter]. Before the introduction of the lamp stations the 'drawer' would have to work the rest of his shift in the dark or attempt to relight the lamp himself, which was often the cause of an explosion" (Tootle, 1995).

low – "light or flame: 'haud about a low'" (Wilson, G'head, 1820s); "low (rhymes with cow) – light" (Dodd, Tanfield Lea); "low – flame, light: 'a cannel... macks a berra low'" (Charles Trelogan, New Herrington); "shine a low – to direct the light of a lamp or candle in a required direction" (Nicholson, 1888); "low (luw) – a flame, (Palgrave, Hetton 1896); "the low it went out, and my marrow went wrang" (Collier's Rant, C18).

low-rope – "a piece of rope lighted at one end: 'Wor low rope'" (Wilson, G'head, 1820s); 'low-rope,' hempen rope steeped in tar, to burn as a torch" (Palgrave, Hetton, 1896); "lowe rope – a piece of tarry rope, used as a torch, in shaft or pump work" (Tootle, 1995).

midgy – "also called a 'Mistress'. These names were given to a kind of lamp used by putter lads. The height of the lamp was about 8 in., width 3 in., with open front. When first invented, they were simply little wooden boxes, with a hole at the bottom, through which the candle was thrust, and another hole at the top to let out the heat. Afterwards tin took the place of wood. The flame was sheltered by a piece of wood or tin about 2 in. high from the bottom of the lamp, and a similar piece from the top. The 'midgy' has now gone out of use" (Palgrave, Hetton, 1896); "mijee – small oil lamp (not safety)" (Dodd, Tanfield Lea); "maggie – flame oil lamp" (McBurnie, Washington, 1970s); "Midgies – an open-flame lamp used by the 'putter'. Its use was restricted to certain areas of the mine" (Tootle, 1995, N.East); "a midgy was an open fronted hand lamp (oil) used by miners when walking in by... The only form of light at the coal face was from wax candles which the miners had to provide themselves" (Walton, W.Auck.); "nothing here to make a muggie with" (Grice, 1960, ch3).

mistress or **midgey** – "an oblong box without a front, carried upright, the use of which is to carry a lighted candle or small lamp in a current of air; a kind of lantern" (Nicholson, 1888); "mistress – an oblong box with the upper half of the front opened. There was a round hole in the base for a candle. The candle could then be raised as it burned down. The 'mistress' allowed the candle to be carried in a strong current of air. Used by 'drawers'" (Tootle, 1995, N.East).

pit-rat – "a candle used in the pit" (*Bell MS*).

pricker – "a tool for trimming the wick on an oil lamp" (Tootle, 1995).

safety-lamp – "a lamp constructed in such a way as to prevent the flame from communicating with the atmosphere by which it is surrounded. The original inventors were Dr. Clanny, Sir H. Davy, and Mr. George Stephenson. Their lamps are still in use as invented, or modified by recent inventors, and the large majority of lamps invented since are simply modifications of the 'clanny', 'davy', and 'stephenson'" (Nicholson, 1888).

sweal – "to gutter, as a candle does in a current of air" (Nicholson, 1888).

weeken – lamp wick (Wade, South Moor, 1966).

Keep Your Lamp Lit Geordie Hinny
(Tune: "Keep yor Feet still Geordie Hinny")

Chorus:
Keep ye lamp lit Geordie hinny
Keep ye lamp lit Geordie lad
An' divvent let it gan oot doon the drift
Keep ye lamp lit Geordie hinny
Keep ye lamp lit Geordie lad
An' ye can test fer gas 3 times a shift.

Now deep doon i' the coal mine dangerous gases lie asleep
An' fra oot o'l gob an' brikkers they dee seep
By the proper use of ye detector
In iviry working sector
Ye'll not leave a wife an' bairns alone to weep.

If ye lamp shoud gan oot hinny divvent leave it way back-by
Cos to pinch it some sly rogue will hev a try
An' hard lines tho' it may be
It's ye that'll hetter pay
£5 or more 'll make ye bonnie missus cry.

(Ernie Taylor, Dawdon)

Chapter 14: Everyday

Everyday terms

The paradox of Pitmatic is that it 's not only a pit language; it drew on, enriched, and informed the spoken dialect in use in the world around it, so it is hard to know, in many cases, whether a term should be reckoned valid pit talk or part of common usage outside.

In the following list, the words are ones certainly used in the pit, but are general rather than technical in tone, and would mostly be equally valid outside the pit. Pitmatic or North East dialect?

barney's bull – "anything broken beyond repair was said to be like barney's bull b------d" (Wade, South Moor, 1966).

bat – "to strike a blow with the fist or a hammer" (Wade, South Moor, 1966).

get-thi-blaw – "to rest, to regain the breath" (Wade, South Moor, 1966).

bonny gan on – "serious trouble" (Wade, South Moor, 1966).

bully – "a brother, comrade" (Tootle 1995 N.East), also **boolies** [keel bully].

bump the set – "get into trouble" (Dodd, Tanfield Lea).

caad – "puttin in kaad – becoming cold" (Dodd, Tanfield Lea).

cant – "anything leaning over is said to be 'on the cant'" (Wade, South Moor, 1966).

chow – "a quid of tobacco" (Wilson, G'head, 1820s); "piece of chewing tobacco (baccy). 'Giz a chow, marra' was an often heard request" (Sharkey); "chewing tobacco was popular in the pits as smoking was prohibitied. A 'chow' was a short flat stick of compressed tobacco" (Trelogan, New Herrington); "chew – a piece of chewing tobacco. A substitute for smoking, also used to keep the mouth moist and free from dust by constantly having to spit out the tobacco juice" (Tootle, 1995).

clag – "to stick" (Wade, South Moor, 1966); "claggy – anything that is sticky" (Tootle, N.East, 1995).

cogley – "unsteady" (Wade, South Moor, 1966).

coin – "to turn from the straight" (Wade, South Moor, 1966).

chum – "empty, e.g. empty tub, empty water-bottle, empty pint-glass, etc." (Johnson, Dawdon).

clarts, clarty – "describes working in mud, or muddy conditions. 'Up to the neck in clarts': an expression used when men are working in wet, muddy conditions" (McBurnie, Washington, 1970s).

cockwood – "bits of wood sawn off of props about 6 inches long which were taken hyem and chopped up into sticks for lighting the fire" (Sharkey).

contraband – "cigarettes, pipe, matches or lighter used for smoking (miners' slang)" (Briscoe, 2003).

crack – "crack can include the news of the day underground, the newest batch of jokes, and most other things" (Douglass, 1973).

cribble – "to curry favour" (Tootle, N.East, 1995, C19); "cryble – to make up to" (South Moor, 2005).

deputy's-end – "the easy or lightest part of the work" (Wade, South Moor, 1966).

dunched – "to run into with force as 'tubs dunching'" (Wade, South Moor, 1966).

ettle – "to intend, appoint, arrange" (Nicholson, 1888).

fast – "if something is said to be 'fast' it means…it cannot move at all" (Douglass, 1973). [OE faest 'firm'.]

femmer – "slender, weak" (Nicholson, 1888); "weak or delicate" (Wade, South Moor, 1966).

fettle – to order, to get ready: 'it tuik some time to fettle them'; 'gat fettl'd up a set of geer – and bun' to hew'; 'the house aw'll fettle up masell'" (Wilson, G'head, 1820s); "fettle, fettled: 'will you fettle this for me?', meaning will you repair this for me. 'Have you fettled that for me?', meaning have you repaired that for me" (McBurnie, Washington, 1970s); "also to be 'in good fettle' meant you were well when asked. There was also a greeting between miners, 'Wot Fettle?' meaning literally 'how are yer gannen on and is owt new?'" (Sharkey).

flackered – "finished, unable to do any more" (Wade, South Moor, 1966). [flacker – to flinch – here influenced by knackered?]

flayed – "frightened" (Nicholson, 1888).

flee – "fly" (Riley, Blyth).

forenenst – "opposite" (Riley, Blyth); "fernenst" (Wade, South Moor, 1966).

gob – "to gob something meant to throw it away" (Riley, Blyth) [goaf].

grathe – "to put in order, to dress; to replace a worn bucket-leather" (Nicholson, 1888); "graithe – to make ready or repair" (Wade, South Moor, 1966); "grathely – tidy, orderly" (Tootle, North, 1995).

hacky – "dirty or filthy" (Wade, South Moor, 1966)

hasky – "rough and dry: My dad was born 1904, and used to say his hands felt 'hasky' when he meant rough and dry" (Adams, Seaham).

haud – "stop" (Wilson, G'head, 1820s).

hillbillies – "miners from West Durham transferred to work in East Durham" (J. Moreland, Dawdon, 1980).

how – "HOW! – To which the reply is HOW AGAIN! – The salutation and response of two pitmen, near to or within hail of each other. It may be friendly of otherwise, but is usually the former" (Greenwell, 1849, p.188); "The reply to 'how' is very generally 'champion'. Another version is 'hoi' a term meaning 'hallo' the return is always the same, 'hoi'" (Douglass, 1973).

how way! – "come away" (Wilson, G'head, 1820s).

howk – "to dig or scoop out…" (Wade, South Moor, 1966).

hunkers – "to sit on one's hunkers is to set with the hams resting on the calves of the legs" (*Bell MS*); "sitting on the hunkers – sitting on the toes with the thighs resting on the calves of the legs, a manner of sitting peculiar to pitmen" (Nicholson, 1888); "miners on thor hunkers sit", "hunkersittin" (Scott Dobson); "hunkers – the buttocks: a favourite posture of pitmen is sitting on their hunkers" (Wade, South Moor, 1966).

insense – "this word means more than to explain: it means the making the person, to whom the explanation is given, thoroughly understand such explanation" (Nicholson, 1888).

jell – piece of wood: "get us that jell" (John Patrickson, Seaham, re C20/mid) [deal].

joggle – "to shake" (Nicholson, 1888).

jooks/dukes – "fists. A challenge to a fight would be, 'get ya jooks up'" (Wilson, North Walbottle).

kelter – "money" (Riley, Blyth) [but in some places "rubbish"!].

leach – "hard-work, great fatigue, a word frequent among the miners in the North" (*Kennet MS*).

led – "in coal mining, any spare article: 'a led prop', 'led trams'" (Brockett, Newc, 1820s).

lippen – "to calculate, depend upon, or expect a thing being done" (Nicholson ,1888).

marrow! – "a favourite salutation among the pit-men" (Brockett, Newc, 1820s); "marrows – two alike, a pair" (Dinsdale, Tees, 1849); "marrows – when workmen form a group to work together either in the same working place, or to follow in different shifts on the same class of work, also all sharing in wages worked for. These men term each other as their marrow when working in the same shift together. They term the men following them at the same work in the next shift their cross-marrows" (McBurnie, Washington, 1970s); "marra – workmate, friend" (Dodd, Tanfield Lea); "marra – when two men work together each calls the other his marra, meaning equal" (Wade, South Moor, 1966).

met – "a measurement marked on a stick" (Wade, South Moor, 1966).

paggered – "tired or worn out. Also means broken" (Wilson, North Walbottle).

penker – "a steel ball bearing out of coal cutters, about 1″ dia." (Geggie, Ashington).

pinch – "a portion of snuff" (Riley, Blyth).

piss nyuk – "urinal" (Dodd, Tanfield Lea).

pityak – "mining talk" (Chessman, Bedlington, Blyth, Cramlington). [Cf. *OED* yack – incessant talk 1958, verb 1960, yacker – chatterbox, gossip, 1959.]

pit-yakka – "one who works underground" (McBurnie,Washington, 1970s); "pit-yakkor – a term of abuse applied to pit men" (Tootle, N.East, 1995); "only pit-yackers spoke the pit-yackers' language" (Hitchin, 1962, p.70).

pitman's pink – "a name given to the single pink, which is a great favourite among the pitmen, who, in general, pay much attention to the cultivation of flowers" (Brockett, Newc, 1820s).

poke – "a sack or bag: 'a poke o' cwols'" (Luckley, Alnwick, 1868).

put yawsel awai – "work harder" (Dodd, Tanfield Lea).

rid – "to clear out or tidy up a place" (Wade, South Moor, 1966).

rive – "to tear; roven – torn" (Wade, South Moor, 1966).

scrush – "crush" (Wade, South Moor, 1966).

shaw'd – "injured by friction" (Wilson, G'head, 1820s).

stramp – "stamp: 'Ooh! Lad, ye've stramped on my foot!'" (*Ashington Col Mag*, January 1938).

tageing – "a hard fatiguing time or job" (Wade, South Moor, 1966).

tew – "to struggle, toil: 'we had to tue on wi' a nasty scabby roof'" (Wilson, G'head, 1820s).

tewed, tewin' – "fatigued as 'it's been a tewing job'" (Wade, South Moor, 1966); "choo-in - exhausting... physically rough" (Dodd, Tanfield Lea).

teeming it bye – "unloading it for future use" (Trelogan, New Herrington) [teem – to pour].

tha – "you" (Hitchin, 1962, p.91)

timmer – "'Just the right timmer', meaning just the right size" (McBurnie, Washington, 1970s).

tume – "empty: 'his bottle's nearly tume'; 'Sall and Aw are byeth fast tuimmin' / The cup of life...'" (Wilson, G'head, 1820s).

varney – "very nearly" (Wade, South Moor, 1966).

"Where's tharat?" – greeting to some one who answers a telephone. Remember calls were not usually routed and making a call meant energising the ringers on every phone in the circuit (Sharkey).

win – "to get: as winning stones, to get stones in a quarry" (Bailey, Durham, 1810).

yakka – "ignorant [variation] of pitman" (Dodd, Tanfield Lea). [pit-yakka.]

Both Fred Wade and Michael Dodd – working alike on Pitmatic – give much wider lists than this…

Clothes

Clothing for the miner, on duty, was a strictly practical concern, a balance between ease of movement, protection and optimum body heat. Work at the face being strenuous and hot, minimal clothing like 'hoggers' (shorts) were traditional.

> A miner can, and always does, regulate the effects on him of warm air by regulating his clothing, and he quite commonly works stripped to the waist.
>
> (*HRCM*, ch.18)

With improved ventilation in the twentieth century, and cooler working conditions, full overalls and wellington-type boots became standard wear, dust being more of a problem than heat. Plus a black donkey jacket for the surface – 'NCB' in white lettering or black lettering on orange panel.

clog – "a sort of shoe, the upper part of strong hide leather, and the sole of wood, plated with iron" (Brockett, Newc, 1820s).

dad – to beat, shake:

His pit claes on the cracket lie
Aall dadded, aired and folded by
Me patient, hard-rowt muthor.

(W.B. Coombs)

duds – "working clothes: 'The duds thrawn on'" (Wilson, G'head, 1820s).

The din and strife of human life.
Awake in 'wall' and 'board',
When, lo! a shock is felt which makes
Each human heart-beat heard.

Each bosom thuds, as each his duds
He snatches and away,
And to the distant shaft he flees
With all the speed he may...

(Joesph Skipsey, *The Hartley Disaster*)

half-shoon – "old shoes with the toes cut off" (Wilson, G'head, 1820s). [The aim being to stop bits of coal getting trapped and hurting your feet.]

hoggers – "stockings with the feet cut off" (Wilson, G'head, 1820s); "stockings without feet, chiefly used by the putters" (Nicholson, 1888); "There is my hoggars, likewise my half shoon" ('The Collier's Rant'). [The aim seems to have been to guard shins while making sure no bits of trapped coal could get lodged under the foot. By origin, from hogger meaning hosepipe, re common cylindrical form.]

hoggers – "shorts miners wear in the pit" (Wade, South Moor, 1966); "pit hoggers – short trousers" (Sharkey).; "with your huggers and your vest" (J. Moreland, Dawdon, 1980); "underground, [the pitman] will usually wear these 'hoggers', his boots, belt battery and knee pads and nothing else" (Douglass, 1973); "hoggers – boxer type underpants worn by aarl fyes wurkers except cutters we used te keep their trousers on mind am tarkin here about when aarl the coals cyem off the showlder" Darby (Co. D'm). [The term develops from 'hoggers' as stockings. As these fell out of use, the word transferred to shorts.]

linings – "pitmen's drawers, fastened at the knee by strings" (Palgrave, Hetton, 1896).

pit claes – "the working clothes of a pitman" (Nicholson, 1888).

> One of my jobs was to dad my Father's pit claes against the wall, to get the dust out; then scrape the clarts off his beuts, and wipe them over with dripping – to keep the wet out, for he was often working in wet conditions underground.
>
> (Florence Merihein, Ashington)

sark – shirt: "He dons his hoggers, badly worn, / His pit sark, and his vest" (W.B. Coombs)

> In the '90s of the last century [i.e.1890s] the pitman's working clothes were usually a thick blue flannel shirt and a red flannel sleeveless body shirt [vest] – no other colour but red would do, as this was considered a safeguard against bodily ills. A checked flannel coat with large pockets, knee breeches tied or open at the knee called pit hoggers, a pair of home made underpants tied at the knee called linings, thick woollen stockings and strong shoes. Some wore a corduroy cap while others wore a flat topped cap with large peak and a tassel.
>
> (Fred Wade, *Annfield Plain*, 1966, p.19)

from *The Fore Shift* (W.B. Coombs)

Subdued, me muthor meks the tea,
And joins him in a cup,
Ne word is spak as he and she
In sulky silence sup.
She packs his bait, its varry smaal,
Just a slice o' breed and butter,
Wi' sugar sprinkled on, that's aall,
Forbye a bottle o' wettor.
His bottle, shot-box, midgy, bait,
Across the tyeble gyeps,

The beggars seem to mock his fate,
The flamin' skitt'rin' yeps. — apes
He watches them wi' baleful eye,
And wunders if he dore,
Wi' one mad final fling, let fly,
And swipe them ont' the floor.
But sanity agyen retorns,
And meekly, as time's pressin',
The divil in 'm draas in his horns,
And he finishes his dressin'.
His pit claes has that special tang
Of oil, and grease, and smoke,
That to colliery hooses aal belang,
And singles oot pit folk.
He reaches for his cap and scarf,
And last of aall his jacket,
Revealin' there that stordy dwarf,
The hyem-med wooden cracket.
He pockets shot-box, bottle, and bait,
Afore he leaves his hyem,
Nods to the wife, and shuts the gate,
She gans t' bed agyen.
The cool neet air the cobwebs shift,
His rank bad temper banishes,
The star-lit sky his spirits lift,
And gloomy thowts syun vanishes.
He gans alang the cobbled street,
His hob-nailed byuts a-clatter,
He faalls in step wi' kindred feet,
and joins in wi' their chatter...

Washing

Once upon a time, the miner carried his dirt home with him:

> A pitman going home after his shift was not the most popular man to sit beside you on a bus. Especially for women dressed for the day. Or even if you sat where he had vacated...
>
> (Trelogan, New Herrington)

> Before pit-head baths were built it was common practice for miners to walk away from the pit covered in coal dust and wearing the clothes in which they had worked. My earliest childhood memories are of such scenes – a neighbour washing in front of a fire, his body black and dirty against the white enamelled bath. While he washed away the dust and the aches his wife tried to clean his pit clothes by banging them against the back yard wall.
>
> (T. Moreland, Dawdon, 1960s)

beuts – boots: "You used to grease the pit boots you know, every night, with fat" (Simpson Wilson, Beamish, 1974/371).

brushes – "men would say 'see you on the brushes', this was a place where boots were cleaned by rotating brushes. Also, where grease could be applied to boots" (Riley, Blyth).

cracket – stool: "They used to bring a crackett home and sit on it to dry themselves in front of the fire when they bathed themselves" (Simpson Wilson, Beamish, 1974/371).

dadding – "dashing dusty pit clothes against a wall" (Colls, 1987); "to beat the dirt out of pit clothes" (Wade, South Moor, 1966); "dad thi klaiz – strike and shake dirty pit clothes on wall" (Dodd, Tanfield Lea).

duds – "clothes" (Wade, South Moor, 1966)

kit – "a small tub for washing in, used by pitmen" (Palgrave, Hetton, 1896).

pit baths – "where men could change and shower" (Trelogan, New Herrington).

poss – "wooden laundry implement used to pound soaking clothes" (Colls, 1987).

pulleys – "short for pulley-wheels and used to describe the black rimmed eyes of miners who didn't get a proper wash" (Sharkey).

stockings – "pit stockings were rubbed out in the water, everything was cleared away, it was routine, stockings to do every day. Back then they brought them every night, we'd rub them out in the water and peg them out in the yard, they had two pairs, to wash and wear". (Simpson Wilson, Beamish, 1974/371).

stour – dust:

On, on they toil; with heat they broil,
And streams of sweat still glue
The stour unto their skins, till they
Are black as the coal they hew...

(Joseph Skipsey)

wesh – "wash" (Dodd, Tanfield Lea):

...when pitmen came off shift, they would bath first – perhaps sitting on a cracket with a tin bath of hot water before them – some miners wouldn't have their backs washed – said it weakened their backs... then ready to eat main meal.

(Eveline Johnson, Trimdon)

And I've seen me and him [younger borther] come home and there were no baths then, we had to wash in the tin bath on the mat. And I've seen me and him strip off there and count each other for the most knots [bruises] on our backs. We used to have the game on. We used to be that tired, we used to get our suppers, my mother used to have the big pan boiling on the hob there. She used to put the cold water in. She used to say, 'Now there's the soap and flannel get washed and get away to bed.' There was many a time, she'd come down at half past seven the next morning, to get the other bairns off to school and we were still lying there black [unwashed], then the game was on. The fire was out, the water was cold, she had to start all over afresh. We got many a rolicking over that.

(Ralph Porter, via *Horden Miners*, ed. Keith Armstrong, Peterlee, 1984)

Food

There is no fixed time allowed for meals, because the nature of the work is desultory, and they have occasional or regular stops from the nature of the work. [Re Killingworth Colliery.]

(*PP*, 1842, CR xvi, p.586)

Brought the Bankhead Firebox and Boiler out of the South Pit, to make room for new air receiver, for Ingersoll engines, on Pay Sat. Sep. 4th, was at work from 12 oclock on the Fri. night, till 3 oclock on the Sat. afternoon, and only had one bate time, owing to our chargeman being afraid of the overman that was there, and there was a few of ours, that was bad with the beer, they had had on the Fri. night, couldn't eat any bate, so with one thing and another, the few that could eat, had to do without.

(J.C. Walshaw's diary, Ryhope, 1908)

bait – "food taken by a pitman to his work" (Nicholson, 1888); "a packed meal" (Wade, South Moor, 1966); "Mid-shift food" (McBurnie, Washington, 1970s); "food carried for work or travel" (Dodd, Tanfield Lea); "my 'bait' of bread and jam" (Hitchin, 1962, p.62); "when we were hevvin our baits" (Hay, Ushaw Moor, C20/2); "Give us plenty bate an' bottle, Plenty beaf an' baccy chews" (Barrass, Consett, 1897). [origin: Old Norse.]

bait box – "lunch box: 'a sandwich outa me bait box'" (Hay, Ushaw Moor, C20/2).

bait poke – "a bate poke is what a workman carries his dinner or corn for his horses [in]" (*Bell MS*); "a bag in which a pit-lad carries his provisions: 'Aw put the bait-poke on at eight'" (Wilson, G'head, 1820s); "Linen bag in which workmen carry their food" (Palgrave); "the bag in which a pitman carries his day's provisions" (Nicholson, 1888); "baitpoke – a bag to carry the meal in" (Wade, South Moor, 1966); "His white bait-poke was slung around his left shoulder, and his jacket pocket bulged with his pit bottle" (Grice, 1960, ch.14).

bate tin – "The tin in which the miner carried his bate. Usually an old army mess tin, where one half fitted inside of the other. The tin was slung on the miner's belt" (Tootle, 1995).

bait time – "a stop for a meal" (Wade, South Moor, 1966).

canteen – "a small flat wooden barrel containing about half a gallon, in which a pitman used to carry water or coffee with him to his work" (Tootle, 1995); "it varies in content from 3 pints to 5, although somehow or other some men manage on less than a pint a day" (Douglass, 1973).

canteen – "In 1942 there was only 59 canteens. With subsidies from the Miners' Welfare Commission, this rose by 1945 to 912, [with] 566 providing full hot meals" (Tootle, 1995); "provided simple, filling meals of the pie-n-chips type" (Barnett, Seaham); "as a little lad I would march down to the canteen to meet my Dad going out of the pit as would many other kids" (Douglass, 1973).

clammin' – "hungry/thirsty: 'clammin for sumthing to eat'" (Charlton, Dawdon).

drouthy – "thirsty" (Wilson, G'head, 1820s).

geysen'd, kizzen'd – "parched with thirst: 'With parched tongues and gyzen'd throats'" (Wilson, G'head, 1820s).

poke – if the miner (and not the pit mice) were to benefit from the 'bait', a bag that could be hung up or a tin box to protect the food was essential. By the 1960s the 'poke' tended to be an ex-army square bag, slung over one shoulder.

tin bottles – "He had a lathe and he used to do jobs for people. In those days there were tin bottles, men used to take into the pit, everybody had a tin bottle and it used to leak at times and they used to bring them down and my father used to solder them. He was taught that by Matt Dawson, he was the tin smith in Crook in those days and he used to make midgeys, bottles, bake tins, everything for the pit" (Mr Carroll, Crook, Beamish, 1991/32).

Tommy box – "Teesside steel workers' food box, but just 'box' at ICI" (Alderslade, Billingham).

Tommee shop – "where miners compelled to shop (now obsolete)" (Dodd, Tanfield Lea). [In the earlier nineteenth century, pay could include credit or tokens, only redeemable at the employer's own shop.]

Tommy ticket – "the pay ticket, otherwise the ticket denoting the deduction for 'tommy', 'tommy' being one of the names for 'truck'" (*M'bro Weekly News*, 21 April 1850).

wallet – "a miner's sack. Filled with food this lasted him the week he was away from home…" (Teward, Teesdale, 2003); "My dad when he worked at Rookhope, he used to go off on a Monday morning, he used to take his wallet, he used to take grub to last him to the Wednesday, it was a pillowcase, used to carry them, a long pillow case, used to put grub in each end and used to carry it over their backs, used to call them a wallet" (R. Graham, Beamish, 1991/112).

watter – water: "two pit bottles full o watter" (Hay, Ushaw Moor, C20/2).

watta bottle – "tin bottle for drinking water in the pit" (Wilson, North Walbottle); "the large tin bottles in which miners carried their drinking water" (Hitchin, 1962, p.42); a hewer can lose 3–4 lbs of sweat per hour – needs to take not only water but salt – else cramp. "this loss has to be made up at the time or afterwards by drinking water, tea, etc." (*HRCM*, ch.18).

yell – ale: "Here, lass says Jack, help this agyen, It's better yell than in the toun" (Wilson, G'head, 1820s).

> When you first went down the pit, especially the youngsters, they used to say, watch out for the pie-wife – and it was if you seen a light coming – oh yes this must be the pie-wife coming up – I mean there was no pie-wife there, but it was just having the youngsters on and that sort of thing…
>
> (Brian Muter, Bates Colliery, Blyth, 1950s)

> In our mining family, Dad went to work about 2am, roused by the pit buzzer – a slice of bread and jam would be left for him for his breakfast, and a kettle on the bar, to make a cup of tea. There would be a tin bottle of water and some jam sandwiches for him to take to work (he loved fig and lemon jam!). Us kids would be up by 7.45 am for school; Dad would be back from the pit about 10.45am, his dinner would be ready for 11am; then we would be home form school for our dinner at 12.15 pm; our tea would be 4 pm. Our big brother also worked at the pit – but he would want his dinner at 5.30 pm. Only on a Saturday and Sunday would our meals coincide!
>
> My Dad would start his dinner with a yorkshire pudding and gravy – it was the size of a sandwich (sponge) tin. Then his main course of meat and veg; and last a rice pudding. And he was only 5 foot!
>
> (Florence Merihein, Ashington)

The old-time miner might have some porridge or a cup of tea on getting up; his bait for work would be left ready – sandwiches in a tin, and a tin bottle with a cork for his tea (black and sugared). He would appreciate meat, cheese or jam in his sandwich; or he might make do with sugar or treacle. In Wheatley Hill, they say that Christmas cake – with cheese – was used to fill sandwiches in the New Year. Some miners would take a small pot of jam down with them as they reckoned it helped clear the throat of dust.

> The meal we had to take to work – our bait – was a couple of slices of jam and bread or sugar sprinkled on bread and a bottle of cold tea and I can tell you it was as good as a meal in the best hotel in Britain.
>
> (Mr Cawson, Kibblesworth, Beamish, 1993/5)

> About 1962 as me and my marra John walked from the bus terminus at Dawdon, heading for the pit about 8 on a cold winter morning, two heroes in front started shouting thus:
>
> 'Is thow sortun yer've left it at yame?? Is thow sortun??'
>
> 'Aye, am tellun yeh, a've left it on tabbble, I've got nee bait marra.'
>
> Just then a coal lorry came past and the first hero threw his bait wrapped in paper onto the coal in the wagon.
>
> 'There we are marra..both the syame!! neee bait!'
>
> (Kenn Johnson)

There are two other words, besides 'bait', current in the North East for food in general, both first noted down by Thomas Wilson in the 1820s: 'belly-timmer' and 'scran'. 'Scran' may derive from the Dutch verb schransen – to gorge oneself, but was also used in the navy for odd bits of anything or lost property. As Jack Gair wrote: "In a book written by Petty Officer Robert Burgess in 1943 he writes: scran bag – a despository for lost articles…In another book *Sailors have a word for it* by Gerald O'Driscoll also 1943 he writes: scran bag – the lost property office of the Royal Navy. It is usually a cell into which all clothing left lying about and all unclaimed belongings are dumped. The tax imposed for the redemption of each piece of clothing is one square inch of soap." Jack also recalls scran bag being used in this sense on scout outings and the like, in Co. Durham, in the mid-twentieth century. The link is this case would seem to be with the Icelandic *skran* – rubbish, odds and ends, and 'scran' may often have the sense of casual food.

Occasionally, a worker might not eat all his food at work: "Steel-workers going home at the end of their shift who had unwanted food in the Tommy boxes and did not want to take it home in case it upset their wives who had shopped for the goods handed it over to children who called to them 'Have you any soreyes?'. I have never heard the word anywhere except in Middlesbrough" (E. Reynolds). Curiously, Umpleby's list of Staithes words from the 1930s has a similar concept: "Wowtin-ceeak – food that is not eaten at sea and returned in a wow-tin" – 'wow' in the North East usually stands for treacle.

Also at Brandon if you were on examining the aerial flight, it was quite the usual thing to look for mushrooms as you were coming over the fields, take them into the canteen at Brandon, and ask them "Could I have some bacon 'n eggs and here's a bag of mushrooms" – and you used to get a wonderful breakfast!

(David James, Brancepeth)

A Tale of the two Slices

Young lad started down the pit. His mother put his bait up consisting of 2 slices of bread and jam. When he finished his work and came home his mother asked him how he had enjoyed his work. He said alright, but he wanted more bait. So she put 4 slices in the next day. She asked him if he had plenty when he returned home, but he said he could eat more, so she cut a loaf of bread into two and put it up for him. On returning home she asked if he enjoyed his work and was his bait alright. The lad replied yes his work was alright but I see you have gone back to the 2 slices.

(Geordie McBurnie, Washington, 1970s)

Talking about 'jam and bread bait sandwiches' reminds me of the story of the miner who on opening his bait one day said 'Jam and breed agyan. I'll kill wor lass if she gives us jam and breed agyan,' and he threw the offending packages on to the conveyor belt. Same thing happened the following day and on to the belt went the sandwiches. On the third day he was sitting with his mate ready to eat his bait when he took the package out of his bait tin and threw it on to the belt unopened. His mate, surprised, asked, 'What's wrang wi thee bait the day then?' and he replied 'Jam and breed agyan, ah canna stand it!' 'But the nivvor oppened it, how's the knaar its jam and breed?' asked his mate. 'Cos ah purrat up mesel!' he said.

(Tony Sharkey)

Young lad – started work, his first day down the pit had not been to his liking. On arriving home his mother put his dinner ready for him, but he just sat in the corner with his head in his hands. His mother asked him what was the matter and did his work not suit him, and the reply she got was: 'NO. I wished I was 65.

(Geordie McBurnie)

Sources

Adams, Seaham – Isabel Adams, formerly of Seaham.

Alderslade, Billingham – George Alderslade.

Allan, 1891 – *Allan's illustrated edition of Tyneside songs* ed. David Harker (Newcastle on Tyne, 1972).

Armstrong, Keith (ed). *Horden Miners* (Peterlee, 1984).

Ashington Collieries Magazine (ACM).

Atkinson Cleve, 1868 – J.C. Atkinson, *A glossary of the Cleveland dialect* (London, 1868).

Atkinson, Frank, *The Great North Coalfield* 1700–1900 (Barnard Castle: Durham Local History Society, 1966).

Bailey, D'm, 1810 – John Bailey *General view of the Agriculture of the County of Durham* (1810).

Baker, A.R.H. & Butlin, R.A., *Studies of the Field Systems in the British Isles* (Cambridge University Press, 1973).

Barnett, Seaham – Steve Barnett, Seaham Colliery.

Barrass Consett, 1897 – Alexander Barrass, *The Pitman's Social Neet* (Consett, 1897).

Bell MS – Newcastle University, Bell-White MS 12 (1815–1830s).

Bell-Harker – Dave Harker (ed.) *Songs from the Manuscript Collection of John Bell* (Surtees Society, vol.196, 1985).

Benson, 1989 – John Benson *British Coalminers in the 19th century: a social history* (London, Longmans, 1989).

Briscoe, 2003 – Diana Briscoe *Wicked Geordie English* (London, 2003).

Brockett, Newc, 1820s – John Trotter Brockett *A glossary of North Country words in use…* (Newcastle: T & J. Hodgson, 1825), 2nd edn, 1829, 3rd edn, 1846. [Brockett died 1842, aged 54; his main collecting seems to have been work of the 1810s, 1820s.]

Brown – Bob Brown, Ryhope Colliery, 1937–74.

Cheesman, Bedlington, Blyth, Carmlington – Phil Chessman.

Chicken, Benwell, 1720s – Edward Chicken *The collier's wedding* (2nd edn, Newcastle, 1764). [Written 1720s re miners at Benwell.]

Colls, 1987 – Robert Colls, *The Pitmen of the Northern Coalfield* (Manchester University Press, 1987).

The Compleat Collier [by J.C.] 1708 (London, Conyers, reprinted, Newcastle, Graham, 1968).

Conn, Seaham – Norman Conn, former Deputy.

Coombs, W.B. – Ashington pit poet, verses published in Northumbriana, etc.

Cuthbert, C15/mid – *The Life or St Cuthbert in English Verse* c. AD 1450 (Durham: Surtees Society, vol.87, 1891).

Darby, Seaham – Geordie Darby.

Davidson, Ashington – Brian Davidson.

Denham Tracts – M.A. Denham, *The Denham Tracts* (London, 1892).

Dinsdale, Tees, 1849 – Frederick T. Dinsdale's, *A Glossary of Provincial Words used in Teesdale in the County of Durham* (London, 1849). "The area covered is from Middleton in Teesdale to Darlington and north of the Tees for 9 or 10 miles along this route."

Dobson, Scott, *Stotty Cake Row* (Newcastle: Graham, 1971).

Dodd, Tanfield Lea – 'Michael Dodd's List of Geordie Words, c.1960–1980' survives as a hand-written card index at Beamish Museum's Regional Research Centre; Dodd (b. 1909) was storeman at Tanfield Lea Colliery, and apparently got his enthusiasm for recording mining dialect from a talk he heard on the subject in the 1950s. The list he constructed covered more than one decade, though individual entries are not dated.

Douglass, 1973 – Dave Douglas, *Pit talk in Co. Durham* (Oxford: History Workshop, 1973).

Durham, 1590s – ed. B.Colgrave and C.E. Wright, 'An Elizabethan poem about Durham' in *Durham University Journal*, vol.32 (n.s.1) 1940, pp.161–168.

Egglestone, Weardale, 1870s – William Egglestone, *Betty Podkin's letter ted Queen on Cleopatra's Needle* (London, 1877).

Elliott, Tyne, 1910 – Thornton Elliott c.1910 in *Scrapbook of Tyneside Songs 1878–1922* (Newc Cen Lib L427.82).

Etherington – John Etherington, Hartlepool (1974).

Freese, 2005 – Barbara Freese, *Coal: a human history* (London: Heinemann, 2005)

Richard Fynes, *The Miners of Northumberland and Durham* (1873).

Geggie, Ashington – Alan Geggie.

Greenwell, 1849 – G.C. Greenwell, *Glossary of Terms Used in the Coal Trade...* (Newcastle, 1849).

Grice, 1960 – Frederick Grice. *The Bonny Pit Laddie* (OUP, 1960).

Griffiths, Bill, *A Seaham Reader 5. The Mines* [1991], *A Seaham Reader 6. Yearly Bonds, etc.* [1991].

Griffiths, Horden – Geoff Griffiths (ex-Horden Colliery mechanic).

Grose, 1787 – Francis Grose's *Provincial Glossary* (1787, repr. Scholar Press, 1968).

Hardy, George, 'A Historical Account of the Londonderry Railway', *Proceedings of Antiquaries of Sunderland*, 17 (1916), 34–35, (repr. Seaham, Amra, 2001).

Dave Harker (ed.) *Songs and Verse of the North-East Pitmen c.1780–1844* (Durham, Surtees Society, vol.204, 1999).

Hatcher, John, *The History of the British Coal Industry* (Oxford, Clarendon, 1993).

Hay, Ushaw Moor, C20/1 – James Hay *Spider and other tales of pit village life* (Seaham, Amra Imprint, 2003). [James Hay 1890–1969, lived at Ushaw Moor and was a miner at Bearpark Colliery all his working life.]

Heslop, N'd, 1880s – R. Oliver Heslop, *Northumberland Words: A glossary of words used in the County of Northumberland and on the Tyneside* (2 vols, English Dialect Society, 1893–4), first appeared as a series of articles in the *Newcastle Evening Chronicle* in the 1880s.

Hill, Harrington – Harry Hill, mining engineer, Harrington, etc. now New Silksworth.

Hitchin, 1962 – George Hitchin *Pit-Yacker* (London, Jonathan Cape, 1962).

Houghton, Thomas, *Rara Avis in Terris: or the Compleat Miner* (London, William Soper, 1681).

Hooson, William, *The Miners Dictionary… explaining that most useful Art of Mineing more esp. of Lead-Mines by Wm Hooson, a Derbyshire Miner* (Wrexham, Payne, 1747).

HRCM – Historical Review of Coal Mining (London, Mining Association of Great Britain, 1924).

Kell, Leasingthorne – John Kell, pitman of Leasingthorne, via Frank Atkinson.

Kennet MS – Bishop Kennet's 'Etymological Collections of English Words and Provincial Expressions', a manuscript dictionary surviving as *BL MS Lansdowne 1033* (vol. 99 of Bishop Kennet's Collection), compiled in the 1690s.

Kerr, George *Practical Coal Mining* (Griffin & Co., 1901).

Leister, I., *The Sea Coal Mine and the Durham Miner* (Durham, 1975).

Johnson, Dawdon – Kenn Johnson: "I was a Mine Surveyor (survivor was our nickname) at Dawdon in late 50s early 60s."

Ivor Lee, Sunny Brow, circa 1910–25.

Lloyd – A.L. Lloyd *Come All Ye Bold Miners* (London, 1952, 1978).

Luckley, Alnwick, 1870s – John Lamb Luckley, *The Alnwick Language* in Newcastle Central Library.

McBurnie, Washington, 1968 – Geordie McBurnie. [Deputy and member of Mine Rescue Team, Glebe Colliery, Co Durham (died 1979). Notes made by him while learning to write again after a stroke in 1968. Preserved by Ada Radford of Darlington.]

McGee, Sherburn Hill, Brandon – Tom McGee.

Makepeace – Michael Makepeace, of South Shields.

Monthly Chronicle of North-Country Lore and Legend (Newcastle, Scott, 1889).

J. Moreland, Dawdon 1980 – Jim Moreland, *Just One Man* (Durham, English Folk Dance & Song Soc., 1980). [Jim had worked at Dawdon Pit for over 20 years.]

T. Moreland, Dawdon, 1960s – Tom Moreland, extracts from his unpublished family history.

Mountford, Seaham – Dave Mountford [song-writer and performer].

Nef, J.U., *The Rise of the British Coal Industry* (Routledge, 1932).

Nicholson, 1888 – W.E. Nicholson, *A glossary of terms used in the coal trade of Northumberland and Durham* (Newcastle: Andrew Reid, 1888). [Nicholson recognises and draws on a previous list of mining words, G.C. Greenwell's 1849 glossary with the same title.]

Northumbrian III – *Northumbrian Words and Ways*, vol.3, compiled by Jean Crocker, 1990.

OED – Oxford English Dictionary.

Orange, Ronald – Bebside (Horton Grange Colliery).

Orr 2005 – Colin Orr a *New Silksworth Childhood* (Houghton-le-Spring, Gilpin Press, 2005).

Oxley, Burradon – Stan Oxley of Burradon Colliery via *Northumbrian Words & Ways III* ed. Jean Crocker, 1990, and by kind communication from his widow, Joyce Oxley.

Palgrave, Hetton 1896 – F.M.T. Palgrave: *A list of words and phrases in everyday use by the natives of Hetton-le-Hole in the County of Durham* (English Dialect Society, vol.74, 1896).

G. Patrickson, Dawdon, C20/mid – Gordon Patrickson, surface worker, Dawdon Pit 1950s–60s.

J. Patrickson – John Patrickson, face worker Dawdon Pit, 1970s.

Phillips, Cullercoats – Joan Taylor Phillips.

Platts, F.N., *The Canny Man* (1970).

PP – Parliamentary Papers, Commissioners Reports [includes Glossary of Pit Terms, *PP,* 1842, CR vol.16, pp.558–562].

J.B. Priestley, *English Journey* (1935).

Raine MS – James Raine: BL MS Egerton 2868 [uses wills of the Diocese of Durham, wills of the Diocese of York, and records of trials held in York Castle, plus some early printed books and diaries].

Ray, John 1674 – Ray 1674 – John Ray, *Collection of English words, not generally used.* (London, 1674). Also 1737 edition.

Richardson, J.B., *Metal Mining* (London, Allen Lane, 1974).

Riley, Blyth – Bill Riley, coal miner at Bates Colliery, Blyth, and later in Midlands. From website www.pitwork.net

Ritson, Joseph (ed.) *The Northumberland Garland* (Newcastle & London, 1809).

Robson, 1849 – J.P. Robson, *Songs of the Bards of the Tyne* (Newcastle ca.1849) [includes glossary].

Robson, 1875 – W.J.Robson, *Life of Billy Purvis* (Newcastle & Sunderland, 1875).

Roxborough swDm – Frank Roxborough, Mainsforth Colliery.

Sanderson – J. Sanderson, Peterlee.

Scrapbook Tyne – *Scrapbook of Tyneside songs* (Newcastle Central Library L427.82).

Sharkey – Tony Sharkey, started work 1942, e.g. at Dean & Chapter and Mainsforth pits, qualifying as a surveyor in 1949; went on to work at a variety of pits in southwest Co. Durham, including posts as undermanager at Dean and Chapter and Leasingthorne collieries.

Shelley, Sth Hetton – Yvonne Shelly.

Smith, Jeffrey, 'George Stephenson and the miner's lamp controversy', *North East History*, 34, 113–135 (2001).

Sterling, Hartlepool – Alf Sterlng's online wordlist at www.hartlepoolslang.bravehost.com

Temple, 1994 – Dave Temple, *The Collieries of Durham* vol.1 (Newcastle: Trade Union Printing Service, 1994).

Teward, Teesdale 2003 – Kathleen Teward, *Teisdal' en how twas spok'n* (Teesdale, 2003).

Tonge, 1906 – James Tonge, *The Principles and Practice of Coal Mining* (London, 1906).

Tootle, 1995 – Harry Tootles online Dictionary of Mining Terms at http://website.lineone.net/~coalmining/

Trelogan, Herrington – Charles Trelogan, New Herrington.

Tweedy, Shilbottle – Jack Tweedy via *Northumbrian Words & Ways III*, ed. Jean Crocker, 1990.

Umpleby, Staithes – A.Stanley Umpleby *The Dialect of Staithes* (1930s).

Wade, South Moor, 1966 – Fred Wade, 'Pitmatic Word List, South Moor, 1966', pp.187–190 in *The Story of South Moor: a mining village situated in the north western part of County Durham*, typescript.

Wade, Fred, *Annfield Plain* typescript, 1966.

Wade, Fred, *The Story of West Stanley*, typescript 1956.

Walton. W.Auck. – Bill Walton from West Auckland.

Wilson, G'head, 1820s – Thomas Wilson, *Pitman's Pay* published in three parts in the journal *The Newcastle Magazine* in 1826, 1828, 1830. [A 'collected' edition, with glossary, was issued with an introduction by the author, in 1843, also used here; the text refers to conditions ca.1800.]

Wilson, 1907 – John Wilson, *A History of the Durham Miners' Association* 1870–1904 (Durham, 1907).

Wilson, Walbottle – Norman Wilson, North Walbottle Colliery, now Newburn.

Woodward, H.B., *Geology of England & Wales* (London, 1876).